LONGMANS' LINGUISTICS LIBRARY

STUDIES IN ENGLISH ADVERBIAL USAGE

LONGMANS' LINGUISTICS LIBRARY

THE LINGUISTIC SCIENCES AND LANGUAGE TEACHING
M. A. K. Halliday, Angus McIntosh and Peter Strevens

GENERAL LINGUISTICS
AN INTRODUCTORY SURVEY
R. H. Robins

A LINGUISTIC STUDY OF THE ENGLISH VERB
F. R. Palmer

WHAT *IS* LANGUAGE?
A NEW APPROACH TO LINGUISTIC DESCRIPTION
Robert M. W. Dixon

IN MEMORY OF J. R. FIRTH
Editors: C. E. Bazell, J. C. Catford, M. A. K. Halliday and R. H. Robins

PATTERNS OF LANGUAGE
PAPERS IN GENERAL
DESCRIPTIVE AND APPLIED LINGUISTICS
Angus McIntosh and M. A. K. Halliday

A SHORT HISTORY OF LINGUISTICS
R. H. Robins

SELECTED PAPERS OF J. R. FIRTH 1952-59
Editor: F. R. Palmer

ESSAYS ON THE ENGLISH LANGUAGE
MEDIEVAL AND MODERN
Randolph Quirk

TOWARDS A SEMANTIC DESCRIPTION OF ENGLISH
Geoffrey N. Leech

STUDIES IN ENGLISH ADVERBIAL USAGE
Sidney Greenbaum

Studies in English Adverbial Usage

Sidney Greenbaum

LONGMANS

LONGMANS, GREEN AND CO LTD
London and Harlow
Associated companies, branches and representatives
throughout the world
© Longmans, Green and Co Ltd 1969
SBN 582 52400 8
First published 1969
Made and printed in Great Britain by
William Clowes and Sons, Limited, London and Beccles

To the memory of my mother and father

Preface

This book is a revised version of a thesis accepted by the University of London for the degree of Ph.D. and prepared at the Survey of English Usage during 1964–1967. The work was supported in part by a grant to the Survey of English Usage by H. M. Department of Education and Science. I am grateful to Professor Randolph Quirk as Director of the Survey for making available the Survey corpus and providing facilities for research, in particular facilities for experiments with informants. I am also deeply indebted to Professor Quirk in his personal capacity for his supervision of the research and for constant advice and practical assistance.

My research has gained immensely through being conducted in the congenial atmosphere of the Survey research room. From Jan Svartvik, whose last year at the Survey coincided with my first, I learned a great deal about methods of analysing a corpus. I have also benefited from discussions with other Survey colleagues: Valerie Adams, Caroline Bott, Judith Carvell, Henry Carvell, Derek Davy, Norman Fairclough, Joan Huddleston and Ruth Kempson. They all deserve my gratitude for willingly and patiently acting as informants. In addition, my thanks are due to Derek Davy for helping in the recording of material for experiments and in the administration of experiments, and to Valerie Adams, Norman Fairclough, and Joan Huddleston for their practical assistance in connection with the experiments. My work has also benefited from discussions with Eugene Winter on his research into clause connection. I owe a special debt to Geoffrey Leech, who gave a careful reading to a preliminary version of this study and commented extensively on it.

I wish to thank Professor T. F. Mitchell (Leeds), Professor F. R. Palmer (Reading), and Professor E. G. Stanley (London) for their interest and advice. Their suggestions have led to a number of changes, which have enhanced the value of the book.

Finally, I wish to thank Peggy Drinkwater of Longmans for help in preparing the book for press and for the care she has taken with it.

University College London   S.G.
July 1968

Contents

6. Attitudinal disjuncts: position, punctuation, and intonation

11. Conclusions

Tables

Figures

Chapter 1

Introduction

1.1 The scope of the study

This book is concerned with some of the functions of the 'Adjunct' in Contemporary English, that is, with some of the functions of those constituents of a clause that are not Subject, Verb, or Complement.[1]

Various form-classes may be Adjunct:

[1] the class of items traditionally termed 'adverbs', e.g.:
David plays chess *well*.
Here they fought their last battle.
David *frequently* gave William money.[2]
[2] prepositional phrases, e.g.:
David plays chess *with great skill*.
On this hill they fought their last battle.
David gave William money *on many occasions*.
[3] finite verb clauses, e.g.:
David plays chess *as his father taught him*.

---

1 For an instance of the recent use of the term 'Adjunct' in this sense, see Hudson 1967. The term 'adjunct' for the function of adverbs may be found in the works of traditional grammarians such as Poutsma 1926, 29ff., 691ff., 1928, 320ff. and Kruisinga 1932a, 123.
2 I have included among adverbs only items that are represented orthographically as single words. There are some marginal cases. For example, *nonetheless* is sometimes written as three separate words and sometimes, like *nevertheless*, as one word. A case could be made for including among adverbs constructions such as *of course* and *at all*, even though they are always spelt as two words, on the ground that they do not allow expansion. By contrast, *in fact* and *at least* would then have to be excluded, since they can be expanded to *in actual fact* and *at the very least*. Both in this respect and also in present spelling practice *in fact* may be contrasted with *indeed*.

They fought their last battle *where the college now stands.*
David gave William money *whenever he needed it.*
[4] non-finite verb clauses, in which the verb is:
  [i] *to*-infinitive, e.g.:
       David plays chess *to please his father.*
  [ii] *-ing* participle, e.g.:
       Standing on this hill, they fought their last battle.
  [iii] *-ed* participle, e.g.:
       Whenever approached by him, David gave William money.
[5] verbless clauses, e.g.:
     David plays chess *when on holiday.*
     Fearless, they fought their last battle.
     Though indignant at his threats, David gave William money.

This book deals in particular with some of the functions of the Adjunct that are realised by adverbs.[1] The functions that have been isolated for detailed investigation are realised by adverbs that have been called by writers on English grammar 'sentence modifiers' or 'sentence adverbs'.[2] Many writers appear to include among these the adverbs that are felt to link sentences, such as *therefore* and *nevertheless,* but some treat linking adverbs as a separate class.[3] Grammarians are not in general agreement on what to include among 'sentence modifiers' or 'sentence adverbs'. Moreover, they either fail to be precise about the criteria to be employed in assigning adverbs to this class or fail to provide any criteria.[4]

Since the terms 'sentence modifier' and 'sentence adverb' have been used imprecisely and in various ways, I shall not make use of them in this book. However, the adverbs on which I am concentrating would probably be designated as such or as linking adverbs by those who employ the terms, though many others would be included as well. I give

---

[1] Adverbs may, of course, have functions other than those of Adjunct. For example, an adverb may modify an adjective, as *surprisingly* in *His proposals had a surprisingly great effect.*
[2] For the term 'sentence modifier', see, for example, Sweet 1891, 125–7; Poutsma 1926, 692–3, 1928, 434–51; Francis 1958, 399, 403–4, 408; Strang 1962, 166–7; Jacobson 1964, 28–33, 48, 51. For the term 'sentence adverb', see Curme 1935, 73–4; H. Palmer 1939, 171, 179, 180; Zandvoort 1962, 204, 249–50. The term 'sentence adverbial' has been used by linguists who write within the framework of transformational grammar, cf. Katz and Postal 1964, 77; and Chomsky 1965, 102.
[3] They are separately treated in Sweet 1891, 143–4 as 'half-conjunctions' and in Curme 1935, 74–5 as 'conjunctive adverbs'.
[4] See Jacobson 1964, 29–32 for an account of some views on the 'division of adverbials into sentence-modifiers and word or word-group modifiers'. Jacobson finds it difficult to apply the criteria that have been proposed and decides against utilising the distinction consistently in his description and explanation of the position of adverbs.

some examples of adverbs with the functions that I shall be considering in detail in this book:

Strangely, he answered the questions.
Frankly, he is not very clever.
David *probably* plays chess.
He *wisely* refrained from smoking.
They enjoyed the film, *though*.
Moreover, they refused to reply to our letter.
He is *therefore* rather unhappy.
Still, he did not charge us for it.
Yet no one has heard of him.

Before we go any further two points need to be made clear. First, by the 'function' of an item I mean the sum of its syntactic features. Syntactic features comprise both those that are present for a particular item in the clause that is being considered and also those that are potential. Furthermore, potential features include both positive and negative features.[1] Some examples will help to make these distinctions clear.

In the sentence *David plays chess very well*, we observe as syntactic features of the adverb *well*:

[1] its ability to appear after the Complement.
[2] its ability to accept *very* as premodifier.

Positive potential features of *well* include:

[1] its ability to serve as response to an interrogative transformation of the sentence introduced by *How: How does David play chess? (Very) well.*
[2] its ability to be the focus of clause comparison with the correlatives *as . . . as: David plays chess as well as William does.*

Negative potential features include:

[1] its inability to be moved elsewhere in the sentence. By contrast, *usually*, for example, can occupy several positions: *Usually David plays chess, David usually plays chess,* and *David plays chess usually.*
[2] its inability to be the focus of *only* in initial position in respect of allowing Verb-Subject inversion: **Only well does David play chess.* In this respect it can be contrasted with, for example, *occasionally*. Thus, for *occasionally* in *David plays chess occasionally* we have *Only occasionally does David play chess.*

---

[1] Cf. Crystal 1967, 45 (note): 'There is no reason why carefully selected negative criteria could not be introduced into the definition of a word class, though these will usually be the corollary of positive criteria used for the definition of other classes.'

The second point I wish to make raises the difficulty of drawing a line between homonymy and polysemy. Homonyms are items that have the same written and spoken form but differ in meaning. *Bear* (denoting an animal species) and *bear* (signifying 'carry') are therefore homonyms, since there does not appear to be any connection between the two meanings. In contrast, *hand* (of a human being) and *hand* (of a clock) can be considered instances of polysemy or multiple meaning. We can see a semantic relationship between the two uses of *hand*, the meaning of *hand* of a clock being a metaphorical extension of the meaning of *hand* of a human being. For some purposes we are justified in regarding these as essentially the same lexical item. In many cases the semantic relationship is tenuous. For example, an etymological connection can be traced between *board* ('long thin piece of sawn timber') and *board* ('committee'), but for present-day speakers of English the two items are probably not connected in meaning. Finally, items may have a semantic affinity while differing syntactically. Thus, there is an obvious semantic affinity between the noun *hand* (of a human being) and the verb *hand* (meaning 'deliver by hand') although there is a syntactic difference between the two items.[1]

Let us see how all this applies to the functions of adverbs. As one of the syntactic features of *well* in the sentence *David plays chess very well*, I have mentioned its inability to be moved elsewhere in the sentence. But let us look as these sentences:

[1] *Well*, David may play chess.
[2] David may *well* play chess.
[3] David may play chess *well*.

For convenience, I shall assign to *well* in each of the sentences a corresponding subscript, so that I shall refer to $well_1$, $well_2$, and $well_3$. The three sentences do not, of course represent a contradiction of what I have just said about the immobility of *well*. The sentences exemplify three different functions. Each item is restricted in its particular function to a particular syntactic position. I shall mention a few of the features that distinguish these three occurrences of *well*:

[i] $Well_1$ and $well_3$ may accompany any form of the verb group, but this is not true for $well_2$. Thus, we can say *Well, David plays chess* and *David plays chess well*, but not **David well plays chess*. $Well_2$ collocates (i.e. co-occurs) obligatorily with certain auxiliaries. For the lexical verb *play* the auxiliaries are restricted to *may* and *might*.

[ii] $Well_3$ can serve as a response to an interrogative transformation

---

1 For a recent discussion of homonymy and polysemy, see Waldron 1967, 47f., 63ff.

of the clause introduced by *How*: *How did David play chess? Well.* This is not true for $well_1$ and $well_2$.

[iii] *Well₁* and *well₂* can collocate with any main verb, but *well₃* is restricted to certain verbs, or perhaps certain classes of verbs. For example, if the verb *play* is replaced in the three sentences by the verb *be* and *chess* by *the leader*, only *well₁* and *well₂* remain acceptable:

[1a] *Well*, David may be the leader.
[2a] David may *well* be the leader.
[3a] *David may be the leader *well*.

The restricted collocability of *well₃* with certain verbs is further highlighted if we substitute *know* for *play*:

[4] David may know chess *well*.

Although *well* in this function and *well₃* share most of the features that have been mentioned, they differ in at least one respect. *Well₄* (as we may call it) cannot serve as a response to an interrogative transformation introduced by *How*: **How did David know chess? Well.* Moreover, if the Complement is a phrase of some length or a clause, *well₄* may precede the main verb, but not *well₃*:

David knows *well* what he wants.
David *well* knows what he wants.
David plays *well* what he wants to play.
*David *well* plays what he wants to play.

The questions now inevitably arise:

[1] Is *well* in each of the four sentences a separate lexical item, so that the sentences display four homonyms? Or do we have one lexical item, with four manifestations that are instances of polysemy?

[2] If there is here only one lexical item, do we ascribe its four manifestations to four syntactic classes, just as we assign the noun *hand* and the verb *hand* to different syntactic classes? Or do we regard them as members of one syntactic class with differences in their syntactic relationship to the other constituents of the clause, just as we speak of adjectives having predicative and attributive relationships?

Let us attempt to see a semantic relationship between the four instances of *well*. *Well₃* may be paraphrased (rather clumsily, it must be admitted) by 'in a manner that is *good* (in the sense of 'skilful')' and *well₄* by 'to a *good* (in the sense of 'thorough') extent'. *Well₃* and *well₄* can thus be said to have related meanings, corresponding to the related meanings of the two instances of *good*. *Well₂* is semantically an intensifier roughly equivalent to *indeed* in that position. As an intensifier, it is semantically related to *well₄*, a degree intensifier. A closer semantic relationship between *well₂* and the others is indicated if we paraphrase the sentence *David may well play chess* as 'There may be *good* reason for saying that David plays chess'. *Well*₁ has a wide semantic range, but there are at least some contexts in which it can be viewed as related in meaning to *well*₂ or *well*₄. Let us imagine a short conversation:

> [A] I am bored.
> [B] Why don't you have a game of chess?
> [A] Is there anybody here who can play?
> [B] *Well*, David plays chess.

It is possible to paraphrase *well* in this last sentence by 'It may *well* be', with *well*₂, or by 'I (or 'we') know *well*', with *well*₄, the different meanings perhaps distinguished intonationally. By these paraphrases we can show some connection between the meanings of the four instances of *well* and regard them, if we wish, as a case of polysemy.[1]

If we assume that the four instances of *well* are related semantically, are we also to consider them members of the same syntactic class? At one level of abstraction they all function as Adjunct, and hence we can assign them all to the class of Adjunct adverbs. However, since the purpose of this book is to investigate in detail some of the functions of adverbs that are Adjunct, it is convenient in the primary analysis to assign the different functions to different classes of items. Items that are identical in their written and spoken forms but that differ syntactically are considered to be 'syntactic homonyms' and when the term 'homonym' is used in the book it is used in this sense. At the same time, if it is possible, I shall indicate underlying semantic relationships between the homonyms.[2]

Some further illustrations will outline the approach. *Strangely* appears in both of these sentences:

> [1] *Strangely*, he answered the questions.
> [2] He answered the questions *strangely*.

On a normal interpretation, the two sentences differ considerably in meaning. We must assume that the semantic difference, reflected by a variation in position, results from a difference in the perception of the function of *strangely* in the two sentences. We can apply syntactic tests to demonstrate that *strangely*₁ and *strangely*₂ differ syntactically. (In applying the tests we must, of course, hold constant the semantic force of each of these items.) For example, if we transform the sentences into

[1] I do not intend to suggest that there are no clear cases of homonymy among adverbs. The classic instance of homonyms among adverbs is *fast*. In Contemporary English the identical form represents two different items, one with the meaning 'quickly' and the other with the meaning 'firmly'.
[2] The syntactic difference between *well* in *They played the game well*, and in *It was a well-played game*, is analogous to the syntactic difference between an adjective in predicative and in attributive relationship.

questions, then we can only retain *strangely* in the interrogative transformation of sentence [2]:

[2a] Did he answer the questions *strangely*?

However, *strangely*$_1$ is not acceptable in a question in any position. The function of *strangely*, it must be said at once, is not determined solely by its position. Thus, *strangely* below is ambiguous between the functions of *strangely*$_1$ and *strangely*$_2$:

[3] He *strangely* answered the questions.

Adapting a distinction made by Chomsky (1965, 16), we may say that the function of *strangely* is not entirely determined by the 'surface structure' (that determines the phonetic and graphetic interpretation) but rather by the 'deep structure' (that determines the semantic interpretation). The semantic relationship between the two homonyms and the relationship between each of them and other constituents in the sentence can be expressed by paraphrases. For example, for the first two sentences with *strangely* our paraphrases might be:

[1b] *It is strange (that)* he answered the questions.
[2b] He answered the questions *in a strange manner*.

The relationship between *It is strange (that)* in [1b] and *strangely*$_1$ and between *in a strange manner* in [2b] and *strangely*$_2$ will be said to be a 'correspondence relationship'. A 'correspondence' may be defined as a paraphrase which retains at least part of the morphemic identity of the item that is being paraphrased. The correspondence *in a strange manner* has the additional characteristic that it shares a number of syntactic features with *strangely*$_2$.[1]

In some cases an item may have the same function in deep structure, as manifested in its correspondence, as its homonym has in surface

---

[1] Sporadic instances of paraphrases of this kind may be found in the work of a number of writers. Sweet (1898, 21) explains the difference between the two uses of *gladly* by stating their correspondences: '*gladly* in *I gladly acceded to his request* means "I was glad to (accede to . . .)", while in *I acceded to his request gladly* it means simply "with gladness".' Similarly, he explains the relationship of *luckily* to the clause that follows: '*Wednesday came, and luckily it was a fine day*, where *luckily* = "it was lucky that . . .".' On the other hand, he also paraphrases the meaning of an adverb without providing a correspondence: 'if we made *he generally failed to explain his meaning* into *he failed to explain his meaning generally*, the adverb would modify *explain* only, and the meaning would be "he succeeded only partially in explaining his meaning".' One other example may be quoted, this time from Jespersen (1949, 84): 'As a typical example [of what he terms 'style tertiaries'] may be given "she fairly screamed", which is = "you may fairly say that she screamed".' For other examples of the use of correspondences, see Poutsma 1928, 440–1; Jespersen 1949, 88; and Zandvoort 1962, 250. A recent and more comprehensive use appears in Davies 1967.

structure. For example, *frankly* appears in both of the following sentences:

> [1] *Frankly*, he wrote to them about it.
> [2] He wrote to them about it *frankly*.

In surface structure only *frankly*$_2$ is a manner adjunct, i.e. can serve as a response to an interrogative transformation introduced by *How*. But in deep structure *frankly*$_1$ can also be shown to be a manner adjunct. One of several possible correspondences for *frankly*$_1$ is:

> If I may speak *frankly*, I would say (that) . . .

In this correspondence *frankly* is a manner adjunct in the clause *If I may speak frankly*.

This book is primarily a descriptive account of some adverbs that have been isolated on the basis of their syntactic features. Individual items are discussed, so that distinctions can be made between homonyms. The adverbs are also analysed with respect to their semantic features. Where it is possible to do so, formalised paraphrases, which we have termed 'correspondences', are established for groups of adverbs.

1.2 Sources of data

For this study I have examined the material in the files of the Survey of English Usage. I have supplemented this information with citations collected over a period of two years from several British newspapers. In addition, I have frequently consulted the data that Jacobson (1964) presents on the placement of adverbs in English. Finally, I have taken into consideration examples that I myself have supplied from introspection.

There are several advantages in making use of a corpus if one is analysing the syntax of one's own language:

(1) a corpus provides information on linguistic performance.[1] Such information is particularly valuable when syntactic differences correlate, or may be thought to correlate, with differences in position, intonation or punctuation. This holds true for the area of syntax that we are considering.[2]

---

[1] For the distinction between competence and performance, see Chomsky 1965, 3–4.
[2] See the discussion of *strangely* (above, pages 6f.) and also, for example, the statement of Curme 1931, 132: 'We sometimes find the sentence adverb at the very beginning of the sentence, or after the verb at or near the end of the sentence; in the former case followed by a slight pause and in the latter case preceded by a pause, which in both cases marks the adverb or adverbial element as a sentence modifier: "*Unfortunately* (pause), the message never arrived," "The

(2) if data is provided only by the introspection of the analyst, important aspects of syntax may be neglected because examples of those aspects fail to be recalled. As a consequence of such failures, invalid generalisations may be formulated.[1]

(3) if the corpus contains samples of varieties of the language, it may be possible to generalise about the frequency of occurrence of particular syntactic structures in such varieties.[2]

On the other hand, a description that is limited to material in a corpus is also inadequate, unless the analyst's aim is no more than a description of the syntax of the corpus or of an aspect of syntax found in the corpus. Inadequacies arise in the description because some syntactic structures are not represented in a finite corpus. The analyst may himself impose a further limitation. He may decide to note only those features that are present in the structures he observes in the corpus, ignoring the potential features that he can supply from his knowledge of the language. By taking into account both features that are present in the corpus and also those that are potential and in addition contributing specimens of language drawn from introspection, the linguist can avoid the disadvantages of a description restricted either to a corpus or to his own introspection.

Unless the linguist's aim is limited to a description of what he finds in a corpus, he is likely to be confronted with problems of acceptability. He may well find in his corpus constructions that he would not wish to include in his generalisations on the syntax of the language.[3] Furthermore, problems of acceptability arise when the linguist applies transformational tests to his material or lists potential features or wishes to supply a series of similar constructions from introspection. After a time his judgment is likely to become unsure and inconsistent. In any case, the linguist is not always reliable as his own informant. He tends to be biased towards a preconceived classification or explanation. Moreover, he is prejudiced in favour of orderly classification and neat rules. It is clear that there is a need for an objective method of assessing acceptability that the linguist can employ when he is in doubt.

---

message, *unfortunately*, never arrived," or "The message never arrived (pause), *unfortunately*." '

[1] Cf. Bolinger's criticism of an article by Lees for 'a certain proneness to skimp the specimen-gathering phase of our science and to base generalisations on insufficient data' (Bolinger 1961b, 366).

[2] See Svartvik 1966, 152–5 for an example of the value for this purpose of a corpus-based study.

[3] 'False starts, deviations from rules, changes of plan in mid-course, and so on' (Chomsky 1965, 4) may be of intrinsic interest as part of a study of performance. They may also tell us something about 'our internal mechanism for constructing sentences'. For some examples of the information they provide about this 'mechanism', see Quirk 1966, 842–8.

1*

For this study, experiments were conducted with informants to in-vestigate the acceptability of structures containing certain types of adverbs. Since it was not possible to conduct an experiment whenever problems of acceptability arose, I at times relied on the views of col-leagues, whom I consulted when I was in doubt. Some of these ac-ceptability experiments indirectly yielded information on differences between types of adverbs. Other experiments were specifically designed for this purpose.

1.2.1 Corpus data

The corpus of the Survey of English Usage comprises material repre-senting a number of varieties of educated British English, both written and spoken. The material consulted for this study was produced be-tween 1950 and 1966. It consists of twenty 'texts', each text being a con-tinuous stretch of about 5,000 words.[1]

In this study, quotations from Survey texts are provided with a re-ference to the number of the appropriate slip in the Survey files. Access to the Survey files at University College London will be possible for interested scholars. The twenty texts, totalling about 100,000 words, are grouped in Figure 1, and supplied with their Survey file references.

The notation of citations from Survey spoken material is a reduction of the system employed by the Survey. The full system is described in Crystal and Quirk 1964. I have omitted the features of the full system that are not relevant to this study. The omission of these features makes the citations easier to read and prevents the distraction of unnecessary detail. The following features are retained in this study, illustrated in the environment of the word *man*:

[1] The boundary of a tone unit is marked: *man#*
[2] The onset of a tone unit is marked: */man*
[3] 7 types of nuclear tone are recognised:
    [i] The simple fall is marked: *màn*
    [ii] The simple rise is marked: *mán*
    [iii] The simple level is marked: *mān*
    [iv] The rise-fall on one syllable is marked: *mân*
    [v] The fall-rise on one syllable is marked: *mǎn*
    [vi] The rise plus fall over more than one syllable is marked: *mán of wàr*
    [vii] The fall plus rise over more than one syllable is marked: *màn of wár*
[4] A pause equivalent to the speaker's rhythm unit is marked: *man* –

---

1 For the principles governing the compilation of material in the corpus, see Quirk 1960, 40–61 and Godfrey 1965, 98–103. Three of the texts (W6.1, 4c.1, and S.1b.6) are composite texts.

[5] Any detectable pause less than – is marked: *man* ·

[6] Words that are overlapped by the words of another speaker are marked: *man*

[7] Uncertainty over the presence of a nuclear tone or about the type of nuclear tone is marked: ?*màn*
The alternative reading is indicated in the margin, accompanied by a query

[8] Words that are unclear on the tape are marked: ((*man*))

[9] Word-fractions ('stammers' and the like) are marked: [*ma*] *man*

FIGURE I *Distribution of Survey texts*

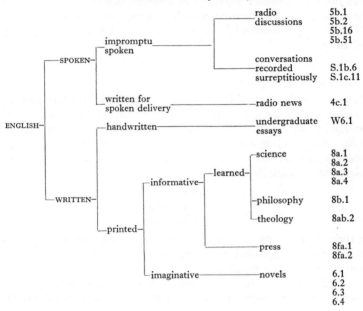

A short extract from a Survey text will illustrate most of the features that have been retained in the notation of spoken material:

```
? –    A  you're /[g] getting rìd of them ( (áre you# */?làter#) ·
? –       /?gòod#) )*
       B  */yès# ə it was /passed* at ði: ?ə ði ə sub committee last
          *Tùesday#*
       A  */that means* that there will be two questions ònly#
                                                        (S.1c.11–65)
```

The citations from British newspapers range over the period October 1965 – September 1967. The newspapers from which most examples have been collected are here listed together with the abbreviations that denote them in this study:

G   *The Guardian* (daily newspaper)
O   *The Observer* (Sunday newspaper)
OM   The magazine supplement of *The Observer*
ST   *The Sunday Times*
STM   The magazine supplement of *The Sunday Times*
TES   *The Times Educational Supplement* (weekly)

References to quotations from these newspapers give the symbol for the title first, followed by the date of publication. A colon follows and then two sets of figures, separated by commas, that refer to the page of the newspaper and to the column on that page respectively. For example, ST 21/8/66: 4, 6 denotes *The Sunday Times* of 21st August 1966, page 4, column 6.

1.2.2   Data from experiments

Material was also derived from experiments with native informants. In the experiments use was made, with some modifications, of techniques devised by Quirk and Svartvik (1966) for investigating linguistic accept- ability. Several groups of informants, mainly undergraduates, partici- pated in each of the three Batteries of tests. The total number of informants for each Battery was:

Battery I —85
Battery II —179
Battery III—117

In these experiments, the instructions were pre-recorded on tape and the informants responded in writing during intervals of silence timed from one instruction to the next.

Each Battery consisted of two sets of tests: (1) a Performance set, followed by (2) a Judgment set. The performance tests constitute an indirect method of eliciting informant reactions, whereas in judgment tests informants are asked explicitly for their reactions. Two types of per- formance tests were employed: (1) compliance tests and (2) completion tests, and two types of judgment tests: (1) evaluation tests and (2) simi- larity tests. Figure 2 represents the composition of Batteries II and III. (Completion tests were not included in Battery I.)

Compliance tests are operational tests. Informants are asked to per- form a simple grammatical operation on a 'test sentence', e.g. to turn in- to a question the test sentence *he will /probably stay làte#*. A mechanical performance of this operation would produce the 'target sentence' *Will he probably stay late?* If the 'response sentence', the sentence written down by the informant, is identical with the target sentence, it is regi-

FIGURE 2 *Composition of test Batteries*

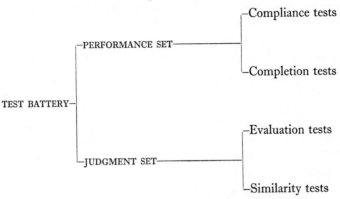

stered as 'compliant', while if it deviates from the target sentence it is registered as 'non-compliant'. Hesitations in response sentences are also recorded. Target sentences that are unacceptable in some way may be expected to evoke non-compliant responses and/or hesitations. Such changes and hesitations would be produced by informants in the course of a re-structuring of the test sentence.[1]

In completion tests, informants were given the opening words of a sentence and were asked to complete the sentence. For example, they were asked to complete the sentence beginning *I /bădly*. This test was intended as an indirect method of discovering what verbs or semantic groups of verbs collocate with certain intensifiers when these are in pre-verb position.[2]

In evaluation tests, informants were asked to judge the acceptability of sentences on a three-point scale of 'perfectly natural and normal', 'wholly unnatural and abnormal', and 'somewhere between'. In many cases test sentences from the compliance set were repeated in the evaluation set, though sometimes informants were presented with the form of the target sentence. In all such cases, it was possible to correlate the results of the two types of tests.

Similarity tests required from informants a judgment of the similarity of meaning of two sentences, again on a three-point scale: 'very similar in meaning', 'very different in meaning', and 'somewhere between'. The tests relevant to this study presented informants with pairs

---

1 See Quirk and Svartvik 1966 for a detailed discussion of principles and methods of investigating linguistic acceptability. For modifications in the techniques that have been introduced subsequently, see forthcoming papers from the Survey of English Usage.
2 For a detailed account of the results of these tests, see Greenbaum 1969a.

of sentences which were identical except that the adverb was in a different position in each of the sentences. For example, informants were asked to judge the similarity of meaning of the sentences:

your /children cértainly dislìked me#
/cĕrtainly# your /children dislìked me#

Because of a technical error, the results of only sixty-four informants are available for the similarity tests in Battery I. In many cases, the similarity test paralleled a compliance test and an evaluation test given earlier in the Battery, as indeed in this particular instance. Informants had previously been asked to perform a grammatical operation on the sentence:

/cĕrtainly# your /children cértainly dislìked me#

They were subsequently required to judge the acceptability of this sentence in an evaluation test. It was hypothesised that in a series of test sentences with repeated adverbs the results would demonstrate that the greater the similarity in function of the two uses of the adverb the greater would be the unacceptability of a sentence in which the two instances co-occur. We might expect a sentence in which the adverb was repeated to be unacceptable on stylistic grounds. When the two instances of the adverb have similar functions, the sentence is unacceptable not only for stylistic reasons but also for semantic reasons, since the repetition of the adverb is tautologous.[1]

---

[1] There is no objection in some cases to a repetition of an adverb if the two instances appear consecutively – either immediately juxtaposed or linked by *and*. The repetition may be intended to convey emphasis, as in the following headline, which probably echoes a popular song:

Mr Macleod triumphs softly, softly   (G 17/3/66: 6, 5)

Or the repetition may indicate a series, as in *They asked him again and again*, or as in the well-known instance from the last act of Shakespeare's *Macbeth:*

Tomorrow, and tomorrow, and tomorrow,
Creeps in this petty pace from day to day,
To the last syllable of recorded time

Chapter 2

Isolation of conjunctive/disjunctive functions of adverb

I shall examine the syntactic features of a range of items that are traditionally classed as adverbs. I shall first isolate those adverbs that appear to be the most 'peripheral' in the clause, though we must bear in mind that there is a gradient of integration of adverbs in the clause and not a sharp break between the integrated and the unintegrated.[1] I shall then contrast some of the adverbs that have been isolated with other items which they resemble in some syntactic features.

2.1 Conjuncts, disjuncts, and adjuncts

Let us start by considering a range of adverbs. Since items that are identical in their written and spoken form may differ in their function, it is not possible merely to list the items. They must be quoted in context, so that it is clear in which function the item is being tested. Both here and elsewhere in this study the item on which attention is to be focused is italicised. Unless the contrary is stated, such italicising does not represent italicising in the original.

I shall apply tests to adverbs in a number of clauses. The tests are designed to determine the presence or absence of certain syntactic features of the adverbs. The result of each test provides a criterion by which some adverbs may be distinguished from others.

For convenience in applying the tests, the citations represent, with one exception, finite verb clauses that are declarative and affirmative. If an adverb appears in other forms of the clause, it is necessary to make

---

[1] See Hudson 1967, 246, who contrasts examples of two types of Adjunct, describing one as a relatively 'integral' part of the clause and the other as a relatively 'peripheral' part. A distinction between nuclear and peripheral parts of the clause has also been advanced by Longacre 1964, 48ff.

the appropriate transformations to a finite verb clause in the declarative and affirmative form before the tests can be applied. For example,
let us suppose that we are looking at the adverb *frankly* in the sentence
Looking her up and down frankly, he expressed his admiration. Let us
further suppose that we are testing whether *frankly* can appear in initial
position in the clause. Before we apply our test, we must transform the
non-finite verb clause *Looking her up and down frankly* into the corresponding finite verb clause *He was looking her up and down frankly.* When
we now apply the test, we see that the initial position is unacceptable for
frankly, if, of course, we hold constant the semantic force of *frankly*.

One clause that is cited is negative. The exception is citation [i], which
contains the negative adverb *never*. I take account of the exceptional
character of the negative adverb in defining some of the criteria.

I have displayed the results of the tests in a matrix table, Table 1
(page 23). Both citations and criteria are numbered. In the matrix table
the criteria numbers are set out at the heads of columns, while the citation numbers are listed at the left of the table together with the items
that are being tested. If an item satisfies a criterion, this is indicated by a
'+' in the cell at which the horizontal level of the item and the vertical
column of the criterion meet. If it fails to satisfy the criterion, a '−' is
entered, and if the test is not applicable, a '/' is used to indicate this. A
query denotes some doubt over the entry that has been chosen.

Items that have a similar pattern of entries are grouped together in the
table. Horizontal lines separate the groups of items. I should emphasise
that the criteria have been selected to isolate the adverbs that are most
peripheral in the clause. Different groupings would result from a different choice of criteria, and additional criteria would separate items that
have been grouped together in the table.

2.1.1   Citations

Quotation marks denote the extent of the citation to which the tests
should be applied, if they are not to be applied to the citation as a whole.

[a]   '*Briefly*, India faces famine' because there are too many people
      and too little food.   (STM 26/3/67: 34, 1)
[b]   He'd *probably* enjoy it.   (6.1.26-3)
[c]   *Again*, the Holy Spirit bears His testimony in and through the
      word of the Church: . . .   (8ab.2.143-4)
[d]   *However*, the analogy is helpful, . . .   (8a.3.32-4)
[e]   M.P.s will *now* have to wait until next year for any rise in their
      salaries.   (8fa.2.7)
[f]   The hair at the back of his neck was *also* an unpleasing sight.
                                                        (6.4.46-4)
[g]   Fights with dragons, chases after damsels are *usually* incidents in
      the main story. . . .   (W6.1b-6)

[h] '*Technically*, it is feasible today' to transmit text and pictures, . . .
          (ST 8/1/67: 11, 8)
[i] an object can *never* be a concept . . .   (8b.1.152-2)
[j] Carfax and Viola had *already* met on this point, . . .
          (6.2.103-3)
[k] I *always* have tea in town on Mondays, . . .   (6.2.91-3)
[l] /I will déal# with /that nòw#   (5b.51.21)
[m] there'll be widespread frost tonìght#   (4c.1-18)
[n] *Outside* the evening was cold and wet, . . .   (6.2.96-2)
[o] They both sat *there*, . . .   (6.4.48-2)
[p] /I've got · *only* twò chíldren#   (5b.16.35)
[q] Centuries before 'it *first* became the cathedral of the new diocese of Bristol in 1542' the church of the Abbey of St Augustine had been a centre of worship and learning.   (8fa.1-48)
[r] it may /wéll be absurd#   (5b.2.4)
[s] I will burn the church *down*.   (8fa.2.39)
[t] /we àre agreed# en/tìrely#   (5b.16.11)
[u] the /government promised · compensǎtion# · /làter#[1] (4c.1a-16)
[v] I've /got some hére#   (S.1c.11–30)
[w] He looked her up and down *frankly*.   (6.4.48-1)

---

[1] There is an ambiguity in the function of *later* in [u], which remains even if one knows the context from which the citation was taken. The more probable interpretation of the sentence is 'The government promised that there would be compensation later' and it is according to this interpretation that the adverb is tested. The other interpretation is obligatory if the adverb is transposed to before the Subject or verb, e.g. 'The government later promised compensation'.

Later, in the first interpretation, is related to the Complement of the clause, *compensation*, rather than to the clause as a whole. Indeed, one can analyse *compensation later* as a verbless clause, itself functioning as Complement.

Another illustration, this time with an adverb of place, can be cited from the Survey corpus:

/this is sómething# that /we condèmn# in /South África# when it /comes to ràces# – we /ought to condémn it# /here in Brìtain# · when it /comes to ìncomes#   (5b.1.14)

We may notice that it is only the context that determines the function of *here*. We can contrast:

In many countries people approve of violence, but we condemn it *here*.

With prepositional phrases that are related to a Complement, there may be neutralisation between Adjunct and postmodifier functions if the Complement has as its head a noun:

We ought to condemn racial violence *in Britain*.

There is indeterminancy in the description of the function of the prepositional phrase. The slight difference in nuance may be conveyed by the paraphrases 'We ought to condemn racial violence *when it occurs in Britain*' for Adjunct function, and 'We ought to condemn racial violence *which occurs in Britain*' for postmodifying function. For those who would accept in their analysis of English the postmodification of pronouns by adverbs, a similar neutralisation would happen in such cases:

2.1.2   Criteria

CRITERION I. To satisfy this criterion, the item must be unacceptable in initial position in the clause, i.e. in a position preceding Subject, Verb, and (if present) Complement. Thus, in the following sentences, *down* satisfies this criterion, but not *probably*:

Down he burnt the church.
Probably he burnt the church.

A condition of this criterion is that it be tested with normal Subject-Verb order. If the item can only occur in initial position with Verb-Subject inversion, then it also satisfies this criterion. For example, *never* and *well* in the following sentences

An object can *never* be a concept.
It may *well* be absurd.

satisfy this criterion because when they are transported to initial position Verb-Subject inversion is obligatory:

Never can an object be a concept.
Well may it be absurd.

The mobility test cannot, of course, be applied mechanically, either for this criterion or for the subsequent criteria, since transposition of an item may result in a change of its syntactic function. For example, the sentence *Well it may be absurd* is acceptable though *well* is in initial position, but we then have a function of *well* that is different from the function of *well* in the sentence *It may well be absurd*. We recognise the difference between the functions of the two instances of *well* because of the semantic difference between the two sentences. In some cases, however, it is not immediately obvious whether the semantic change result-

---

We ought to condemn it *here*.
We may refer here to the example cited by Chomsky:
I read the book *in England*.
He interprets this as deriving 'from an underlying structure very much like the one that underlies "I read the book while (I was) in England"' (Chomsky 1965, 219). If we replace *read* by *have*, there must be a very different interpretation:
I have the book *in England*.
This carries the implication that 'I' am outside England while the book is in England.
Verbs like *promise* in that they will allow a relationship of an adverb of time and place to the Complement as exemplified in [u] have two semantic features: [1] they constitute an act of saying or thinking, and [2] they contain a future reference. Verbs in this class include: *advise, announce, anticipate, ask for, await, contemplate, declare, desire, expect, forecast, foresee, hope for, invite, look for, look forward to, offer, pledge, predict, prepare for, prophesy, promise, propose, suggest, threaten, urge, want, warn of, wish*.

ing from transposition is sufficient to warrant ascribing different functions to the items in the two positions. For example, we may be in doubt whether the two instances of *certainly* have identical functions in the pair of sentences:

> *Certainly* we ought to condemn it.
> We *certainly* ought to condemn it.

Problems of this nature are discussed later in this study (pages 127ff.).

CRITERION 2. To satisfy this criterion, the item must be unacceptable in initial position when the clause is negated. For the purpose of this criterion, clause negation is limited to negation by *not* or enclitic *n't*. Thus, *always* satisfies this criterion, but not *probably*:

> *Always he doesn't want it.
> *Probably* he doesn't want it.

The negative adverb *never*, which cannot co-occur with this form of clause negation, also satisfies the criterion.

To satisfy this criterion, the item must be unacceptable in front of the particular negated clause produced by a transformation of the clause cited. It is possible, for example, that in certain restricted contexts *already* may appear in front of a negated clause. In the particular clause cited, however, this position is unacceptable for *already*:

> *Already Carfax and Viola had not met on this point.

Hence, *already* satisfies the criterion.[1]

CRITERION 3. To satisfy this criterion, the item must be unacceptable in initial position if it is in an independent tone unit and carries a rising, falling-rising, or level nuclear tone. For example, *again* with the meaning 'once more' satisfies this criterion because it cannot appear in initial position under these conditions. On the other hand, *again* with the meaning 'furthermore' fails to satisfy the criterion. It can appear in initial position under these conditions, e.g.:

> a/gǎin# he /played quite wèll#

An item fails to satisfy this criterion if it can take any one of the three

---

[1] Some instances occur in the material I have examined of adverbs preceding negative clauses contrary to normal usage with such adverbs, e.g.:

> *Phlegmatically*, Samkange doesn't know who to blame, 'our rivals? our opponents?' (G 28/2/67: 8, 6)

> Quite a few other lordly members are saying flatly that this isn't the sort of business their House should be tackling: *conservatively*, they don't like aping the Commons; *proudly*, they don't like doing re-runs of waning controversies; *patriotically*, they don't like talking too much about this security business. (G 1/7/67: 6, 6)

nuclear tones that have been specified. For example, the transitional conjunct *now* fails to satisfy the criterion even though it does not seem possible to give it a falling-rising nuclear tone (cf. §3.3.3.2 pages 55ff.).

CRITERION 4. To satisfy this criterion, the item must be able to serve as the focus of clause interrogation. The focus of clause interrogation is that part of the clause that is being questioned. An item is shown to be capable of serving as the focus of clause interrogation if it can be contrasted with another item in alternative interrogation, the two clauses otherwise being identical. For example, *politely* in the sentence

He replied to them *politely*.

satisfies the criterion, since it can be contrasted in alternative interrogation:

Did he reply to them *politely* or did he reply to them *rudely*?

Since the two clauses are identical except for the replacement of *politely* by another item in the second clause, it is clear that the only part of the first clause that is being questioned is *politely*. On the other hand, *probably* cannot serve as the focus of clause interrogation.

For the purpose of the test, it is not essential that the items should be completely antonymous. For example, *sometimes* satisfies the criterion because it can be contrasted with, among others, *never*:

Did he *sometimes* reply politely or did he *never* reply politely?

The alternative interrogation may be more acceptable if the second item is restricted by *only*, e.g.:

Did he *usually* reply immediately or did he *only occasionally* reply immediately?[1]

CRITERION 5. To satisfy this criterion, the item must be able to serve as the focus of clause negation. We apply a test similar to the test for Criterion 4. We see whether the item can be contrasted with another item in alternative negation. For example, *always* in the sentence

He *always* replied politely.

satisfies this criterion, since it can be contrasted in alternative negation:

He did not *always* reply politely, but he did reply politely *sometimes*.

---

[1] Contrastive focusing may be a useful method of establishing semantic sets of adverbs. For example, the alternative interrogation

*Did he reply *politely* or did he reply *immediately*?

is semantically unacceptable in English, indicating that the two adverbs belong to different semantic sets.

Once again, *probably* fails to satisfy this criterion.

If the verb group in the second clause does not have an auxiliary, the sentence may be more acceptable when the emphatic auxiliary *do* is supplied.

CRITERION 6. To satisfy this criterion, the item must be able to be focused by *only* in initial position and allow in consequence Verb-Subject inversion. An item is focused by *only* when the semantic restriction indicated by *only* applies to that item alone. Thus, *occasionally* satisfies this criterion, but not *usually*, e.g.:

> *Only occasionally* did he reply politely.
> *Only usually did he reply politely.

Like several of the other criteria, this is a composite criterion. Some adverbs, including *usually*, cannot be focused by *only* even when positioned elsewhere.[1]

CRITERION 7. To satisfy this criterion, the item must be able to serve as the sole focus of a 'cleft sentence' (cf. Lees 1963a, 371ff.). An item is the sole focus of a cleft sentence when it is the only item selected in the focal clause. Thus, from the sentence

> *Yesterday* John replied politely.

we may select *yesterday*, among other items, for sole focus when we transform the sentence into a cleft sentence:

> *It was yesterday that* John replied politely.

Yesterday therefore satisfies this criterion. On the other hand, if the sentence is

> *Usually* John replied politely.

we cannot select *usually* for sole focus:

> **It was usually that* John replied politely.

Therefore *usually* does not satisfy the criterion.[2]

---

[1] Some adverbs will allow Verb-Subject inversion when focused by other restrictives, e.g.

> *Particularly politely* did he reply on that occasion.

or when focused by some additives, e.g.

> *Equally politely* did he reply on that occasion.

[2] Some adverbs, including *usually*, cannot be the sole focus of a cleft sentence, yet may appear within the focal clause when another item is the focus, e.g.:

> *It was usually John who* replied politely.

The transposition of *usually*, in our example, to initial position does not appear to affect the meaning of the sentence:

CRITERION 8. To satisfy this criterion, the item must be able to serve as a response to an interrogative transformation of the clause introduced by *When, Where, How,* or *Why, i.e.* to a *wh-* question. For example, from

> *Yesterday* he replied politely.

we may formulate the question and answer

> *When* did he reply politely? *Yesterday.*

Thus, *yesterday* satisfies the criterion. On the other hand, from the sentence

> *Usually* he replied politely.

we cannot formulate the question and answer

> *When* did he reply politely? *Usually.*

Therefore *usually* does not satisfy the criterion.

CRITERION 9. To satisfy this criterion, the item must be able to accept premodification by *How* in an interrogative or exclamatory transformation of the clause. For example, *politely* satisfies this criterion, but not *yesterday*:

> *How politely* did he reply?
>
> *How politely* he replied!
>
> *How yesterday* did he reply?
>
> *How yesterday* he replied!

CRITERION 10. To satisfy this criterion, the item must be able to serve as the focus of clause comparison with the correlatives *more . . . than.* For the second clause a contrasted Subject is to be supplied, and also an auxiliary, to be determined by the verb group in the preceding clause. For example, in the following sentence *politely* satisfies the criterion, since we can expand the sentence

> He replied *politely.*

> *Usually* it was John who replied politely.

Some adverbs can be the sole focus as well as the accompaniment of the focus, e.g. *often*:

> *It was often that* John replied politely.
>
> *It was often John who* replied politely.

On the other hand, other adverbs may be the sole focus but normally they cannot accompany the focus, *e.g. yesterday*:

> *It was yesterday that* John replied politely.
>
> *It was yesterday John who* replied politely.

into

He replied *more politely than she did.*

On the other hand, *usually* does not satisfy the criterion, as we can see from the unacceptability of the sentence:

*He replied *more usually than she did.*

For the application of this test there is no need, of course, to supply comparative *more* if the item is inflected for comparison, e.g. *oftener*, or if there is a suppletive form, e.g. *better*.[1]

TABLE I *Matrix for range of adverbs*

		1	2	3	4	5	6	7	8	9	10
[a]	briefly	−	−	−	−	−	−	−	−	−	−
[b]	probably	−	−	−	−	−	−	−	−	−	−
[c]	again	−	−	−	−	−	−	−	−	−	−
[d]	however	−	−	−	−	−	−	−	−	−	−
[e]	now	−	−	−	−	−	−	−	−	−	−
[f]	also	−	−	+	−	−	−	−	−	−	−
[g]	usually	−	−	−	+	+	−	−	−	−	−
[h]	technically	−	−	−	+	+	?+	?+	−	−	−
[i]	never	+	+	−	+	−	−	−	?−	−	−
[j]	already	−	+	−	−	−	−	−	−	−	−
[k]	always	−	+	−	+	+	−	−	?−	−	−
[l]	now	−	−	−	+	+	−	+	+	−	−
[m]	tonight	−	−	−	+	+	+	+	+	−	−
[n]	outside	−	−	−	+	+	+	+	+	−	−
[o]	there	−	?+	−	+	+	+	+	+	−	−
[p]	only	+	+	+	−	−	/	−	−	−	−
[q]	first	+	+	+	−	−	−	−	−	−	−
[r]	well	+	+	+	−	−	−	−	−	−	−
[s]	down	+	+	+	−	−	−	−	−	−	−
[t]	entirely	+	+	+	+	+	−	−	−	?+	−
[u]	later	+	+	+	+	+	−	−	−	−	−
[v]	here	+	+	+	+	+	+	+	+	−	−
[w]	frankly	+	+	+	+	+	−	+	?+	+	+

[1] Certain degree intensifiers can serve as the focus of clause comparison with the correlatives *as . . . as*, though not with the correlatives *more . . . than*. *Totally* is an example:

He rejected the suggestion *as totally as she did.*

*He rejected the suggestion *more totally than she did.*

2.1.3 Classification

Table 1 demonstrates that items [a] – [e], the top group, may be isolated from the other items in the Table by their failure to satisfy the first
three criteria plus either Criterion 4 or Criterion 5. Consequently, we
can regard the failure to satisfy the first five criteria as diagnostic for
membership of the top group. We can reduce the number of diagnostic
criteria by setting up a composite criterion to embrace the first three
criteria. On the basis of this composite criterion and Criteria 4 and 5 we
can then separate items that are to be classed with [a] – [e] in the Table
from those to be classed with [f] – [w].

An adverb that satisfies at least one of the three diagnostic criteria to
be listed will be said to have an 'adjunctive' function in the clause:

Diagnostic Criterion 1. The item must be unacceptable in initial
position in an independent tone unit with a rising, falling-rising, or level
nuclear tone when the clause is negated (Criteria 1, 2, and 3, pages 18ff.).

Diagnostic Criterion 2. The item must be able to serve as the focus of
clause interrogation, as demonstrated by its ability to be contrasted with
another focus in alternative interrogation (Criterion 4, page 20).

Diagnostic Criterion 3. The item must be able to serve as the focus of
clause negation, as demonstrated by its ability to be contrasted with another focus in alternative negation (Criterion 5, page 20).

Adverbs having an adjunctive function in the clause are said to be
ADJUNCTS of the clause.

As a corollary, an adverb that satisfies all of the following diagnostic
criteria is not an adjunct:

Diagnostic Criterion 1a. It is acceptable in initial position in an independent tone unit with a rising, falling-rising, or level nuclear tone when
the clause is negated.

Diagnostic Criterion 2a. It cannot be the focus of clause interrogation,
as demonstrated by its inability to be contrasted with another focus in
alternative interrogation.

Diagnostic Criterion 3a. It cannot be the focus of clause negation, as
demonstrated by its inability to be contrasted with another focus in
alternative negation.

Let us look again at citations [a] – [e], which contain adverbs that
satisfy Diagnostic Criteria 1a, 2a, and 3a:

[a] '*Briefly*, India faces famine' because there are too many people and
      too little food.   (STM 26/3/67: 34, 1)
[b] He'd *probably* enjoy it.   (6.1.26-3)
[c] *Again*, the Holy Spirit bears His testimony in and through the
      word of the Church: . . .   (8ab.2.143-4)
[d] *However*, the analogy is helpful, . . .   (8a.3.32-4)

[e] M.P.s will *now* have to wait until next year for any rise in their
salaries. (8fa.2.7)

Semantically, *briefly* in [a] and *probably* in [b] express an evaluation of
what is being said with respect either to the form of the communication
or to its content. On the other hand, *again, however*, and *now* indicate
some connection with what has been said before. By analogy with the
terms 'adjunctive' and 'adjunct', the class of items represented by
briefly and *probably* is said to have a 'disjunctive' function and the items
are designated DISJUNCTS (a term suggesting their lack of integration
within the clause to which they are subordinate), while the class of items
represented by *again, however*, and *now* is said to have a 'conjunctive'
function and the items are termed CONJUNCTS.

The two classes are differentiated syntactically by a simple test: disjuncts can serve as a response to a *yes-no* question, though sometimes
they require to be accompanied by *yes* or *no*; conjuncts cannot serve as a
response to a *yes-no* question even if accompanied by *yes* or *no*. Thus,
briefly in [a] is a disjunct because it satisfies Diagnostic Criteria 1a-3a
and because it may serve as a response:

Does India face famine? *Briefly, yes.*

On the other hand, *however* is a conjunct because it satisfies Diagnostic
Criteria 1a-3a but cannot serve as a response:

Is the analogy helpful? **However, yes.*

2.2 Immobile conjuncts and immobile items of other classes

Some conjuncts are restricted to initial position. These are designated
'immobile conjuncts'. It is necessary to distinguish these from items of
other classes that are likewise restricted to initial position. Initial position, it will be recalled, is defined as a position preceding Subject, Verb,
and Complement.

2.2.1 Immobile conjuncts

There are two sub-classes of immobile conjuncts:

[1] *yet, so* – sole members of the sub-class
[2] *besides, hence* – which may be taken as representative of the second
sub-class (comprising all immobile conjuncts apart from *yet* and
so)

Their use is illustrated in the following citations:

[1a] it is evident that we cannot completely 'kill' the eddy-currents
and *yet* keep the ferro-magnetism. (8a.3.32-1)

[1b] In a kind of world like that of a dream there is no future, no conceivable progression, and *so* all the emphasis must be on the
present, . . .   (W6.1-11)

[2a] 'Isn't there a *man* [ital. sic] about?' cried Dinah, breaking to
voice all this. 'Are there *no* [ital. sic] men in this village? Can't
you fetch your *gardener* [ital. sic]?'

  'He's seventy-three,' said Madeleine. '*Besides*, he's gone to the
football match. I think everybody has.'   (6.1.26-2)

[2b] The addition-complex then becomes a chain-carrier, leading to
kinetics of the type expressed by equation (14), and *hence* this
modification is consistent with the observed kinetics.

               (8a.4.38-5)

The two sub-classes are distinguished by one syntactic feature: only
yet and *so*, members of the first sub-class, will allow the ellipsis of the
Subject of the clause they introduce when the Subject is identical with
that of the previous clause. This is a feature that they have in common
with the conjunctions *and*, *or*, and *but*. Thus, we can omit *and* from
citation [1a]:

It is evident that we cannot completely 'kill' the eddy-currents *yet*
keep the ferro-magnetism.

Though *and* has been omitted it is still possible to have the ellipsis of the
Subject. On the other hand, if we adapt citation [2a] containing *besides*,
we see that the second Subject cannot be omitted although it is identical
with the first:

*He's seventy-three, *besides* has gone to the football match.

We can omit the Subject only if we add one of the conjunctions that
allow such ellipsis:

He's seventy-three, *and besides* has gone to the football match.

We may add as a contrast:

He's seventy-three, *yet* has gone to the football match.[1]

---

[1] We are concerned here with finite verb clauses. A zero Subject is possible in
non-finite verb clauses and in verbless clauses to a much greater extent. Most
conjunctions (excluding *for* and causal *as*, causal *since*, and *whereas*) may introduce non-finite verb and verbless clauses with zero Subject. This also seems
possible for *hence*.

 The Subject is probably less often elided with *so* when it introduces a finite
verb clause, but this is one of several instances in the Survey corpus:

On the other hand, regions such as FGH are found to correspond to *maxima*
[ital. sic] of *g* [ital. sic], *so* are analogous to points such as Z in fig. 3(a), and,
can, therefore, in no circumstances be physically realisable.   (8a.3.28-2)

This distinctive feature of *yet* and *so* is reflected in punctuation. Like the traditional class of conjunctions (with which they are sometimes placed), *yet* and *so* may be separated from the previous clause merely by a comma, and sometimes no punctuation is inserted. All other conjuncts in initial position (when not following a conjunction) are normally preceded by a more major mark of punctuation. There is some slight evidence of this punctuation difference in the Survey corpus, but the numbers involved are very small. Table 2 shows that there are eleven instances where a conjunct is preceded by a comma or is not preceded by any mark of punctuation, in all such cases the conjunct being in initial position without a preceding conjunction. In the six instances involving *then*, the previous clause is subordinate to the clause headed by the conjunct. Since comma or zero punctuation would be common anyway in such circumstances, the punctuation is not necessarily related to the presence of the conjunct *then*, and therefore can be discounted for our purpose. That leaves five instances, three with *so*, one with *yet*, and one with *meanwhile*.

TABLE 2 *Punctuation preceding initial conjuncts*

Full-stop	Semi-colon	Bracket	Dash	Comma	Zero	Total	
104	5	1	1	8	3	122	all conjuncts
13				4	2	19	*then*
8				2	1	11	*so*
9	1			1		11	*yet*
3				1		4	*meanwhile*

2.2.2 Immobile conjuncts and other immobile items

Several classes are restricted to initial position:

[a] immobile conjuncts
[b] conjunctions, e.g. *and, for, if*
[c] reaction signals, e.g. *no, yes* (including variants such as *yeah* or *yep*), *m* (including its many variants, e.g. /mhm̀#/ or /hm̆#/)
[d] initiators,[1] e.g. *well, oh, ah*

In Table 3 the following criteria are applied to members of these four classes:

[1] they may serve as initiators of conversations
[2] they may serve as response utterance, i.e. sole item in a response

---

[1] The term 'initiator' is employed to differentiate them from the reaction signals. As Table 3 indicates they also function as reactions to a previous utterance.

TABLE 3 *Classes of items restricted to initial position*

	1	2
[a] immobile conjuncts	−	−
[b] conjunctions	−	−
[c] reaction signals	−	+
[d] initiators	+	+

Both conjunctions and immobile conjuncts fail to satisfy these two criteria. Their failure to do so reflects their common function as connectives.

2.2.3 Conjunctions

Before we can differentiate between immobile conjuncts and conjunctions, we shall have to look at some of the ways in which conjunctions differ from each other. I exclude, for the present, correlative conjunctions (cf. pages 33f.).

And, or, but, for, and *so that* (meaning 'with the result that') differ from other conjunctions in not allowing a conjunction to precede them. Thus, these sentences are unacceptable:

[1] *They sold the land *and, but* he objected, they gave away the money.

[2] *At first they decided to postpone the launching, *but, for* the President insisted, they launched it later that day.

[3] *He asked to be transferred to a new bank *because, and* the new machine worked well, there was nothing for him to do at his present post.

On the other hand, the remaining conjunctions will allow another conjunction to precede them, as becomes clear if we substitute them for the second conjunction in each of the above sentences:

[1a] They sold the land *and, although* he objected, they gave away the money.

[2a] At first they decided to postpone the launching, *but, since* the President insisted, they launched it later that day.

[3a] He asked to be transferred to a new bank *because, if* the new machine worked well, there was nothing for him to do at his present post.

In this respect *although, since,* and *if* are typical of all the conjunctions apart from the five we have specified.[1]

---

[1] I am, of course, considering cases where the conjunctions are linking clauses. *And,* for example, will readily link two conjunctions:

I shall be ready for him, *if and when* he comes.

A corollary of what has been said is that clauses introduced by these five conjunctions cannot be linked to each other by another conjunction. Thus, the following sentence is unacceptable:

[3b] *He asked to be transferred to a new bank, *for* he was unhappy *and for* there was nothing for him to do at his present post.

However, if *for* is replaced by *because*, the sentence becomes acceptable:

[3c] He asked to be transferred to a new bank, *because* he was unhappy *and because* there was nothing for him to do at his present post.

Similarly, the following sentence is unacceptable

*He saved a lot of money *so that* he had plenty to spare *and so that* I felt I could ask him for a loan.

though we may have the two sentences:

He saved a lot of money *so that* he had plenty to spare.
He saved a lot of money *so that* I felt I could ask him for a loan.

Another feature that the five conjunctions have in common is that a clause introduced by one of them cannot be transposed. In the sentence

[1b] They gave away the money, *but* he did not receive any.

the clause introduced by *but* is sequentially related to the previous clause and cannot be transposed to a position before or within that clause.[1] On the other hand, clauses introduced by other conjunctions are usually mobile. Thus, the clause introduced by *although* in [1a] can be transposed to follow its superordinate clause:

[1c] They gave away the money, *although* he objected.[2]

And, or, and *but* have in common that they allow ellipsis of the Subject of the clause they introduce when the Subject is identical with that of the

---

[1] The expression 'sequentially related' is borrowed from Svartvik 1966, 32.
[2] The distinction that we have made is not invalidated by the fact that such subordinate clauses may be immobile in certain circumstances. The point is that clauses introduced by *and, or, but, for,* and resultative *so that* are never mobile. For the term 'superordinate', see Crystal and Quirk 1964, 52. The criteria I have mentioned so far are to be found in Jacobson 1964, 25 note 36: 'The criteria here used to define coordinating conjunctions as opposed to conjunctive adverbs are the following: coordinating conjunctions always stand between the elements they connect and they never immediately precede each other. The first of these criteria also applies to such a conjunctive adverb as *so,* but not the second, for we can very well say *and so.*' Jacobson includes among coordinating conjunctions what I term the concessive conjunct *only* (cf. page 62). It seems to me possible for *but* to precede *only* in this function.

previous clause. This is a feature that they share with *yet* and *so* (cf. page 26). In their inability to allow ellipsis of the Subject, *for* and *so that* differ from the other three conjunctions. We may contrast:

> He did not contribute, *but* objected to the way they distributed the money.
> *He did not contribute, *for* objected to the way they distributed the money.
> *He did not contribute, *so that* had plenty of money to spare.

In this respect, *for* and *so that* are like all the other conjunctions.

Conjunctions that may be preceded by *and* or *or* do not, in such cases, allow ellipsis of the Subject, e.g.:

> *He sang a song *because* he wanted to please the guests *and because* felt happy.

In this respect, these conjunctions differ from immobile conjuncts like *hence* and *besides* that allow ellipsis of the Subject when preceded by *and*, *or*, or *but*, e.g.:

> He felt happy *and besides* wanted to please the guests.
> He wanted to please the guests *and hence* sang a song.

And and *or* differ in several respects from all the other conjunctions, including *but*. Halliday has pointed to one feature. He asserts that only *and* and *or* are 'pure' co-ordinators, whereas *but* is one of several 'portmanteau items', defined as 'those that contain the component *and*, such that *a b but c* is interpreted as "a and b, but c", etc.' (Halliday 1967b, 220). Thus, the sentence

> I shall phone him, I shall write to him, *or* I shall visit him.

is interpreted as

> I shall phone him, *or* I shall write to him, *or* I shall visit him.

whereas the sentence

> I shall phone him, I shall write to him, *but* I shall not visit him.

is interpreted as

> I shall phone him, *and* I shall write to him, *but* I shall not visit him.

And and *or* may link two clauses introduced by any conjunctions apart from *and*, *or*, *but*, *for*, and resultative *so that*. For example, *and* may link two *if*-clauses:

> They will sell the land *if* they get the money *and if* he doesn't object.

However, usually *but* cannot perform this function:

*They will sell the land *if* they get the money *but if* he doesn't object.[1]

And and *or* may link two interrogative clauses, e.g.:

Did she wash the dishes *and* did he dry them?
Shall I wash the dishes *or* shall I dry them?

But may not generally link two interrogative clauses. In an evaluation test only 45 per cent of the informants accepted the sentence:

/did she wash the cúp# but /he refuse to drínk from it#

On the other hand, linkage by *but* appears to be acceptable if the two clauses have the same Subject and the Subject and auxiliary are omitted from the second clause. Thus, 74 per cent of the same informants accepted the sentence:

/did John break the wíndow# /but refuse to páy for it#[2]

In Table 4 the gradient from co-ordination to subordination is displayed.[3] Six criteria are used in constructing the matrix:

[1] the conjunction is immobile in front of its clause
[2] the conjunction with its clause cannot be transposed before a previous independent clause[4]
[3] the conjunction (when introducing a clause) does not allow another conjunction to precede it
[4] the conjunction allows the ellipsis of the Subject of the clause it introduces when the Subject is identical with that of the previous clause
[5] the conjunction may link two interrogative clauses[5]

---

[1] The sentence would become acceptable if *not* or an additive such as *equally* or a restrictive such as *only* is added before the second *if*, e.g.:

They will sell the land *if* they get the money *but only if* he doesn't object.

The second *if*-clause is not now linked to the preceding clause but to *only*, which is here a verbless clause, with zero items shared with the superordinate clause. Restoration of the ellipted items produces the sentence:

They will sell the land *if* they get the money *but they will only sell the land if* he doesn't object.

One exceptional case has been noticed. *But* can link two clauses introduced by conjunctions if one is headed by *before* and the other by *after*:

They will sell the land *after* he comes *but before* she arrives.

[2] For a detailed analysis of the experimental evidence relating to this problem of acceptability, see Greenbaum 1969b.
[3] For the concept 'gradience', see Bolinger 1961a, and Quirk 1965, 208ff.
[4] The registration of ± in the matrix table takes account of cases where the conjunction does not satisfy this criterion, although it does so in other environments.
[5] The registration of ± for *but* takes account of the result of the evaluation test for one form of such a sentence.

[6] when the conjunction appears in the sequence 'clause *a*, clause *b*, conjunction clause *c*', the meaning is the same as 'clause *a* conjunction clause *b* conjunction clause *c*'

TABLE 4 *Co-ordination-subordination gradient*

	1	2	3	4	5	6
and, or	+	+	+	+	+	+
but	+	+	+	+	±	—
for, so that	+	+	+	—	—	—
other conjunctions	+	±	—	—	—	—

We can see from this matrix table that there is a gradient from the 'pure' co-ordinators *and* and *or* to the 'pure' subordinators, such as *if* and *because*, with *but, for*, and *so that* on the gradient. In this study the term 'co-ordinator' will only be applied to *and, or*, and *but*. Other conjunctions will be termed 'subordinators'.

2.2.4 Immobile conjuncts and conjunctions
We are now in a position to differentiate between immobile conjuncts and conjunctions. We may remember that, apart from immobility in initial position, they have in common two negative features (see pages 27f.):

[i] they may not serve as initiators of conversations
[ii] they may not serve as response utterances

The first two columns of Table 5, columns i and ii, register entries for these two features. Columns 1–4 register entries for the first four features set out above in Table 4. Column 7 registers whether the item allows ellipsis of the Subject if it is preceded by one of the co-ordinators *and, or*, and *but*, which allow ellipsis when the Subject is identical in both clauses (cf. pages 29f.). This criterion is not applicable to the five conjunctions that may not be preceded by another conjunction.

TABLE 5 *Immobile conjuncts and conjunctions*

	i	ii	1	2	3	4	7
and, or, but	+	+	+	+	+	+	/
for, so that	+	+	+	+	+	—	/
other conjunctions	+	+	+	±	—	—	—
yet, so	+	+	+	+	—	+	+
hence, besides	+	+	+	+	—	—	+

Distinctions can now be made between immobile conjuncts and conjunctions:

[a] an immobile conjunct differs from the five conjunctions *and, or, but, for,* and resultative *so that* in that it may be preceded by a conjunction (cf. Column 3)

[b] an immobile conjunct differs from the other conjunctions in two features:

[i] the conjunct with its clause can never be transposed before a previous independent clause (Column 2)

[ii] the conjunct allows ellipsis of the Subject if it is preceded by one of the three co-ordinators, which allow ellipsis when the Subject is identical in both clauses (Column 7).

It may be added that the immobile conjuncts *yet* and *so* allow ellipsis of the Subject in their own right, without the presence of an immediately preceding *and, or,* or *but.* In this respect they are like these three conjunctions and differ from other immobile conjuncts.[1]

The distinctions that have been made between conjunctions and immobile conjuncts do not apply to the initial items in correlative constructions which have a fixed sequence of clauses, e.g. *neither . . . nor, as . . . so, although . . . yet.* Let us take as our example a sentence with an immobile conjunct at the head of the second clause:

Although they did not like the music, *yet* they applauded vigorously.

The sentence becomes unacceptable when we insert *and* between the two clauses:

*Although they did not like the music *and yet* they applauded vigorously.

Thus, the criterion that an immobile conjunct may be preceded by a conjunction is not applicable.

There is a similar constraint if the second correlative is a mobile conjunct. For example, the following sentence with the correlatives *although . . . nevertheless* is unacceptable:

*Although they did not like the music *but* they *nevertheless* applauded vigorously.

If the first correlative is omitted, the sentence is perfectly acceptable:

They did not like the music *but* they *nevertheless* applauded vigorously.

There is another constraint with correlative constructions which

---

[1] The distinction between conjunct and conjunction is blurred with *though* and, to a lesser extent, with *although* (cf. pages 67ff).

applies specifically to the immobile conjuncts *yet* and *so*. It will be re-
membered (cf. page 26) that these allow the ellipsis of the Subject if it is
identical with the Subject of the previous clause, e.g.:

They did not like the music, *yet* applauded vigorously.

However, the Subject cannot be omitted if there is a previous correlative:

*Although they did not like the music, *yet* applauded vigorously.

A full treatment of conjunctions would necessitate a separate study.
However, two types of conjunctions have not been taken into account in
this chapter and they ought to be mentioned. They can be distinguished
from immobile conjuncts without much difficulty.

1. Conjunctions that introduce clauses functioning as Subject or
   Complement, e.g.:

   '*That* he wants it' does not interest me.
   I asked '*whether* she was ill'.

2. Conjunctions that function as Subject or Complement of the clause
   they introduce, e.g.:

   '*What* puzzles me so much', they never complained.

Chapter 3

Conjuncts

In the previous chapter we distinguished conjuncts from items of other classes. In particular, it was necessary to distinguish them from conjunctions, since the connective function of conjuncts is very evident. It is convenient to begin this chapter with a semantic classification of conjuncts and then to attempt some generalisations about syntactic features. We shall continue with a consideration of individual items, which will be grouped according to their semantic classes. Finally, we shall examine the positions occupied by conjuncts in the Survey corpus.

3.1 Semantic classification

Several conjuncts belong to more than one semantic class. The differences will be discussed when the individual items are considered in §3.3, pages 44ff. A comprehensive list of conjuncts can be given because, as defined in this study, they constitute a closed class.

It is convenient to note here which conjuncts are thought to be immobile in initial position, though this feature is not related to the semantic classification. Such conjuncts are distinguished by the asterisk which immediately follows them.

[1] Conjuncts in this semantic class express one of the most obvious meanings of the conjunction *and*, namely they indicate that what is being said is an addition to what has been said before. These LISTING conjuncts may be divided into two sub-classes: ENUMERATIVE and ADDITIVE.

[1a] ENUMERATIVE: These denote a cataloguing or inventory of what is being said. There are clearly-defined sets, though a member of one set may replace a member of another set in

the appropriate position. The order in which they appear is crucial.[1]

first, second, etc.; *first(ly), secondly,* etc.; *one, two,* etc.; *next*; *then; finally; last; lastly*

[1b] ADDITIVE: Besides indicating an addition to what has been said before, these either [i] convey an incremental effect, suggesting a reinforcement of what has been said before, or [ii] indicate a similarity with what has been said before.

[i] *again*; also*; further*; furthermore; more*; moreover*
[ii] *equally*; likewise*; similarly**

[2] TRANSITIONAL: These mark some change from what has been said before, while indicating a continuance of the discourse.

incidentally: now

[3] SUMMATIVE: These indicate that what is being said is a summary of what has gone before.

altogether*; overall*; then; therefore; thus

[4] EXPLICATORY: These indicate that what is being said is some explanation or gloss on what has been said before.

namely; thus

[5] CONTRASTIVE: Conjuncts in this semantic class indicate that what is being said is in contrast to what has been said before. These conjuncts may be subdivided into three sub-classes: SUBSTITUTIVE, ADVERSATIVE, and CONCESSIVE.

[5a] SUBSTITUTIVE: These indicate that what is being said is a reassessment of what has been said before, a preferred reformulation.

better*; rather

[5b] ADVERSATIVE: These indicate that what is being said is at variance in some way with what has been said before. They may be divided into two sub-classes:

[i] REPLACIVE: These indicate that what is being said is a replacement of what has been said before.

(or) again*; alternatively; better*; instead; rather; (but) then*; worse*

---

[1] We may quote from the first scene of Act 5 of *Much Ado About Nothing* Dogberry's confusion of the order and the parody by Don Pedro:

Don Pedro: Officers, what offence have these men done?

Dogberry: Marry, sir, they have committed false report; *moreover,* they have spoken untruths; *secondarily,* they are slanders; *sixth* and *lastly,* they have belied a lady; *thirdly,* they have verified unjust things; and, *to conclude,* they are lying knaves.

Don Pedro: *First,* I ask thee what they have done; *thirdly,* I ask thee what's their offence; *sixth* and *lastly,* why they are committed; and, *to conclude,* what you lay to their charge.

[ii] ANTITHETIC: These indicate that what is being said is in complete opposition to what has been said before.
contrariwise; *conversely*; *oppositely*

[5c] CONCESSIVE: These indicate that what is being said is related to what has been said before in the way defined by Quirk: 'the concessive relation may be said to exist between two parts of an utterance when one part is surprising in view of the other' (Quirk 1954, 6).[1]
anyhow; *anyway*; *besides**; *(or) else**; *however*; *nevertheless*; *nonetheless*; *notwithstanding*; *only**; *still**; *though*; *yet**

[6] ILLATIVE: These indicate that what is being said is a consequence or result of what has been said before.
accordingly; *consequently*; *hence**; *now*; *so**; *somehow*; *therefore*; *thus*

[7] INFERENTIAL: These indicate that what is being said is a consequence of a condition that has been stated or implied.
else; *otherwise*; *then*

[8] TEMPORAL TRANSITIONAL: These indicate that what is being said overlaps in time with what has been said before.
meantime; *meanwhile*

3.2 Syntactic features

Let us first consider the constraints on the appearance of conjuncts in certain types of clause and then examine other syntactic features that they exhibit.

3.2.1 Appearance in clause types

[1] *Questions*. All conjuncts may appear with questions, whether *yes-no* questions or *wh*-questions. Some conjuncts may appear in front of questions. These certainly include conjuncts from the semantic classes that have been termed listing (with the probable exception of *more*), explicatory, transitional, and temporal transitional. Summative conjuncts are probably unacceptable in front of questions. It is not possible to generalise about contrastive and illative conjuncts. Some, e.g. *alternatively*, *anyway*, *yet*, *so*, are fully acceptable before questions, while others, e.g. *instead*, *however*, *therefore*, are dubious in that position.[2]

[2] *Indirect questions*. Most mobile conjuncts will readily appear in indirect questions. The exceptions are of interest in displaying differences between members of the same semantic class. For

---

1 For a discussion of the differences between the concessive and adversative relations, see Quirk 1954, 4ff., 51ff.
2 For *however*, see pages 66ff.

example, we may contrast the acceptability of *nevertheless* with the unacceptability of *however*, which also belongs to the concessive sub-class:

He asked whether$\left\{ \begin{array}{c} nevertheless \\ *however \end{array} \right\}$they would stay.

Similarly we can contrast *thus* and *therefore*, which both belong to the illatives:

She wondered if she should$\left\{ \begin{array}{c} therefore \\ *thus \end{array} \right\}$approve of it.

Immobile conjuncts are not acceptable in indirect questions, e.g.:

*He asked whether$\left\{ \begin{array}{c} further \\ better \\ altogether \\ still \\ so \end{array} \right\}$they would stay.

These immobile conjuncts must be distinguished from homonyms that may be acceptable in this position, e.g. temporal *still*. Distinctions between immobile conjuncts and their homonyms are made when the individual conjuncts are discussed (§**3.3**, pages 44ff.).

[3] *Other subordinate finite verb clauses.* Most conjuncts may function in certain types of subordinate finite verb clauses, though particular conjuncts may be precluded from functioning in clauses introduced by particular conjunctions. Instances of conjuncts functioning in subordinate clauses are rare in the Survey corpus. There are only five instances out of 410 conjuncts in finite verb clauses. Four of the five are in restrictive or non-restrictive relative clauses:

Instead, the party was acting as a safety valve – a function that *otherwise* might be undertaken by right-wing groups. (8fa.1-13)

'I have invited all the village, except, of course, the two Misses Umbrage, who wouldn't have come *anyway*.'   (6.3.203-3)

Apart from the inward attestation of the Spirit, which is sovereign, and cannot *therefore* be controlled by human factors, it is all that they can see.   (8ab.2.146-3)

It was found that satisfactory agreement between observed and calculated intensities was obtained for structure I, or for structure IV when $z = 0.25 \pm 0.03$ which, apart from this permissible spread of the parameter value, is *then* identical with structure I.   (8a.2.183-3)

The fifth instance functions in a clause introduced by resultative *so that*:

> but the spontaneous magnetisation is actually zero at the transition temperature so that the magnetised and unmagnetised phases are *then* identical.   (8a.3.29-1)

The five instances function in clauses that are immobile. Some conjuncts may also function in clauses that are mobile, particularly in clauses denoting cause or reason, e.g.:

> I saw him, because *otherwise* he would have complained.
> Because *otherwise* he would have complained, I saw him.

With clauses of time and place, it appears that conjuncts are acceptable only in what might be termed 'non-restrictive' clauses, but are not acceptable in what might be termed 'restrictive' clauses, e.g.:

> I met him in the park, when, *however*, it was raining heavily.
> *I met him when, *however*, it was raining heavily.

When a conjunct appears in a time, place, or conditional clause preceding a superordinate clause, the conjunct is in reality functioning in the superordinate clause, as in the following instance of *however*:

> This is the general situation when we have a transition of the first order involving a latent heat, and corresponding finite jumps in one or more of the parameters such as the density and entropy specifying the assembly. When, *however*, the latent heat vanishes, the situation shown in fig. 3(a) is no longer possible.
>   (8a.3.28-3)

It will be observed that if *however* is transposed to the beginning of the sentence or to some position within the superordinate clause, the meaning is not materially affected, although there may be some difference in the distribution of emphasis in the sentence. Moreover, it is not possible to move the subordinate clause with *however* retained in it.

The immobile conjuncts *so*, *only*, and *yet* are exceptional in that they may not be preceded by subordinators. There are also constraints on their appearance after co-ordinators. None of the three may appear after *or*. *So* may follow *and* but not *but*, *only* may follow *but* but not *and*, while *yet* may follow either *and* or *but*.

[4] *Imperative and optative clauses*. Conjuncts may appear even in initial position in imperative and optative clauses, e.g.:

$$\left.\begin{array}{l} \textit{Furthermore,} \\ \textit{Incidentally,} \\ \textit{Therefore,} \\ \textit{Meanwhile,} \end{array}\right\} \begin{array}{l} \text{tell him about it.} \\ \text{don't tell him about it.} \\ \text{let's not tell him about it.} \end{array}$$

The summative conjuncts, e.g. *overall* and *somehow* are probably exceptions. They seem unacceptable in these types of clauses.

[5] *Subordinate non-finite verb clauses.* Some conjuncts may function in subordinate non-finite verb clauses, e.g.:

He refused the first offer, expecting *however* another offer.
They left the meeting, determined, *though*, to return later.

Further investigation is needed to determine the range of clauses and the individual conjuncts that may function in them.

We must distinguish the examples just given from instances of conjuncts in elliptical clauses, e.g. *hence* in the following citation:

An annular muscle runs round just above the lips of the sucker and presumably serves to narrow the margin and *hence to release the fish.*

Hence is not functioning in the non-finite verb clause, but in the ellipted superordinate finite verb clause: *the annular muscle serves.*

[6] *Verbless clauses.* Conjuncts may function in verbless clauses. *However, otherwise, altogether*, and *then* illustrate this use in the following citations.

Regrettably, *however, inevitably*, there is far too much goading of star players by inferiors these days.   (G 22/11/66: 13,1)

The odds are considerable that if he would concentrate the play upon the morality of bombing 'The Soldiers' is a work that would be suitable for the National Theatre. *But not otherwise.*   (ST 7/5/67: 47, 3)

Indeed, he doesn't seem much surprised at being chosen for the tribunal and teaming up again with an old acquaintance, Edmund Davies, a Glamorgan barrister when Lawrence was county prosecuting solicitor, thirty years ago. *Altogether, a formidable team.*   (G 27/10/66: 8, 6)

F   we've got /two minutes lèft in which to answer this
    quéstion# /Victor Mìshcon#
V   ((well)) | *very quìckly thén#* · you /knów# · there /àre
    fixed penalties#   (5b.16.71)

[7] *Clauses with equative verb 'be'.* Conjuncts may appear in clauses where the Verb is the equative verb *be.* In this feature they differ from homonymous manner adjuncts. For example, *so, thus,*

and *somehow* (which may be manner adjuncts in initial position) must be interpreted as conjuncts in the following sentences:

So he was the spokesman.
Thus they were the losers.
Somehow she was very hysterical yesterday.

It seems that conjuncts freely co-occur with any verb. Adapting the terminology of transformational grammar, we can say that manner adjuncts play a part in the subcategorisation of verbs (cf. Chomsky 1965, 103), but not their homonymous conjuncts.

3.2.2 Function in the clause

Conjuncts fail to satisfy the criteria listed in §2.1.2 (pages 18ff.) and displayed in Table 1 (page 23). I summarise the features applying to conjuncts that can be abstracted from that section and add others to them.

[1] They are acceptable in initial position in the clause. As has been indicated, some are restricted to that position (cf. pages 35ff.).

[2] They are acceptable in initial position even if the clause is negated. It is possible that the conjunct *instead* rarely precedes the clausal negative particle, but it does not seem unacceptable to position it in front of a negative clause.

[3] They are acceptable in initial position even if they are in an independent tone unit and carry a rising, falling-rising, or level nuclear tone. As has been pointed out (cf. page 19), the potentiality for this feature distinguishes the conjunct *again* (meaning 'furthermore') from the adjunct *again* (meaning 'once more').

[4] They cannot be the focus of clause interrogation. Thus, this sentence is unacceptable:

*Did he reply *therefore* or did he reply *nevertheless*?

[5] They cannot be the focus of clause negation. Thus, this sentence is unacceptable:

*He did not reply *therefore*, but he did reply *anyway*.

[6] They cannot be the focus of clause comparison. Thus, these sentences are unacceptable:

*He replied *more nevertheless than she did*.
*He replied *as meanwhile as she did*.

[7] They cannot be focused by *only* in initial position and allow in consequence Verb-Subject inversion. Thus, this sentence is unacceptable:

Only anyway did he reply to my letter.

2*

Furthermore, they cannot be focused by *only* even when positioned else-where. Thus, in the sentence

He *only* replied to my letter *occasionally*.

only can be interpreted as referring specifically to *occasionally*. If, how-ever, we substitute the conjunct *nevertheless* for *occasionally*

He *only* replied to my letter *nevertheless*.

then *only* cannot be interpreted as referring to *nevertheless*. In the same way, conjuncts cannot be focused by other restrictives, e.g. *just* and *merely*, or by additives, e.g. *also* and *again*. This is true even when the conjunct is in initial position and is immediately preceded by the re-strictive or the additive.

Meantime and *meanwhile* are probable exceptions to these generalisa-tions. They are marginally acceptable in such a sentence as the following:

?Only $\left\{ \begin{array}{l} \textit{meantime} \\ \textit{meanwhile} \end{array} \right\}$ are they taking drugs.

In addition, in the sentence

They are *only* taking drugs $\left\{ \begin{array}{l} \textit{meantime.} \\ \textit{meanwhile.} \end{array} \right.$

only can be interpreted as referring specifically to *meantime* or *meanwhile*.

[8] They cannot serve as the sole focus of a cleft sentence. Thus, this sentence is unacceptable:

*It was nevertheless that they asked for it.

Most conjuncts may appear within the focal clause when another item is the focus, e.g.:

It was nevertheless on Sunday that they asked for it.

[9] They cannot serve as a response to an interrogative transforma-tion of the clause introduced by *When, Where, How,* or *Why.* For ex-ample, from the sentence

They are *therefore* taking drugs.

we cannot formulate the question and answer:

*Why are they taking drugs? *Therefore.*

[10] They cannot accept premodification by *How* in an interrogative or exclamatory transformation of the clause. For example, for the con-junct *similarly* in the sentence

Similarly, they wrote to him.

we do not have the interrogative transformation

How similarly did they write to him?

or the exclamatory transformation

How similarly they wrote to him!

For the manner adjunct *similarly* in the sentence

They wrote to him *similarly*.

we have both these transformations.

[11] They cannot serve as a response to a simple interrogative transformation of the clause, i.e. a *yes-no* question. This applies even if they are accompanied by *yes* or *no*, e.g.:

They are taking drugs *therefore* every day.
→ Are they taking drugs every day? *No, *therefore*.

Meantime and *meanwhile* are marginal in this respect. They may be acceptable when accompanied by *yes* or *no*, e.g.:

They are $\left\{\begin{array}{l} \textit{meantime} \\ \textit{meanwhile} \end{array}\right\}$ taking drugs every day.

→ Are they taking drugs every day? $\left\{\begin{array}{l} \textit{?Meantime, yes.} \\ \textit{?Meanwhile, no.} \end{array}\right.$

3.2.3 Other syntactic features

[1] Conjuncts do not accept premodification or postmodification. Thus, *conversely enough* and *very alternatively* are unacceptable. The replacive conjuncts *better* and *worse* are exceptions. They allow modification by *even* and *still*. *Better* is modified by *still* in the following citation:

> Brown transformed things with startling abruptness. First he found a length and direction which prompted wary defence on the instant. *Still better*, his pace off the pitch compelled hurried shots.   (G 8/11/65: 11, 5)

It does not appear to be acceptable to modify the substitutive *better*.

[2] Conjuncts are not usually co-ordinated, apart from listing conjuncts. With these, appositional co-ordination is perfectly normal, e.g. *firstly and most importantly* or *thirdly and finally*. It is less usual to find co-ordination among other conjuncts. An example occurs in the material I have examined:

> He believes that as fairy tales can worry children, adult versions of them should as well. 'And as you bring in real things and people when you're reading a fairy story to your child, like

saying that house is just like Aunt So and So's, so you should
with a grown-up story.'
However and notwithstanding, the BBC don't like it. It was
scheduled for New Year's Eve. Now it's been put back indefi-
nitely.   (ST 30/10/66: 13, 2)

We should regard the co-ordinated phrase *however and notwithstanding* as an intentional deviation, jocularly suggesting the
pompous paternalism of the BBC.

3.3 Individual conjuncts

We shall now turn to a consideration of individual conjuncts. These
have been grouped according to the semantic classes set out on pages
35ff. Other form-classes with a similar conjunctive function are mentioned when the particular expressions occur frequently. By 'a similar
conjunctive function' I mean that the diagnostic criteria for conjuncts
(cf. pages 24ff.) are applicable.

3.3.1 Enumerative conjuncts

The relationship between an enumerative conjunct and the clause it
refers to corresponds to the structure:

I would say conjunct (*that*) clause.

Since actual citations are rather long and, therefore, inconvenient for this
purpose, it is easier to demonstrate this by an invented example:

There are two objections against asking him to do the job:
first, he is too old, and, *second*, he is ill.

In this example, *first* has the correspondence *I would say first* (*that*) and
second the correspondence *I would say second* (*that*).
      Enumerative conjuncts may be preceded by a statement of intention
to list, e.g.:

I do not disagree with this view though *I would make two quali-
fying points. One,* interest may well flare up again (however
briefly) when the promised new plant replacement incentives
are announced next month. *Two,* I rather feel two shares have a
reasonably good chance of doing better than the average:
Churchill and Staveley.   (G 25/10/65: 11, 2)

There may, however, be no previous indication of such an intention, as
in the next citation. It will be noticed that only the second in a sequence
of enumerative conjuncts has been given.

the real real real reason why [rɔ) ə Burns is so · ə wŏrshipped# is
/because of course he was a self made măn# who /got thére# · /from

being a fàrm lábourer# and was ac/knowledged as a pòet# · /in his own lifetime# and /sècondly# and /far mòre impórtant# he was a /terrific lòver# a/mongst these dour Presbytérian Scòts# (5b.1.31)

The addition of *and far more important* in the previous citation makes explicit that the points being made are listed in ascending order of importance. They may, however, appear in chronological order:

Two suggestions were subsequently put forward to account for the changes. *First*, Pauling (1930) suggested that the change from Phase III to Phase II was brought about by the onset of free rotation of the ammonium ion with increasing temperature. *Secondly*, Frenkel (1935) had suggested that an order-disorder transformation between two possible orientations of the ammonium ions and this proposal had been treated mathematically by Nagamiya (1942). (8a.2.173-2)

Although there is a sequence in time between the points mentioned, *first* and *secondly* are enumerative conjuncts, as the first sentence in the citation makes clear. For contrast, a series of time sequence adjuncts is displayed in the next citation:

Brown transformed things with startling abruptness. *First* he found a length and direction which prompted wary defence on the instant. Still better, his pace off the pitch compelled hurried shots. *Then*, before hint of his last menace had dawned, he had Kelly leg before on the back foot to one which whipped back. He *next* beat Inverarity's back shot no less comprehensively and forced the left handed Cowper into edging an outswinger. *Finally* he had Inverarity caught low at backward short leg from an involuntary deflection at an inswinger. (G 8/11/65: 11, 5)

Time sequence adjuncts differ in syntactic features from enumerative conjuncts. For example, they may be the focus of clause interrogation or the sole focus of a cleft sentence.

Additive conjuncts easily fit into an enumerative system, as *moreover* in the following citation exemplifies:

So regarded, they at least secure the consequence which Geach's definitions fail to secure, viz. that an A-expression can never be a B-expression. *Moreover*, they do not exclude what Frege explicitly allowed, viz. that an A-expression can be part of a B-expression. *Finally*, in certain simple cases, given a sentence to be exhaustively divided into an A-expression and a B-expression, these descriptions force us to make the division in the way in which we wish to be forced to make it. (8b.1.147-4)

The function of an enumerative conjunct is also performed by a

numeric digit or an alphabetic letter. These may be enclosed by brackets
and set out in separate paragraphs, e.g.:

> We might, therefore, ask two things about a new theory of a
> change of state:
> (a) Does it give a satisfying physical picture of what is probably
> happening?
> (b) Is the numerical agreement with the observed facts in keep-
> ing with the number of adjustable parameters, or is the theory
> unduly 'forced' in this respect? (8a.3.22-1)

Prepositional phrases may be used in place of conjuncts in an enumerative series, e.g.:

> But this is not to say that Mr Wilson's journey is unnecessary,
> even if he is likely to return empty handed. *In the first place*, it
> is a reassertion of Britain's legal responsibility for the future of
> Rhodesia. *In the second place*, it is a demonstration of Britain's
> willingness to continue exploring every possibility of peaceful
> negotiation. (O 24/10/65: 10, 2)

The non-finite-verb clause *to begin with* may function as the first in a
series of enumerative conjuncts. In the next citation it is followed in the
series by *then*:

> All these things we know about in India. But China has similar
> problems of development; some may be even greater. *To begin
> with*, each year millions more additional mouths need to be filled
> than in India, and millions more additional hands need to have
> work created for them. *Then*, for a variety of reasons (some of
> which, but not all, are the result of conscious choices by the
> Chinese Government), China is trying to provide the food and the
> jobs without help from outside. (G 27/5/66: 12, 1)

The clause has the same type of correspondence as the conjunct *first*. On
the other hand, *to begin with* in the next citation is a time adjunct contrasting with *later* in the same sentence:

> This time next year Leeds University will have welcomed its
> first students in a new subject – computational science. Under-
> graduates will be able to take it as one of two main subjects for a
> combined studies B.Sc. degree in which honours may be awarded.
> *To begin with*, the second subject is to be mathematics or
> physics but *later* an engineering subject will be added.
> (TES 5/11/65: 963, 1)

We may also refer to the clause *to conclude*, which appeared as an item in
the series of enumerative conjuncts misused by Dogberry (cf. page 36,
note 1).

3.3.2 Additive conjuncts

As with the enumerative conjuncts, the relationship between an additive conjunct and the clause corresponds to the structure:

I would say conjunct *(that)* clause.

3.3.2.1 *Again*

The additive conjunct *again* indicates that a new point is being added in an exposition, and the new point is a reinforcement of what has been said before. Two examples from written English will exemplify this function:

> But the efficacy of the inward witness is not necessarily proportionate to the powers and resources available. If the Spirit uses the things of this world, as He does, He can just as well use the weak and despised things, the things which are not, to confound the wise and mighty [note 2: 1 Cor. 1:27-8]. The real power of Church and Word and Sacrament may well be in reverse ratio to their human and historical efficacy. 'God's strength is made perfect in weakness' [note 1: 2 Cor. 12:9].
>
> *Again*, the mere presence of the human and historical witness is not itself a guarantee of the efficacious witness of the Spirit.
>
> (8ab.2.145-3)

> The psychologist can assist in detecting those children who may specially require such experiences. Other children may benefit from the many regular tasks which the routine of the classroom has to offer.
>
> *Again*, it is often possible for the psychologist to observe the child at work and at play in a social setting more natural than that of the clinic.   (TES 15/10/65: 758, 4)

The additive conjunct has two homonyms, an additive adjunct and a temporal adjunct. We can illustrate the differences between them with a simplified version of the sentence in the last citation:

> [i] *Again*, the psychologist can observe the child at work and at play.
> [ii] The psychologist, *again*, can observe the child . . .
> [iii] The psychologist can *again* observe the child . . .

Again in [i] is an additive conjunct, indicating no more than that another point is being made. *Again* in [ii] is an additive adjunct, implying that someone besides the psychologist can observe the child at work and at play. *Again* in [iii] is a temporal adjunct, paraphrasable by 'once more'.

The temporal adjunct *again* may occupy initial position, e.g.:

Meanwhile, Private Patrick Siddle, of Westbury Crescent, Dover,

handed the sergeant £200 to get out. *Again* Elms arranged leave,
and Private Siddle, thinking himself free, went job-hunting.

(8fa.2.25)

'Is he *frightened* [ital. sic] of it?' asked Madeline. 'He seems
frightened of it. No wonder.' *Again* she said: 'We'd better go
away.' (6.1.24-1)

Because the temporal adjunct can occupy initial position, the additive
conjunct would require to be followed by a comma in written English
to avoid ambiguity.

Let us examine some examples of *again* as an additive conjunct in
spoken English:

> [i]   /I've been campaigning for this ever since Cânning
>   was · moderator# /ten yêars ago# · /and ə *there agāin*#
>   /how do you get òn with this fellow Hart#   (S.1c.11-67)
>
> [ii] /no *agâin* you see# /this is simply untrùe# /you will
>   not study the èvidence#   (5b.51.21)
>
> ?' [iii] /yèah# /I I sàw that · /but a?gàin I say# /we have ,
>   no pówer#   (5b.1.51)
>
> [iv] and /âll this business# about /selling the pàss# you
>   /knów# a/gain with grèat respéct# it's /quite
>   unrealìstic#   (5b.1.51)

In [i] the additive conjunct is *there again*. This is a unit, since *there*
does not have this function unless accompanied by *again*, which
cannot be omitted in this context. In [ii] *again* is associated by intonation with parenthetic *you see*. It is just possible to regard it as an adjunct
in the clause *again you see*, but this seems an unlikely interpretation.
Similarly, it could be analysed as an adjunct in *again I say*, but
the wider context, too long to quote here, suggests that this is an im-
probable analysis. *Again* in [iv] is ambiguous. It may be an additive
adjunct, so that the contents of the tone unit can be paraphrased by 'I
am saying this with great respect just as I said the previous part with
great respect'. In this interpretation *again* is focusing *with great respect*.
On the other hand, *again* may be an additive conjunct, in which case the
interpretation is 'I am making another point and I am making it with
great respect'.

In the next citation there is an ambiguity between *again* as additive
adjunct and as temporal adjunct:

> ə his /own párty# a/gáin# · is /rìft# – – they /àre# – at
> ?' ?/variance with one anóther#   (5b.16.25)

The context from which the citation comes suggests that it is a temporal adjunct meaning 'once more'.

Again may appear as a temporal adjunct in initial position:

> B I can · ə I can /spend the whòle of thát time# on /those
>   two pápers# · if they /happen to *còme# – and /then
>   agāin# ((from the /[e]))* – from the /eighth of Julȳ# ·
>   un/tīl# ·
> A */Ì see# ((/I'm /I'm /I'm it's)) /very kind of you Sám#
> B what/ever time your Council meeting îs# *·*
> A */m̀#*
> ?' B a/gàin# /I can spend the whole time ?òn *them#*
>   (S.1C.11-13)

In cases of ambiguity, the additive conjunct can be distinguished from
the temporal adjunct by intonational means. If the word is in an independent tone unit and carries a falling-rising nucleus it would be
interpreted as a conjunct. It is probable that this would be the interpretation if the nucleus were a rising or level tone.

3.3.2.2 *Also*

The conjunct *also* is restricted to initial position:

> I nearly always serve the same Cypriot food, which I learnt to
> cook in Nicosia. It's jolly good, easy to cook and it's a bit
> individual: something that my guests probably wouldn't get at
> home. *Also*, this menu isn't harassing to cook and it's ready to
> eat when you are. (OM 10/10/65: 53, 3)

Like the conjunct *again*, the conjunct *also* indicates that an additional
point is being made, but *also* seems less insistent.

As a contrast to the conjunct, some instances of the additive adjunct
are cited:

> [i] */may* · /nôw may I# · /may I hàlt you# – but /âlso
>   in that period# · between /nineteen forty éight# –
>   /ànd# · /nineteen fifty nìne# – /crímes# · of /vïolence#
>   · e/nôrmously# in/crèased# · /as I've dèmonstrated#
>   (5b.51.28)

> [ii] He looked her up and down frankly. Their eyes, like two
>   advance posts of opposing armies, crossed each other as she
>   *also* completed her equally frank and undisguised survey.
>   (6.4.48-1)

> [iii] When his face wasn't split open in a frank, clean-toothed smile,
>   or composed into an I-follow-you-through-all-these-argu-
>   ments-and-I-sympathise-more-than-I-dare-say look of the junior
>   politician, it sagged badly, just where, Sir James sighed, it

should most burgeon out into bone and muscle and tensity. The hair at the back of his neck was *also* an unpleasing sight.

(6.4.46-4)

In [i] *also* is specifying *in that period* . . . as an addition to a period previously mentioned. A separate tone unit for *also* with a falling-rising nucleus would merely have indicated that an additional point was being made (cf. the remark on the intonation of *again*, page 49).

In [ii] *also* specifies *she* as an addition. We may paraphrase the effect as 'she in addition to him completed . . .'. The completion of the looking at her has not been explicitly mentioned, but is implied in the un-marked meaning of the past tense of *looked*. Similarly, the words 'an unpleasing sight' have not been mentioned in the previous sentence, but they are implied in the description of the face.

What is being added to may have appeared several sentences, or even paragraphs, before. An instance occurs in the Survey corpus:

Under *a Bill published on Saturday* local authorities would be able to collect three-quarters of any increase of land values brought about by the granting of planning permission.

   Called the Town and Country Planning (Land Values) Bill, it is a private member's measure, . . .

[Three intervening paragraphs]

The text was also published on Saturday of the House Buyers' Pro-tection Bill, introduced last month under the 10-minute rule by Mr Harold Lever.   (8fa.1-17)

The results of evaluation and similarity tests in experimental Battery I suggest that informants were aware of the difference between *also* as additive conjunct and as additive adjunct. In an evaluation test, informants were confronted with the sentence:

/ălso# your /children álso disliked me#

Nineteen informants (22 per cent) thought the sentence 'perfectly natural and normal' and a further twenty (24 per cent) were dubious about it. Nearly half the informants, therefore, were not prepared to reject the sentence despite the repetition of *also*.

   When the same informants were presented with the pair of sentences:

/ălso# your /children dislìked me#
your /children álso dislìked me#

the majority either thought them very different (twenty-seven, or 42 per cent) or 'somewhere between' (fifteen, or 23 per cent). Only twenty-two (34 per cent) considered them very similar in meaning. Accordingly, we may assume that some who evaluated the sentence as abnormal did so for stylistic reasons, objecting to the repetition of *also*. It is probable that if the two instances had been distanced further apart then there would be less objection to their co-occurrence:

Also, your children disliked me *also*.

Certainly, if a synonym were substituted for one of the instances the sentence would be more acceptable, if not fully acceptable:

In addition, your children *also* disliked me.

An example of the co-occurrence of *also* the conjunct and *also* the adjunct appears in the material that has been examined. Because of the distance between the two instances, it may well be that the co-occurrence would pass unnoticed if attention were not drawn to it:

> But according to the cannons [sic] of Socialist realism, the purpose of art is determined by society, not by the individual artist. This is one reason for the conflict between the modern and the classical in Russian art – for the Modern, the Abstract, the Cubist, or for that matter Pop art is a rebellion against the past, which in the Soviet is a political act.
>
> If rebellion is allowed in art, then why not in history, in philosophy and, finally, in politics? *Also*, the self-assertion of the individual artist, through the modern and therefore wayward form of his work, against the uniform classicism of official art, is *also* an act of rebellion, which has to be nipped in the bud before the heady feeling of freedom spreads to others. (G 15/2/67: 7, 6)

3.3.2.3 *Then*

Then as an immobile additive conjunct is roughly synonymous with *furthermore*. It can be easily distinguished from the adversative conjunct *then* (page 62), which is also immobile, since it must be preceded by *but* whereas the additive conjunct may not be preceded by *but*. I cite some instances of the additive conjunct:

```
B  /wèll I mean# *we've /got we've* we've /gòt the
A  *( (2 or 3 syllables) )*
B  people there already# *to do* the /lìterature#
A  */m̀#*
B  /you sée# and /then there's Márley there# /there's ə ·
      Lògan · and /probably Tìllman# you sée#        (S.1c.11-20)
```

/if we are going to prevent that kind of thing happening agáin# we've /got to keep our eye on what might bè# – and /thên# as to /old āge# · əm · /medical scíence# is /keeping people going a véry lóng tíme nów#   (5b.2.25)

'But there are three obvious objections to that, aren't there?'
said Emma cruelly. '*One* is that your process inhibits action; that
is you weigh intellectually, instead of being a moral being and
acting and letting your morality come out of your action. And *then*
one can scrupulously rob or murder or commit perversion. *And* it
offers nothing for other people.'   (6.2.95-1)

In the last citation, *then* is in a series initiated by *one*.

3.3.2.4   Others

More and *further* and their mobile counterparts, the compounds
furthermore and *moreover*, seem to have greater force than the three
additive conjuncts we have considered so far. They strongly imply
that the new point being made reinforces what has already been said.
The following citations exemplify the use of these conjuncts:

> Stone had begun his attacks on McCarthy in the pages of
> *The New York Compass,* and he took them up with redoubled en-
> ergy in the *Weekly.* But he was never subpoenaed by McCarthy's
> committee, though he was prepared for such an occurrence.
> He was small fry, though uncommonly aggressive and well-
> informed, and anyway such a summons could do him no
> damage. *Furthermore,* his criticism of McCarthy and his advocacy
> of the civil rights of Communists was completely open. 'I was
> the Gypsy Rose Lee of the Press. I exposed myself completely.'
> *Finally,* since there was no suggestion of subversion or secret
> infiltration in his behaviour, his case would have lacked the
> elements necessary to a good, dramatic witch hunt.
>
> (STM 16/7/67: 34, 3)

Two of the walls are a foot thick and the others are made of
plaster-board. The roof, *moreover,* is of corrugated iron, which
puts an intolerable burden on the artists when it rains; . . .

(G 25/10/65: 3, 1)

Modernisation, he said, begins at home, and the country is
ready for a more dynamic programme of parliamentary modernisation. So it is. *More,* to bring the system of government up
to date – at Westminster, in Whitehall, and in the town halls – is
an essential preliminary to bringing Britain up to date.

(G 22/4/66: 12, 1)

In my idiolect *too* cannot occupy initial position and only functions
as an additive adjunct. Some people, however, seem to be able to use it
in that position as an immobile additive conjunct, e.g.:

> Hitler was *too* romantic for that: no man who tied up the
> railway system of his country in wartime transporting non-

combatants merely to murder them could be accused of having a head for business. And, *too*, Hitler's reputation is so bad that it seemed really rather amazingly unnecessary for the American narrator (who sounded like Peter Cook's Karl J. Pipesucker) to try to make young Hitler look like some kind of beatnik as well. (G 21/9/67: 5, 6)

In my idiolect, *also* would have been used instead of *too* for this position.[1]

Equally, *likewise*, and *similarly* are additive conjuncts indicating that an additional point is being made that is similar to what has been said before. Some examples are cited:

In principle the whole field of organic chemistry is filled with problems which can be solved by neutron diffraction investigation of the position of hydrogen atoms. *Equally*, there are wide fields of investigation in the crystal chemistry of the compounds of heavy elements. (8a.2.162-2)

Inspection should be no problem if the goodwill is there, as it seems to be; officers from the other side can just be invited to look. *Likewise*, the absence of a Bangkok agreement need not prevent the resumption of trade relations, since both sides recognise the benefits. (G 2/6/66: 10, 1)

A similar effect can occur in certain models of liquid helium II (p. 303) because the occupation number of an energy level cannot be less than zero, and it may happen that a 'natural end' to a free energy curve arises in *this* [ital. sic] way. *Similarly*, it might arise, in an assembly obeying Fermi statistics, through a set of levels becoming completely filled or completely empty.
(8a.3.30-3)

Movement of the conjunct is not possible without changing it into an adjunct, either an additive adjunct or a manner adjunct.

Prepositional phrases that function like additive conjuncts include *in addition* and *by the same token*:

These fibres apparently mostly end within the organ, in contact with ganglion cells whose axons run to unequal right and left habenular ganglia. *In addition* there are supporting and pigment cells in the retinas. (8a.1.103-3)

These ways of drawing the distinction, then, enable us to understand some of the things that are said about the items of List II. *By the same token*, they enable us to understand some of the things that Frege says about the items of List IV. (8b.1.152-1)

---

[1] Some account of the environments in which *too* will replace *also* is given in Lee 1965.

The finite verb clause *what is more* has a similar function:

> Today and tomorrow the public can see, at the Cambridge
> Senate House, an exhibition of prints, etchings and lithographs.
> *What is more* they can buy them from as little as three guineas
> upwards. (TES 5/11/65: 954, 1)

More corresponds to *what is more*, but unlike *more* the clause is mobile.
More than this can also be conjunctive, e.g.:

> And at the weekend Father McCabe was informed from Rome
> that by order of the Dominican Master-General, the Spanish
> Father Fernandes Aniceto, he was forbidden to edit or write
> for 'New Blackfriars' again.
>   *More than this*, he has temporarily been suspended from
> his priestly functions. (G 15/2/67: 6,4)

More than this does not have the correspondence *What is more than this*.
More and *what is more* do not have the correspondence *What is more
is (that)*, cf. pages 214, 216.

3.3.3 Transitional conjuncts

Incidentally and *now* are the only conjuncts that have been classed as
transitional conjuncts.

3.3.3.1 *Incidentally*

Incidentally marks a digression in the subject-matter and is intended
to suggest that the digression was not premeditated. The prepositional
phrase *by the way* has a similar function. It is of psycho-linguistic
interest that in fact the digression is often carefully planned.[1]
   Two examples of the conjunct function of *incidentally* are cited:

> Norway welcomes children, and here, as usually elsewhere,
> there is a 70 per cent reduction for those up to three, 50 per cent
> from three to 12, provided they sleep in an extra cot, not in a
> separate room. You are half-price, *incidentally*, until you are 15
> on Norwegian trains and most buses and steamers.
>   (TES 5/11/65: 971, 1)

> I /have incidéntally# · ɔːm per/suàded# /ðiː · British
> Musèum# – to /purchase · microfílms#   (S.1b.6-60)

The citation from a speech text contains an illuminating intonation
pattern. Presumably because the position between the auxiliary and the
lexical verb is also possible for the adjunct *incidentally*, the conjunct is

---

1 Cf. Feldman 1959, 16–25, for a discussion by a psycho-analyst of some instances of the use of *incidentally* and *by the way*.

separated from the verb by a tone unit boundary and a slight pause. In the next citation, where there is no such separation, there is some ambiguity about the function of *incidentally*. The context, however, suggests that it is to be interpreted as an adjunct and may be paraphrased 'occurring as an attendant circumstance':

> M and it was /only when he stabbed ((a)) sérgeant# that they
> /let him gò# (haha)
> F and I sup/pose *incidentally* became very popular with the
> other rànks# (haha)   (5b. 1.9)

The acceptability of *incidentally* in front of a question was tested in the course of Battery II. Informants were required to turn into a *yes-no* question the sentence:

> inci/děntally# /he is the chàirman#

122 informants (68 per cent) complied fully with the instructions. In a subsequent evaluation test there was a more decisive majority in favour of the acceptability of the transformed sentence:

> inci/děntally# /is he the cháirman#

167 informants (93 per cent) endorsed this sentence as 'perfectly natural and normal'. Indeed, it appears that the initial position is considered more acceptable, since there was a distinctly smaller majority when informants were asked to evaluate a question with the conjunct in final position:

> /is he the cháirman incidentally#

This time 136 informants (75 per cent) fully accepted the question, while as many as 23 (13 per cent) rejected it completely and 20 considered it 'somewhere between' the two extremes. There had only been four rejections and eight queries when the conjunct was in initial position. We may contrast the acceptability rating for *incidentally* in initial position with the rating for *however* in the same position before a question (cf. page 67). It is clear that there was considerable uneasiness about the retention of *however* in that position.

3.3.3.2 *Now*

Now marks a transition in exposition. All the sixty-eight instances in the Survey corpus occupy initial position, but it can occur elsewhere:

> Harris: What time do you get up on a typical day? How does
> it go from then on?
> P.M.: Well, let me see *now*. Most days in the year I wake
> at 7.30, ... (OM 24/10/65: 22, 3)

Presumably *now* in this example is not a temporal adjunct; it could occupy initial position with its collocate *well*: 'Well *now*, let me see.' We interpret *now* as a conjunct because that is the more plausible interpretation in the context and not because there are formal criteria of position or punctuation to distinguish the conjunct from the adjunct.

Let us examine a few instances of *now* in initial position:

[i] you /can't have informed opìnion# · /on this vital
   mátter# · with/out being kept vèry much up to dáte# · with
   the /látest fàcts of defence# – *now* /what ìs wróng# with
   a /coalition gòvernment#   (5b.16.22)

[ii] – əːm you're /very kind old Sám# – – /blèss you# well /that
   finishes thàt# · əːm ((*now*)) /what was the òther thing I
   wanted to ask you#   (S.1c.11–15)

[iii] A lot happens in this cemetery. *Now* keep back, for God's sake.
                                                                  (6.1.27-3)

Now in [i] might be paraphrased by 'following from what I say', though its meaning is vaguer than the paraphrase suggests. In [ii] *now* is roughly equivalent to 'let me see'. This might be isolated as the ruminative use of *now*. In [iii] *now* is admonitory. This admonitory use of *now*, customary with imperatives, may have been the source of the admonitory *now now*:

   so /whŷ do you say# · /now we've tried all these others we must
   fall back on thìs means# because our /whole *argument is
   that it ìsn't a means#*
N *now now I /don't* – now /just a mòment Mr Williams#
   /why fall bàck# – – /Î'm not ə# · /falling băck# on
   /ànything# – – –   (5b. 51.43)

In this last citation an admonitory *now* introduces the 'imperative' *just a moment* when the speaker resumes the thread of his argument after the anacoluthon.

In speech the conjunct *now* in initial position will only carry the nucleus when it is at the end of a tone unit or followed by a pause. These instances of *now* show the conjunct with nuclear tone:

   well /nòw# [w] /whàt I wanted to ask y* ((ou))#   (S.1b.6-58)

   /well nōw# · /whý not#   (S.1c.11-60)

On the other hand, in these citations *now* is a temporal adjunct:

   /nôw may Î# · /may I hàlt you# –   (5b.51.28)

   /well *now* we àre# be/ginning to divèrge from this quéstion#
                                                            (5b.16.11)

and /*now* here agàin# are the /main points of the néws#

(4c.1-18)

The temporal adjunct may be in initial position with or without the nuclear tone. A falling-rising nucleus does not seem possible for the transitional conjunct, though it is possible for the illative conjunct *now* (cf. §3.3.7.4, page 73).

3.3.4 Summative conjuncts

The summative conjuncts *altogether* and *overall* are restricted to initial position. *All in all* and *in all* have a similar function. Some citations are given to illustrate their use:

> An appendix provides useful mathematical tables. *Overall*, this is a useful book, . . . (TES 5/11/65: 988, 5)

> *All in all*, then, it is not difficult to see why Mr Wilson retains his grip so far and why Mr Heath cannot dislodge him.
> (ST 16/7/67: 8, 6)

Then may function as a summative conjunct to indicate the conclusion of an exposition. It corresponds to 'one may then say' in which *then* is a temporal adjunct meaning 'by this time'. An instance of this use of *then* appears in the following citation:

> It must be emphasised that this conclusion does not apply to homologues of benzene and their derivatives, since these compounds contain 'aliphatic' hydrogen atoms, which are much more susceptible to abstraction by free radicals. Polynuclear hydrocarbons such as naphthalene are also exceptions to this rule. Apart from these exceptions, *then*, the main reaction of aryl radicals from diaroyl peroxides with simple benzene derivatives is that of straight-forward substitution, . . . (8a.4.35-4)

Therefore and *thus* may be used in a similar manner. Both of them can replace *then* in the last citation, though it would be necessary to position *thus* at the beginning of the sentence.

3.3.5 Explicatory conjuncts

Namely and *viz.* (the Latin abbreviation that represents *namely*) point to some kind of appositional relationship between two linguistic units. The relationship may be between two nominal groups with identical function, e.g.:

> but the expression 'is wise' demands a certain kind of completion, *namely* completion into a proposition or propositional clause. (8b.1.153-1)

The relationship may, however, be between a nominal group and a clause, e.g.:

> /if you lòok# · at the /totals · of floggable offěnces# · that
> is of/fences which between eighteen sixty one and
> nineteen forty èight# wére pùnishable# · /by judicial
> bèating# – you dis/cóver# · a /very remarkable fàct# –
> ?ˑ /nàmely# that /when it was ?abòlished# · in · /nineteen
> ?ˇ forty ?èight# – the /number of these crìmes# con/tinuously
> decrèased#   (5b.51.27)

Namely may also indicate a reformulation of what has preceded, e.g.:

> sta/tistical evidence shows that this ìsn't a detérrent# *namely*
> /people in this státe# · will /nòt be deterred# /by this form of ·
> N /well I don't think you're really əm · [m] · corrèct on those
> grounds Mr Williams#   (5b.51.59)

Similar functions are performed by the clauses *that is* (and the Latin abbreviation *i.e.* that represents it) and *that is to say* and by the prepositional phrase *in other words*, though this last is more usually used for reformulation. A more open class of introducers of explication is represented in the next citations:

> But – to borrow a phrase of W. E. Johnson's – the expression
> 'is wise' not only introduces being wise, it also carries the asser
> tive or propositional tie; or, *in still older terminology*, it not only
> introduces its term, it also copulates it.   (8b.1.151-2)

> But of course one book cannot contain everything. Suffice it to
> say that Mr Frewin has ranged extensively in time and space over
> the world of English and Commonwealth cricket. Or, *in simpler
> words*, has scored another boundary.   (TES 15/10/65: 780, 5)

Exemplification is a form of explication. The most common introducers of exemplification are the prepositional phrases *for example* (and the Latin abbreviation that often represents it, *e.g.*) and *for instance*. *Thus* may also introduce exemplification, e.g.:

> The brain itself (Fig. 64) is built on the typical vertebrate
> plan, as an enlargement of the front end of the spinal cord, with
> thickenings and evaginations corresponding to the various
> organs of special sense. Although we know little of its internal
> functional organisation in lampreys, it is probably not far wrong to
> regard it as chiefly consisting of a series of hypertrophied
> special sensory centres; *thus* the forebrain is connected with
> smell, midbrain with sight, hindbrain with acoustico-lateral and
> taste-bud systems. (8a.1.101–1)

3.3.6 Contrastive conjuncts

Contrastive conjuncts are divided into three sub-classes: substitutive conjuncts, adversative conjuncts, and concessive conjuncts.

3.3.6.1 Substitutive conjuncts

Both *rather* and *better* may be used to introduce a reformulation of what has been said. However, they add the notion of a preferential reformulation. There is therefore a contrast with what has been said before. *Rather* corresponds to *one should rather say (that)* or *I should rather say (that)*, while *better* corresponds to *it would be better to say (that)*. Only one example of substitutive conjuncts has been observed:

> The only common denominator that unites the parties on the issue of reunification is the absence of a policy. Or *rather*, there is a policy, but this only states that the Federal Republic is in favour of reunification on the basis of self-determination – which is about as helpful as being against sin. (G 23/4/66: 8, 1)

Better may replace *rather* in this context.

3.3.6.2 Adversative conjuncts

Adversative conjuncts may be divided into two sub-classes: replacive conjuncts and antithetic conjuncts.

3.3.6.2.1 Replacive conjuncts

Replacive conjuncts indicate that what is being said is a replacement for what has been said before. They differ from substitutive conjuncts, since the latter indicate merely a linguistic replacement or reformulation. Replacive conjuncts cover some of the range of the conjunction *or*, except for *instead*, which is closer semantically to *but*.

Or again may constitute a unit with the meaning 'or on the other hand':

> For I might pronounce the words 'Socrates is wise' is [sic] an interrogative tone of voice and thereby ask a question instead of making an assertion. Or I might use the words 'is wise' in framing a different kind of question, in asking 'Who is wise?'. *Or again* I might make a remark which begins with the words '*If* [ital. sic] Socrates is wise ...' or '*If* [ital. sic] Raleigh smokes ...'
> (8b.1.149-3)

This attraction to *or* does not happen with other conjuncts that have an additive meaning. *Or also*, for example, would mean 'or in addition' and not 'or on the other hand'.

Or again indicates that what follows is one of several choices in the citation. *Alternatively* in the next citation suggests a contrast with various possibilities that are considered together as the first alternative:

Are Mr Wilson's measures adequate? How and when shall we regain speed? Shall we ever get back to the old (expansionist) course? And what if, *alternatively*, the July storm turns into an autumn hurricane? (G 8/8/66: 8, 1)

On the other hand can usually be used in place of the conjuncts (*or*) *again* and *alternatively*.

Rather and *better* indicate an alternative, but with the added denotation that it is preferable, e.g.:

Perhaps if you feel up to it, you wouldn't mind waiting here and holding Gwilym. Or *rather*, start walking on home – I should. (6.1.28-3)

Princes Street station, though it has a dignity and character of its own, is by no means the only station with great possibilities. St Enoch's, Glasgow, due I think for closure, has a terrace high above St Enoch's Square which would be a splendid site for statuary or a restaurant or both. *Even better, perhaps*, you could extend the station roof across the bridge over the Clyde and diners could gaze up and down those sombre Victorian vistas which are just coming into their own. (G 18/4/67: 14, 8)

Worse indicates an unfavourable alternative, e.g.:

A commonly expressed view among delegates here is that if Britain condones U.D.I., which she herself has branded as treason, or, *worse still*, agrees to let Mr Smith have his way, good will for Britain will be destroyed. (O 24/10/63: 1, 2)

The replacive conjuncts *better* and *worse* correspond to *What is better* and *What is worse* respectively, though in some contexts it might be more appropriate to replace *is* by other forms of the verb *be*, such as *would be* or *may be*. It is possible, indeed, to analyse *better* and *worse* as elliptical clauses with ellipted *What is*. However, unlike the adjectives to be discussed later (cf. pages 213), they cannot be interpreted as elliptical clauses with ellipted *It is*. It should be noticed that *good* and *bad*, the positive forms of the comparative adjectives *better* and *worse* cannot, of course, function as conjuncts.

Like the previous three conjuncts, *instead* implies a substitution rather than an unbiased alternative. *Instead* is a replacive conjunct when it refers back to a previous clause. We can demonstrate its reference by expanding it, e.g.:

He did not use the octet and the sestet, but *instead* divided the sonnet into three quatrains and a concluding couplet . . .
(W6.1-1)

Instead can be expanded into *instead of his using the octet and the sestet*, a prepositional phrase denoting the positive alternative of what is expressed in the preceding clause. On the other hand, in the following citation it refers back to a nominal group:

> When, however, the latent heat vanishes, the situation shown in fig. 3(a) is no longer possible. *Instead*, we must have some such situation as that shown in fig. 3(b), ... (8a.3.28-3)

The adjunct *instead* in this sentence can be expanded into *instead of the situation shown in fig. 3(a)*, a prepositional phrase with a nominal group as its complement that is identical with the Subject of the preceding clause.

Both the conjunct and the adjunct may appear in initial position, but it seems that only the conjunct may precede the clausal negative particle. No examples have been observed of the conjunct *instead* in front of a negative clause, and indeed it may be rare for it to appear in such a position. But the following invented example seems to be acceptable:

> He used to arrive very early in the morning. Now, *instead*, he doesn't come before eleven.

In contrast, in the following sentence the adjunct *instead* (expandable into *instead of an early visit*) is unacceptable:

> I expected an early visit. **Instead*, he didn't come before June.

The normal indivisibility of the fossilized prepositional phrase *instead* is infringed in the next citation:

> The RAF won. Mr Healey cancelled the Navy's big carrier programme – again for perfectly good reasons – and accepted *in its stead* an alternative pared to such fine levels in requirement and in numbers of aircraft that only perfection can sustain it.
> (ST 21/8/66: 8)

Such infringement is only possible with the adjunct *instead*.

3.3.6.2.2 Antithetic conjuncts

Conversely and *contrariwise* indicate a complete opposition to what has gone before. An example of the more common *conversely* is provided:

> One is aware of masses of verbiage that can be very economically expressed in a mathematical formula, and *conversely* of very graphic and telling phrases that are extremely difficult to quantify.
> (TES 5/11/65: 947, 3)

It is interesting that *oppositely* has appeared in a recent issue of a British weekly, *The New Scientist*, with a very similar function to *conversely*:

Any normal person is depressed when circumstances (such as the loss of a loved companion, or threat of bankruptcy) give a proper cause for depression. *Oppositely*, normal people show unusual excitement in the face of a big win on the pools, or when a first novel is accepted for publication. (*The New Scientist* 11/8/66: 324)

The O.E.D. marks this function of *oppositely* as obsolete. It is not referred to in this function in the third edition of Webster's New International Dictionary.

But then can constitute a unit with the meaning 'but on the other hand', e.g.:

'I didn't realise that would be your area. It absolutely isn't mine. *But then* I haven't got any area ...' (6.1.20-3)

A number of prepositional phrases indicate an antithesis. They include *on the contrary*, *in contrast*, *by contrast*, and *by way of contrast*. A milder antithesis is indicated by *in comparison*, *by comparison*, and *by way of comparison*. *On the other hand*, which can indicate replacement, can also indicate antithesis. It always does so when it is the second of a correlative pair with *on the one hand*. Of all the adversative conjunctive prepositional phrases *on the other hand* has the widest range.

3.3.6.3 Concessive conjuncts

The semantic feature common to the concessive conjuncts has been mentioned earlier (page 37). Concessive conjuncts occupy areas of the semantic range of the conjunction *but*.

3.3.6.3.1 *Only*

The immobile conjunct *only* corresponds to *the only thing is* (*that*). No example appeared in the material examined, so I may be permitted to invent an example:

I in/tènded to gó# /ŏnly# I /didn't feel wèll#

If *only* were in the same tone unit as *I* and *I* carried the nuclear tone, then *only* would be interpreted as a restrictive focusing *I*.

The conjunct *only* appears to be limited to informal spoken English. Some native speakers of English regard the use of *only* as a conjunct as unacceptable.

3.3.6.3.2 *Else*

It is probable that the concessive conjunct *else* always follows immediately the conjunction *or*, as in the following citations:

Countries in Canada's massive physical league, with similar built-in jealousies, have achieved a sprawling coherence before now. But to do so they have had to fight a war of their own or lead a faction or throw up a distinctive culture, like the States. *Or else*, like Australia, they have had to be splendidly isolated with an obvious choice of rôles going begging; Western outpost or Asiatic helpmate. (G 30/6/67: 10, 4)

'To do nothing would lead either to the cathedral becoming a ruin *or else* place our children in the position of having to pay many times more if they could not bear the shame of our neglect', he wrote. (8fa.1-48)

The concessive conjunct *else* is equivalent to *even if not*. There are contexts, as in the first of the above citations, in which it is difficult to distinguish the concessive conjunct from the inferential conjunct *else*, equivalent to *if not*. The inferential conjunct *else* is synonymous with *otherwise*.

The conjunctive function of *else* is, of course, easily distinguished from its function as a postmodifier of certain pronoun-like items, e.g. *all, everybody, anything, somebody*.

3.3.6.3.3 *Yet*

The immobile conjunct *yet* is often equivalent to 'although that is so', e.g.:

So no A-expression can be a B-expression, or vice versa. *Yet* an A-expression can be part of a B-expression. (8b.1.151–3)

It may, indeed, reinforce the effect of the subordinators *although* or *though* that introduce the previous clause. For example, we might transform the previous clause in our last citation into a subordinate clause introduced by *although* and still retain *yet* in the superordinate clause:

So *although* no A-expression can be a B-expression, or vice versa, *yet* an A-expression can be part of a B-expression.

Many of the concessive and illative conjuncts are related in this way to subordinators and can be used to reinforce the effect of the subordinator in the preceding clause.

Not every instance of *yet* can be related to the subordination of the preceding clause by *although* or *though*. For example, it is not possible to establish such a relationship for *yet* in the next citation:

The Conservatives will not let the colour question be forgotten. They are constantly talking about it, particularly before elections. *Yet* once you teach race hatred it is very difficult to teach love.
(8fa.1-3)

However, it is possible to express the general force of *yet* in this passage by a concessive clause implied in the context, which might be phrased 'though they are teaching race hatred only for a time and only in order to win the elections'.

The adjunct *yet* cannot be confused with the conjunct, since it cannot occupy initial position.

3.3.6.3.4   *Nevertheless*

Nevertheless can often replace *yet* with a very similar force. In the next citation it reinforces the effect of the concessive subordinator *while*:

> '*While* I do not say we have won a victory – that can only come about if the Government decides to withdraw the Bill, or at least find some excuse for not proceeding with it – *nevertheless*, we have not been defeated.'   (8fa.2.23)

After the long parenthesis, *nevertheless* reminds us of the relationship of the two clauses.

Nevertheless, unlike most of the conjuncts, has no homonymous adjunct. Variation in position in the clause does not affect its function. In the course of Battery I, informants were confronted with the pair of sentences:

/neverthelĕss# /some people attèmpted it#
/some people neverthele`ss attempted it#

Fifty-three informants (83 per cent) judged these sentences to be very similar in meaning, while only seven (11 per cent) thought them very different and another four (6 per cent) 'somewhere between' these extremes. The synonymity of the sentences in the view of a large majority of the informants reflects the similarity of function of *nevertheless* in the two positions. The results of the similarity test are largely corroborated by the results of the corresponding evaluation test given earlier in the Battery. Informants were asked to judge the acceptability of the sentence:

/neverthelĕss# /some people neverthele`ss attempted it#

Of the eighty-five informants who responded, only eleven (13 per cent) accepted the sentence as 'perfectly natural and normal', while another twenty-one (25 per cent) were in doubt. On the other hand, fifty-three informants (62 per cent) rejected it completely. A larger number were in doubt in the acceptability test than in the similarity test. The results for these tests may be contrasted with those for the corresponding sentences with *also* (page 50).

3.3.6.3.5   *Still*

The immobile conjunct *still* is semantically close to *nevertheless*. Only one instance occurs in the Survey corpus:

'It's a big room and fairly cheap. Only one bathroom in the building but the other tenants refrain from baths till Saturdays, so it's not too bad. *Still*, the stairs are endless and there's not a square inch of garden to let him out in. I might move now.'

(6.1.19)

Still may appear in a non-initial position with a meaning close to *nevertheless*, but it also retains some of its temporal meaning:

It is only mediately and as a testimony that these acts are the redemptive acts of God. To that extent they cannot be compared directly with either the miracles or the death and resurrection of Jesus Christ. But they are *still* the works of the attesting Spirit, conforming to the incarnational pattern as we have it in the life and activity of Jesus Himself. (8ab.2.144-2)

Colleagues have paraphrased *But they are still* by 'But it remains true that they are' and 'But they nevertheless remain'. They have not felt that there is a temporal meaning about the conjunct in initial position. Temporal *still* may occupy initial position, e.g.:

We're sorry. We did our best. Stopped it going on dying, shovelled it into limbo. There's nothing more to be done, we'll go away. Darkness, close up this fissure; dust under roots and stones, consume our virulent contagion; silence, annul a mortal consternation. We must all recover.
But *still* the stones seemed rocked, the unsterile mounds, reimpregnated, exhaled dust's fever; a breath, impure, of earthbound anguish. (6.1.29-4)

3.3.6.3.6 *However*

However expresses some reservation with respect to what has been mentioned previously. Sometimes there is a contrast between units in the two clauses, so that *however* may be very similar to *on the other hand* though adding concessive meaning. The positioning of *however* may focus the unit being contrasted, e.g.:

Those who owned cars without safety harness were always about to have it fitted. Those with safety harness, *however*, admitted that they did not always use it. (OM 24/10/65: 53, 4)

In the Survey corpus, *however* appears mostly in scientific texts. Of thirty-five instances in the corpus, twenty-six are in scientific texts. The adjunct *however* may occupy initial position, e.g.:

However he reacts, Mr Wilson ought to take the risk of speaking plainly. (G 25/5/66: 10, 2)

However did you manage to persuade him to do it?

However may also be a premodifier, e.g.:

But we should still foster it it, *however* much of an embarrassment it
may be to us. (6.2.107-1)

The context will normally show whether these are conjuncts or not.
In cases of ambiguity, intonation and punctuation separation will
make it clear that *however* is a conjunct.

The acceptability of *however* in front of a question was tested in
Battery I. Informants were required to turn the following sentence
into a *yes-no* question:

how/ĕver# he /started a new bùsiness#

Seventy-one informants (84 per cent) produced non-compliant responses. Forty-eight (56 per cent) transposed the conjunct, twenty-
eight putting it before the lexical verb and twenty at the very end.
There are therefore clear signs of dissatisfaction with the target sentence. But there are also indications that some informants felt uneasy
about retaining *however* in the sentence. Fourteen informants (16 per
cent) omitted it altogether. We may contrast the results of this test with
those for similar tests on sentences containing *today* and *suddenly*,
which are likewise unacceptable in front of a question. The same informants were asked at different stages of Battery I to turn these into
yes-no questions:

to/dăy# the mu/seum was òpen#
/sŭddenly# he /opened the dòor#

We may now compare the number of non-compliant responses, the
number of sentences in which the initial item was transposed, and
the number of sentences in which it was omitted.

	non-compliance	omission	transposition
however	71 (84)	14 (16)	48 (56)
today	82 (96)	0 (0)	80 (94)
suddenly	84 (99)	3 (4)	82 (96)

We see that in the tests involving *today* and *suddenly* almost all the
informants produced a non-compliant response and in virtually
all cases the non-compliance was realised in the transposition of the
initial item. Since there is no doubt about the acceptability of *today*
and *suddenly* in a question, the deviance that would have resulted from
compliance was merely positional. Transposition of *today* and *suddenly*
was an easy and obvious rectification of the deviance, and it was considered a sufficient rectification by nearly all the informants. As we have
seen, fourteen of the informants did not consider it a sufficient rectification for the question involving *however*, since they preferred to omit
the conjunct.

An evaluation test in the same Battery provides confirmation of the unacceptability of *however* before a question. Twenty-five informants (29 per cent) judged this sentence 'wholly unnatural and abnormal':

how/ĕver# /did he start a new busíness#

Another thirty-seven informants (44 per cent) accepted it unreservedly, while the remaining twenty-three (27 per cent) were undecided. Thus, as in the compliance test, only a minority were prepared to show their complete acceptance of *however* in front of a question, though there is a greater tolerance in the evaluation test.

3.3.6.3.7 *Though*

The conjunct *though* in the second of a sequence of two clauses may be logically equivalent to the subordination of the first clause with the conjunction *though* as subordinator, e.g.:

His food is rather a problem. He looks fit *though*, doesn't he?

(6.1.18)

→ Though his food is rather a problem, he looks fit, doesn't he?

Often such a transformation is not possible, e.g.:

    A ((it)) /dôesn't contribute to ði candidate's ability# ·
?'   /to · write · or · read · corréctly# /I don't ?thìnk#
     – /that's
    B *m/hṁ#*
    A the most dùbious gróund ((*though*))#   (S.1c.11-73)

We can, however, imagine an implied concessive clause, such as 'though I am offering it as one of the reasons'.

A concessive clause introduced by *though* is often mobile with respect to the superordinate clause, e.g.:

Though he is poor he is happy.
He is happy *though he is poor*.

In these two instances *though* is undoubtedly a conjunction. We can, however, juxtapose the clauses and place *though* at the end of what had before been the superordinate clause:

He is poor. He is happy, *though*.

Though is now a conjunct. The relationship between the two clauses is preserved if we place *though* at the beginning of the clause, provided we separate the clauses by a major mark of punctuation, e.g.:

He is poor – *though* he is happy.

In speech a special kind of intonation would be needed, e.g.:

he is /pòor# – though he /is hăppy#

Though in this instance is nearer to the mobile conjunct than to the subordinating conjunction.

A clear example of the conjunct *though* in initial position appeared in a London evening newspaper:

> If the Government really insists on maintaining some sort of contact with China despite its obvious futility, it is possible to do so without actually having representations there.
>
> TOLERATED TOO LONG
> *Though* the country would probably gain a good deal more respect abroad if we stopped playing this childish game of tit-for-tat. If we instead told the Chinese to release our diplomats immediately in return for sending their representatives home.
>
> *(Evening Standard* 30/8/67: 6, 1)

This initial *though* is mobile. If we were to place it after *the country* we would not have altered the meaning of the sentence nor changed its relationship to the rest of the paragraph. It is significant that the sentence with initial *though* heads a new paragraph separated from the previous paragraph by a headline.

Two other citations are brought to exemplify the conjunct *though* in initial position:

> We'd better hurry back and ring up the vet – *though* I doubt if we'd get him on a Saturday evening.   (6.1.25-3)

> My favourite poster is, I think, a French one for Nesquik, which shows a sophisticated-looking small boy leaning nonchalantly against something and saying that thanks to Nesquik he went back on to milk. He really looks a nice child. *Though* there are some Adchildren that one would feel quite ashamed to have around the house.   (G 27/10/66: 6, 5)

In contrast, *though* in the next citation is a conjunction and cannot be moved from initial position:

> it's got the /right to keep its great · industrial – armaments fàctory# because it can be /turned into armaments any moment *though* the armaments part has been destroyed at Krúpps#
>
> (5b.1.46)

When *although* is separated from a preceding superordinate clause by a major mark of punctuation in written English, it approaches the semantic effect of the conjunct *though* in initial position. For example, *although* in the next citation can be replaced by *though*, and *though* can be moved elsewhere in the clause with little change of meaning:

The plain fact is that Martins can never hope to catch up with the others in size. If ever its deposit growth slips seriously behind it must know that its days are numbered (*although* any bidder would have to get Martins' agreement to make it work).

(ST *Business News* 16/1/66: 3, 3)

In spoken English a pause and a special kind of intonation would be needed, as for the initial conjunct *though*. It is possible to regard *although* in this use as nearer to an immobile conjunct. It will be noticed that *although* can replace *though* in the examples that have been given of the conjunct *though* in initial position.

3.3.6.3.8 *Besides*

Besides indicates that an addition is being made to a process of reasoning. It suggests that even if a previous reason were not sufficient, the reason being offered should be taken into account. This connotation of *besides* is exemplified in the following citations:

> The worthy citizen stays to face the plague in London because he believes it to be God's will, and *besides* he has a warehouse full of valuable merchandise. (W6.1-12)

> The call for a Royal Commission, though tempting, is only a call for more delay. As for a filibuster, this is neither honourable, nor dignified, or democratic. *Besides*, the Government has wisely indicated that it will provide extra time if necessary.

(G 1/6/67: 8, 2)

In addition to the conjunct, there is a preposition *besides* and an additive adjunct.

3.3.6.3.9 *Anyhow, anyway*

Anyhow and *anyway* are similar to *besides*, except that they are mobile. An instance is given of the use of *anyway*:

> 'Yes, dear,' replied his mother in a worried sort of way; 'I have invited all the village, except, of course, the two Misses Umbrage, who wouldn't have come *anyway*.' (6.3.203-3)

Anyway in this passage has the general force of 'even if I had invited them' or perhaps 'whether or not I had invited them'.

3.3.6.3.10 Prepositional phrases

A number of prepositional phrases have concessive force. *All the same* is analogous to *nevertheless*, *at the same time* to *still*, and the three phrases *at any rate*, *in any case*, and *in any event* to *anyhow* and *anyway*. Others include *in spite of that*, *for all that*, and *at all events*.

3.3.7   Illative conjuncts

Illative conjuncts primarily indicate that what is being said is a consequence or result of what has been said before. *Somehow* is exceptional in that the cause is never made explicit in the preceding context.

3.3.7.1   *So*

Sometimes the immobile conjunct *so* has the meaning of 'because of that', e.g.:

> Only one bathroom in the building but the other tenants refrain from baths till Saturdays, *so* it's not too bad.   (6.1.19-1)

Often its reference is much vaguer, and it may be virtually equivalent to 'it follows from what we have said', e.g.:

> Now we can say that terms referred to and terms predicated are alike *introduced* [ital. sic]. So expressions of the two classes distinguished in List II, i.e. A$_2$s and B$_2$s are alike in introducing terms, even though they introduce them in different ways, being used respectively to refer to them and to predicate them. The failure of Geach's definition to distinguish these ways of introducing terms consists essentially in the fact that an assertion may, depending on the context, be said to be *about* [ital. sic] any term introduced into it, and not merely about the term or terms introduced in the referring way.
>
> *So*, then, the expression 'Socrates' and 'is wise' ('Raleigh' and 'smokes') have in common the fact that each serves to introduce a term into the remark 'Socrates is wise' ('Raleigh smokes'); ...
>
> (8b.1.146-3)

In the next citation *so* is partly continuative, partly summative. The final sentence might be paraphrased 'So you see that's the situation we're in'.

> He asked me if I could look after him till he came out, so I went down last Spring and collected him. But I don't think he will ever come out. . . . He's worse. *So* there we are.   (6.1.18)

In our final citation for the conjunct *so*, we see it virtually weakened to sequential *and*:

> a /girl went into a chemist's shōp# and /asked fōr# ·
> /contracèptive tablets# – – ((*so* he said)) /well I've got · all
> kînds# and · /all prîces# what do you wànt#   (S.1c. 11-29)

Several homonyms of the conjunct *so* may occupy initial position. Closest to the central meaning of the conjunct is the use of *so* in the compound conjunction *so that*, equivalent to 'with the result that':

The lower part of the scale will be affected by the central pay settlement, but not the top, *so that* by 1966, when their minimum will have risen to £2,888, the span of the scale will have fallen from £432 to £162. (8fa.1-37)

A clause introduced by *so that* is sequentially related to the previous clause when *so that* has the meaning 'with the result that', i.e. the clause cannot be transposed. If *that* is omitted, we are left with the immobile conjunct *so*, which can be preceded by *and*, unlike the compound conjunction.

There is another compound conjunction *so that* with the meaning 'in order that':

With a ball-point pen, he wrote it all down in the weather pro-forma – the oblong card which chimed the hours on the dar-kened flight-deck – and passed it back *so that* the engineer could add the fuel available, . . . (6.4.59–1)

That can be omitted here too, but *so* would remain a conjunction since it cannot be preceded by *and*. Moreover, when *so that* and *so* have the meaning 'in order that', their clauses are mobile. An example of this use of *so* is cited:

'Makes a nice week's holiday for you, Mr Brocklehurst,' Payton suggested, craning his neck round Cavendish's bulk *so* he could see and be seen. (6.4.55-3)

So may be the second of a correlative pair of which the first is *as* or *just as*, e.g.:

/*just as* Eŭrope# must /put aside · old habits of wár# and
/doctrines fórmed# at the /height of the East West cónflicts# – –
/*so* Britain and Nigèria# must cast òff# /old ways of thìnking#
(4c.1b-9)

In this function, *so* has the meaning 'likewise'.

So may function as a pro-form:

After Mass, the 66-year-old Pontiff spoke to the convicts. Wardens and prisoners wept during his speech. *So* did the Pope.
(8fa.2.27)

Together with *did*, *so* is substituting for *wept during his speech* present in the previous clause. Verb-Subject inversion takes place when the Subject alone is different from that of the previous clause. Verb-Subject inversion and initial placement of *so* are obligatory unless an adjunct is added, e.g. *The Pope did so too*. *So* in this function can only appear in initial position when in an affirmative clause.

The manner adjunct *so* may occupy initial position:

'Life was very hard in those days.' *So* he began his story.

If the second sentence occurred in isolation, we would be in doubt whether *so* was the immobile conjunct or the mobile manner adjunct. However, if we were confronted with the sentence

So he didn't begin his story.

we would be sure that *so* was a conjunct, since manner adjuncts do not precede the clause negative particle.

3.3.7.2 *Hence*

The immobile conjunct *hence* can be paraphrased 'it follows from that (what has been said before)', an analogy in discourse of spatial movement conveyed by the adjunct *hence* ('from here'). We may compare the analogy with temporal succession implied in the conjuncts *still*, *yet*, *nevertheless*, *then*, and *now*. Some of the conjunctions, e.g. *while*, *since*, and *as*, are used both for temporal and logical succession.

Hence can sometimes be replaced by the conjunct *so*:

The dimerisation reaction (13c) has been shown not to occur, and *hence* chain-termination must take place by a reaction of radicals R'' with the solvent giving products which do not enter into the chain process.   (8a.4.37-3)

It cannot be replaced by *so*, however, in the verbless clause in the next citation:

The animal often comes to rest, attaching itself with the sucker to stones (*hence* the name, 'suck-stone') or to its prey.
                                                                        (8a.1.84-3)

The parenthesis can be paraphrased 'from this (characteristic) derives the name "suck-stone" '.

3.3.7.3 *Therefore*

The mobile conjunct *therefore* often indicates that what is being said is a consequence or result of a previous statement, e.g.:

And because the Church is human, and *therefore* fallible, there are constant tensions, . . .   (8ab.2.145-1)

When *therefore* appears within the clause and is followed by intonation or punctuation separation, it tends to focus on the previous linguistic unit, e.g.:

The hydrogen atoms also, *therefore*, must occupy positions appropriate to these same unit cells.   (8a.2.183-3)

In the Survey corpus *therefore* usually occupies initial position in texts drawn from spoken English, while in written English it is prevalent before the lexical verb or after the equative verb *be*.

The conjunct *therefore* has no homonymous adjuncts. In the course of Battery II informants were presented with the sentences:

/thĕrefore# /many seats are booked a week befòre#
/many seats are therefore booked a week befòre#

156 informants (87 per cent) judged the sentences to be very similar in meaning. Only twelve (7 per cent) thought them very different, while another eleven (6 per cent) considered that they were 'somewhere between'. It is clear that the variation in position of *therefore* was not semantically significant for the vast majority of the informants. The same informants had been asked earlier in the Battery to judge the acceptability of a sentence with two instances of *therefore*:

/thĕrefore# /many seats were therefore booked a week befòre#

127 informants (71 per cent) rejected the sentence, twelve (7 per cent) accepted it fully, while forty (22 per cent) were in doubt about its acceptability. We may assume that the perception of a similarity of meaning between the two instances of *therefore* contributed to the size of the majority who rejected the sentence or were dubious about it (cf. pages 50f., 64).

3.3.7.4 *Now*

There is an illative conjunct *now* which might be paraphrased 'since that is so', though temporal force is not entirely absent. The following citations exemplify this use of *now*:

> Come, Winifred, we have done what we can. *Now* the affair will have to be left in the hands of the police.   (6.3.208-1)

> /there's been a change of jŏckey# for the /fàvourite# · in the /Lincolnshire Handicap this afternòon# – ə /Lester Pìggott# will /now ride Solar Chárge# · in/stead of the Irish apprĕntice# /Vivien Kĕnnedy# · /who was taken ìll this morning#   (4c. 1-16)

The illative conjunct may co-occur with a temporal adjunct indicating a time other than the present, e.g.:

> Lester Piggot will *now* ride Solar Charge *tomorrow*.

The potentiality for such co-occurrences distinguishes the illative conjunct from the temporal adjunct *now*. The relationship to the conjunction *now* (*that*) will be noticed. For example, in the second sentence of the first citation, the general force of *now* could be conveyed by the subordination of the previous clause with the conjunction *now* (*that*) as subordinator:

3*

Now (that) we have done what we can, the affair will have to be left in the hands of the police.

3.3.7.5   *Thus*

The illative conjunct *thus* can usually be replaced by *therefore*:

> Presumably the action of this muscle deepens the oral cavity and is *thus* the main agent securing attachment of the sucker.
> (8a.1.88-2)

All twenty-three instances of the illative conjunct *thus* in the Survey corpus appear in either the scientific texts or in the philosophical text.

The manner adjunct *thus* cannot appear before the clausal negative particle, though it can occupy initial position in an affirmative clause. We contrast *Thus he began his story*, in which *thus* is ambiguous between conjunct and manner adjunct, with *Thus he didn't begin his story*, in which *thus* can only be a conjunct (cf. page 72 for the same contrast between conjunct *so* and manner adjunct *so*).

3.3.7.6   *Somehow*

The illative conjunct *somehow* has the meaning 'for some reason'. It is exemplified in this invented example:

> *Somehow*, he seems happier than he used to be.

The manner adjunct *somehow*, meaning 'in some way', may also appear in initial position, e.g.:

> It was in Tarquin's third year that the supply of nannies gave out. After that they would not come even for two weeks at a time. *Somehow* word had got round among the nannies of England, primly debated over large black perambulators in Regent's Park, furtively whispered between nursery maids having a secret cigarette in the lavatories, coldly knitted into jumpers by lonely love-sick governesses in countless schoolrooms, that Bidcombe was no cop.   (6.3.199-3)

If we negate the sentence headed by *somehow* in this citation, then *somehow* is interpreted as the conjunct:

> *Somehow* word had *not* got round among the nannies of England . . .

3.3.7.7   *Accordingly, consequently*

Accordingly and *consequently* can usually be replaced by *therefore*, though *therefore* is probably less acceptable at the end of the clause. Their use as illative conjuncts is exemplified in the following citations:

> American drama teaching leaves him cold, too – 'lacking discipline, lacking organisation'. *Accordingly*, Fernald is spending

some of his summer recess over here organising a quiet drama
brain drain, ... (G 30/6/67: 10, 6)

The constitutional position of the Prime Minister will be something of a paradox: the colony has been self-governing for
forty years, but Mr Wilson refuses to admit that Britain is
consequently relieved of direct responsibility. (O 24/10/65: 1, 5)

The manner adjunct *accordingly* only appears in some position after
the verb. Its use is illustrated in the following invented sentence:

The dying man told the solicitor what he wanted and he drew
up the will *accordingly*.

O.E.D. and Webster's Third New International Dictionary record
as obsolete a manner adjunct *consequently* with the meaning 'in succession'.

Prepositional phrases with a similar function to illative conjuncts
include *in consequence, as a consequence, as a result*.

3.3.8 Inferential conjuncts

Two of the inferential conjuncts, *else* and *otherwise*, have a negative
implication.

3.3.8.1 *Then*

The inferential conjunct *then* is semantically equivalent to 'if so' or
'in that case', as illustrated in the following citations:

F we've got /two minutes lèft in which to answer this quéstion#
/Victor Mìshcon#
V ((well)) /very quìckly *thén*#   (5b.16.71)

'In fact, half my days seem to be spent in taking personal
cognisance of Louis Bates.'
    '*Then* you must realise that he's egocentric to the most extrava-
gant degree. He's irrepressible, ...' (6.2.106-3)

In half of the thirty-six instances in the Survey corpus, it appears in
a superordinate clause following a conditional clause, e.g.:

so I begin to feel that if I ought to marry Mr. Eborebelosa *then*
probably I ought to marry him too. (6.2.92-1)

Indeed, in mathematics the use of *then* after an *if*-clause has become
institutionalised.

The conjunct *then* and the temporal adjunct are not, it appears,
differentiated by position or by features of intonation or punctuation.
There seems, however, to be a potential difference in pronunciation.
The temporal adjunct is always pronounced /ðɛn/; the illative conjunct

may be pronounced /ðɛn/, as in the citation from the spoken text above, but it may be reduced to /ðən/ or /ðɪn/. A criterion for the illative conjunct would be that it was either pronounced in the reduced forms or was capable of being replaced by them.

An instance of *then* that cannot be replaced by 'if so' or 'in that case' may be conveniently noted here:

'Yes, I know,' said Treece, 'and I . . . well, I apologise.' 'Well, what is it, *then?*' said a brisk voice; it was the waitress.

(S.1b.6-20)

In this passage the waitress is interrupting Treece. *Then* is related to the previous situational context and suggests that the woman has been waiting impatiently for the meal to be ordered. *Now*, on the other hand, would suggest a departure from the previous linguistic or situational context:

Well, what is it, *now?*

3.3.8.2 *Else*

The inferential conjunct *else* is semantically equivalent to 'if not'. It can be distinguished semantically from the concessive conjunct *else*, meaning 'even if not', cf. pages 62f. Unlike the concessive conjunct, it need not be preceded by *or*. I borrow an example from Jacobson (1964, 250), who cites a sentence from Victor Bonham-Carter's book *The English Village* (published by Pelican Books, 1952, page 62):

To meet the needs of the new situation, agriculture had to undergo a drastic change – that was indisputable, *else* the country would have starved.

The inferential conjunct *else* may be added to reinforce the implication of a conditional relationship in a sentence consisting of an imperative clause linked to a following declarative clause by *or*, e.g.:

Hand over your money, or *else* I'll shoot.

3.3.8.3 *Otherwise*

The inferential conjunct *otherwise* is also equivalent to 'if not', but is more likely to occur in non-initial position than *else*. An example is given:

/what about the màsses of people# /who go down to the hóliday camps# · /who might not ŏtherwise# /ever have the chance of sèeing the beautiful countryside#   (5b.16.65)

In some contexts the conjunct can be more accurately paraphrased by 'apart from that', though even in such contexts we can indicate the negative condition implicit in *otherwise* by a conditional clause such as 'if it were not for that', e.g.:

> The vagrants are the dramatic element, the press of the thorn, in Father Fehily's weekly round. *Otherwise* his life follows the orderly pattern of devotional grind that is imposed on all Dublin priests by weight of numbers and the amenability of the congregations to the discipline of the faith. (STM 9/7/63: 27, 1)

The conjunct *otherwise* is to be distinguished from the manner adjunct meaning 'differently' or 'in a different manner', e.g.:

> It is only in the light of fulfilled revelation that we can see the Father and know the Holy Ghost. And that revelation means Jesus Christ.
>   There is, of course, a temptation to have it *otherwise*.
>   (8ab.2.135-2)

It does not seem possible for the adjunct to appear in initial position. If the conjunct occupies a position open to the adjunct, the appropriate interpretation is usually resolved by the context. In cases of ambiguity the item is likely to be interpreted as conjunct if separated from the verb by comma punctuation in written English and by being in a different tone unit in spoken English.

3.3.9 Temporal transition conjuncts

Meantime and *meanwhile* can be substituted one for the other, though there may be idiolectal preferences for one or the other. An example of *meanwhile* occurs in the following citation:

> B ((it'll /only)) be seven years by the time thát comes round#
> A /m̀# – is the /readership going thrōugh# · *méanwhile*#
>   (S.1c.11-21)

It is significant that *meanwhile* can readily appear in front of a question, e.g.:

> /mĕanwhile# is the /readership going thróugh#

In general, temporal adjuncts are not acceptable in front of a question (cf. the tests involving *today*, page 66).

Despite their temporal significance, the two conjuncts do not have an effect on the time-relationship of the verb. They do not 'specify' the tense of the verb.[1]

The prepositional phrases *in the meantime* and *in the meanwhile* have a similar function to the conjuncts.

---

[1] For a discussion of time-relationships as a product of the specification of the tense by a temporal adjunct, see Crystal 1966. In fact, Crystal considers these two conjuncts among the temporal adjuncts that have this effect. However, they do not seem to me to affect the time relationship of the verb.

3.4 Positions of conjuncts in the Survey corpus

Some conjuncts are restricted to initial position in the clause. These
have been marked by an asterisk in the list of conjuncts set out on
pages 36f. Table 6 (page 79) states the positions of conjuncts in the
Survey corpus according to their text category.

In the list that follows, the symbols F, M, and E denote the positions
of conjuncts in the declarative form of a finite verb clause, except when
they are preceded by another alphabetic symbol.

F   – the conjunct is in front of a finite verb clause; conjunctions,
yes, *no*, and *well* may precede it, and so may other conjuncts
(the two instances of this last are noted); numbers in brackets
denote immobile conjuncts and are included in the previous
total

IF   – in front of an imperative clause

QF   – in front of an interrogative clause

VF   – in front of a verbless clause

NF   – in front of a non-finite verb clause

M1   – between adjunct and Subject

M2   – between Subject and Verb where no auxiliary is present

M3   – between Subject and auxiliary

M4   – between auxiliary and another auxiliary

M5   – between auxiliary and Verb

M6   – between auxiliary *be* and *-ed* form of Verb

M7   – between Verb *be* and Complement

M8   – between transitive Verb and Complement

E   – after intransitive Verb or after Complement (it need not be
immediately after either)

QE   – at end of interrogative clause

VE   – at end of verbless clause

NE   – at end of non-finite verb clause

NGp – parenthetic insertion within nominal group

The left-hand column of Table 6 gives the text categories. The number of words in each category is given in brackets below the category
name.

Table 6 demonstrates that the favoured position for conjuncts in the
Survey corpus is in front of the clause. Approximately, three out of every
four conjuncts occupy that position. Even if we only take into account
those that are mobile, and hence are free to occupy other positions,
nearly twice as many conjuncts are in front of the clause as appear
elsewhere.[1]

---

[1] Two instances of *then* recorded for F position in the Philosophy text occur
after the immobile conjunct *so*.

TABLE 6 *Positions of conjuncts in Survey corpus*

	F	IF	QF	VF	NF	M1	M2	M3	M4	M5	M6	M7	M8	E	QE	VE	NE	NGp	Total
SCIENCE (20,000)	77 (12)			5 (1)	3 (3)	4	9	3	2	7	6	20		2					138
PHILOSOPHY (5,000)	26 (15)			1			3					1	1	2					34
THEOLOGY (5,000)	11 (7)			1					1										13
NOVELS (20,000)	14 (2)	3												4	1				22
NEWSPAPERS (10,000)	12 (3)							1		1			1	1					16
STUDENT ESSAYS (5,000)	14 (10)					2					1								17
DISCUSSION (20,000)	68 (4)	3	7 (1)	1				1	1	1		1		11	1	1		1	97
CONVERSATION (10,000)	45 (15)	1	4 (1)	1 (1)	1					2			1	13	1				69
BBC NEWS (5,000)	3									4	1						1		9
Total	270 (301)	7	11	9	4	6	12	5	4	15	8	22	3	33	3	1	1	1	415

Bracketed foot-totals: {301} (F–NF), {75} (M1–M8), {38} (E–NGp), {114} (M1–NGp).

The evidence from the Survey corpus suggests that conjuncts act as style markers. Some individual conjuncts seem to be restricted to particular varieties of the language or occur more commonly in these varieties, e.g. *only* (page 62), *however* (page 65), and *thus* (page 74). Furthermore, the frequency of conjuncts as a whole varies considerably with the kind of English. Table 7 is derived from the right-hand column of totals in Table 6. It shows the relative frequency of conjuncts in the text categories. The digits opposite each text category denote the number of conjuncts per 1,000 words in the category.

TABLE 7 *Frequencies of conjuncts in text categories*

Science	6·9	Student essays	3·4
Philosophy	6·8	Discussion	4·9
Theology	2·6	Conversation	6·9
Novels	1·1	BBC News	1·8
Newspapers	1·6	TOTAL	4·2

Table 7 demonstrates that there are far fewer conjuncts in narration, a type of discourse which includes the news texts (non-fiction) as well as the novels (fiction). The small number of conjuncts in novels are confined to dialogue, so that no conjuncts occur in the narrative parts of the novels. On the other hand, there are many more conjuncts in conversation and discussion and in the scientific and philsophical texts. This difference is to be expected, since most of the conjuncts are logical connectives, required more in exposition and argument than in narration.

Finally, we refer back to Table 6 for two points about positional frequencies with respect to the text categories. It is striking that of the seventy-five conjuncts in M positions fifty-one come from scientific texts. Twenty of these are confined to M7, the position between the Verb *be* and the Complement. The other point to notice is that the majority of conjuncts in E positions come from the discussion and conversation texts.

Chapter 4

Style disjuncts

In Chapter 2 we distinguished disjuncts from conjuncts by a single test: disjuncts can serve as a response to a *yes-no* question, though some require to be accompanied by *yes* or *no* (cf. page 25). A sub-class of disjuncts can be isolated which I shall term STYLE DISJUNCTS.[1] Style disjuncts refer to what Poldauf has called the 'form of the communication' (Poldauf 1964, 245). Some citations will illustrate the items to be included in this sub-class:

Seriously, we haven't heard much of our two heroes lately, have we?   (G 5/8/66: 12, 2)

What does it give you? *Quite simply* it gives you faster, more efficient internal communications.   (O 24/10/65: 3)

The Conservatives, who have a majority of two, claim that the Minister should not grant the dispensation as it would be contrary to accepted practice. This, *broadly*, is that such a dispensation is granted only if its absence would make it impossible for the majority on the council to carry its business.   (G 8/8/66: 2, 5)

But *strictly*, all the Old Testament is prophetic of Jesus Christ.   (8ab.2.136–2)

but /*quite frănkly*# as a /man who has to pay high tăxes# for my/self and my fămily# as I'm /sure everybody here ((is)) in the àudience# · I /strongly dèprecate# · /fòreigners# /coming to this còuntry# · and being /ăble# · to to /ùse# /our sérvice# · with/òut paying# /ănything# /for it at àll#   (5b.16.51)

---

[1] The term is an adaptation of 'style tertiaries', a designation coined by Jespersen (1937 and 1949, 88).

Later, when it was learned that the NLC had been restored, the crowds shouted for joy, *quite literally.* (ST 23/4/67: 6, 3)

But isn't the mating of fact and fiction loading the dice? And, *more specifically,* were not the politics in 'Cathy' naive and negative? (G 12/1/67: 7, 1)

Briefly, India faces famine because there too are many people and too little food. (STM 26/3/67: 34, 1)

And as California goes today, so goes the nation tomorrow and, *parenthetically,* so may go the rest of the world ten to twenty years hence. (STM 7/4/68: 22, 2)

4.1 Correspondences

The relationship of a style disjunct to its clause can be expressed by a corresponding clause in which a verb of speaking is present. Let us take as an example the sentence:

Confidentially, she is very stupid.

We can show the relationship of *confidentially* to the rest of the sentence by a number of correspondences:

I am speaking confidentially when I say (that) she . . .
I am putting it confidentially when I say (that) she . . .
I tell you confidentially (that) she . . .
I would say confidentially (that) she . . .
If I may speak confidentially [I would say (that)] she . . .
If I may put it confidentially [I would say (that)] she . . .

This list of correspondences is not intended to be exhaustive.

If *confidentially* is in front of a question, then it has somewhat different correspondences. Let us take as an example the question:

Confidentially, is she very stupid?

The relationship of *confidentially* to the question that follows is ambiguous. In one meaning of the sentence, *confidentially* has the correspondence:

I ask confidentially: is she very stupid?

In the other meaning, it has the correspondence:

Tell me confidentially: is she very stupid?

As with the declarative sentence there are other correspondences to *confidentially* in either of the two interpretations. For example, in the first interpretation, correspondences include

I put it to you confidentially: is she very stupid?

while in the second interpretation a possible correspondence is:

I ask you to tell me confidentially: is she very stupid?

We can regard *confidentially* as a truncated clause, sole unit in surface structure of one of several correspondences in deep structure. In surface structure its function is that of style disjunct; in deep structure its function is that of adjunct in a corresponding clause. (For a discussion of the status of correspondences in the light of transformational grammar, see Chapter 10.)

Many style disjuncts have an additional type of correspondence, in which the adjective base of the disjunct appears and not the homonymous adjunct. Let us take as an example the sentence:

Frankly, she isn't very stupid.

A possible correspondence for *frankly* would be:

If I may be frank, [*I would say (that)*] she isn't very stupid.

Slightly different forms are required when the style disjunct relates to a question:

Frankly, isn't she very stupid?

In one interpretation of the sentence the disjunct has the correspondence:

If I may ask you to be frank, tell me: isn't she very stupid?

In the other interpretation, the disjunct corresponds to:

If I may be frank, [*I would ask:*] isn't she very stupid?

Those style disjuncts that have this additional type of correspondence will also have its non-finitisation as correspondence. Thus, for the conditional clause in the sentence

If I may be frank, [*I would say (that)*] she isn't very stupid.

we have:

To be frank, [*I would say (that)*] she isn't very stupid.

Let us, however, replace *frankly* by another style disjunct, *relatively:*

Relatively, she isn't very stupid.

In this case, we have only the correspondences with the adjunct, e.g.:

If I may speak relatively, [*I would say (that)*] she isn't very stupid.

There is no corresponding finite-verb clause with the adjective *relative*:

If I may be relative, [*I would say (that)*] she isn't very stupid.

Hence, there is no corresponding non-finite verb clause:

*To be relative, [I would say (that)] she isn't very stupid.[1]

The structures with conditional clauses are presumably the closest correspondences since their subordinate status reflects the subordinate status of the style disjunct. Nevertheless, it is significant that *I would say quite truthfully* in the text to be cited has the force of the style disjunct *quite truthfully*:

> we were /asked what our vìews were# *I would /say quite trŭthfully#* until /two minutes agó# I /didn't hàve any#

(5b.1.6)

We can compare:

> we were /asked what our vìews were# /*quite trŭthfully#*
> until /two minutes agó# I /didn't hàve any#

As with previous correspondences containing conditional clauses, we must assume that the conditional clause is subordinate to an implied clause with a verb of speaking. It is not subordinated to the clause to which the style disjunct relates, as can be demonstrated by a simple test. When a conditional clause precedes its superordinate clause, the latter can accommodate an inferential *then*, equivalent to 'in that case' or 'it follows from that'. Let us apply this test to *If I may be frank, she isn't very stupid*. It is clear that by inserting inferential *then* in the second clause we produce an unacceptable sentence: *If I may be frank, then she isn't very stupid*. This indicates that *If I may be frank* is not conditional to *she isn't very stupid*. On the other hand, there is no doubt that it is acceptable to insert *then* in the sentence *If I may be frank, then I would say (that) she isn't very stupid*. In the acceptable sentence *If I may be frank, she is very stupid* we must assume a suppressed apodosis to the conditional clause, such as *I would say*.

4.2 Syntactic features

Since style disjuncts share many of the syntactic features of other disjuncts, we avoid repetition by including them in our account of the syntactic features of attitudinal disjuncts (§5.2, pages 111ff.). Nevertheless, several generalisations about style disjuncts can conveniently be stated here:

[1] they may freely appear in front of questions, e.g.:

---

[1] *Confidentially* is evidently an exception. *If I may be confidential* is acceptable but there does not seem to be a corresponding *To be confidential*.

Seriously,⎫
Candidly,⎬how do I look?[1]

Personally seems to be an exception.

[2] many may freely appear in front of imperative and optative clauses, and even when the clauses are negated, e.g.:

Honestly,⎫don't tell him about it.
Confidentially,⎬let's not tell him about it.

Other style disjuncts seem to be unacceptable in these types of clauses, e.g. *truly* and *logically*.

[3] most style disjuncts may be premodified by *very*, *quite*, *less*, and *more*. Examples will be found in the citations given on pages 81f. Some style disjuncts only occur when premodified by a comparative, e.g.:

Miss Toklas was eighty-nine when she died. For three years she had been bedridden, cared for by a pair of ancient servants, in her flat in Rue de la Convention.
   More cheerfully, a figure whom vaguely one had thought probably dead because certainly historic, has been in the news. (G 11/3/67: 7, 8)

More cheerfully, will commute in this context with 'turning now to a more cheerful subject' or 'speaking more cheerfully'. *Truly* seems to be exceptional in not allowing modification.

4.3 Homonyms

As with other disjuncts, features of position, punctuation and intonation may be needed to distinguish style disjuncts from homonyms (cf. Chapter 6). Since the Survey corpus contains very few instances of style disjuncts, it is not possible to bring evidence of the positions in which they usually occur. Intuitively, however, style disjuncts seem to favour initial position. Of the seven style disjuncts in the Survey corpus, five are in initial position.

4.3.1 Manner adjuncts and intensifiers: *honestly* and *frankly*
Some style disjuncts have two homonyms, one a manner adjunct and

---

[1] The acceptability of the style disjunct *confidentially* was tested in the course of Battery 1. Informants were asked to turn into a *yes-no* question the sentence:
   con/fidĕntially# he is a /fòol#
Seventy-two informants (85 per cent) complied with the instruction. A similar majority of seventy-one informants (84 per cent) judged the question to be perfectly acceptable when it was presented to them in an evaluation test:
   con/fidĕntially# /is he a fóol#

the other an intensifier. We can illustrate the homonyms with *frankly* and *honestly*.

[1a] *Frankly*, I have never set out to educate my readers.
                                                    (G 19/8/66: 9, 1)
[1b] 'It is, *frankly*, unfair to many people.'   (ST 10/4/66: 3, 2)
[1c] *Honestly*, I don't care.
[2a] He was, he said, '*frankly* puzzled' by his Government's attitude to reform movement. (G 25/10/65: 9, 4)
[2b] But I don't think I'm deceiving myself like that, Professor Treece; I *honestly* don't.   (6.2.93-1)
[3a] He looked her up and down *frankly*.   (6.4.48-1)
[3b] He *frankly* admitted that he would not like to be headmaster of a two-year sixth-form college.   (TES 5/11/65: 960, 4)
[3c] 'I can *honestly* and sincerely say it was no deliberate attempt on our part.'   (G 8/9/66: 9, 1)

Sentences [1a]–[1c] contain style disjuncts. In sentences [2a] and [2b] *frankly* and *honestly* are intensifiers, roughly synonymous with *really*, whilst the last set of sentences display the manner adjuncts.

Intensifiers differ syntactically from style disjuncts in that they are restricted to positions before the auxiliary or the lexical verb.

Intensifiers differ syntactically from manner adjuncts in several ways:

[1] intensifiers cannot appear after the verb, e.g. *frankly* in *He admitted that frankly* cannot be an intensifier.
[2] intensifiers can appear before the clausal negative particle; thus, 'He *honestly* answered her question' is ambiguous between the intensifier and the adjunct, whereas 'He *honestly* hasn't answered her question' must be the intensifier.
[3] intensifiers have a wider collocational range with verbs than manner adjuncts. Thus, *honestly* in *He can honestly say he didn't do it* will be probably interpreted as a manner adjunct, but it could be an intensifier. On the other hand, in *He honestly deceived me* it will be taken as an intensifier.[1]
[4] intensifiers do not come within the focus of clause interrogation, negation or comparison.

Experimental evidence can be brought from tests in Battery 1 to

---

[1] The intensifier *honestly* may well tend to co-occur with clausal negation. There are, however, only two examples in the corpus, though both happen to be in negative clauses. One is given above in citation [2b], and the other is:

/I *quite honestly* don't knôw#   (5b.1.40)

The collocational range of *frankly* is referred to later in a comparison of similarity tests with *really* and *frankly* (pages 144f.).

show that the distinction between the three homonyms of *honestly* is perceived by native informants. In a similarity test, informants were confronted with the following pair of sentences:

/hŏnestly# /Mr Jones believed our stòry#
/Mr Jones honestly believed our stòry#

Forty-six informants (73 per cent) judged these to be very different in meaning, ten (17 per cent) were in some doubt, and merely eight (13 per cent) thought them very similar. In collocation with the verb *believe*, *honestly* is not a manner adjunct but an intensifier, as some informants indicated in a compliance test, when they were asked to make the verb present in the sentence:

/hŏnestly# Mr Jones honestly believed our stòry#

Two informants replaced the second *honestly* by *really* and one by *completely*, evidence of their interpretation of it as an intensifier.

When, on the other hand, informants were confronted with the pair of sentences:

/ hŏnestly# /Mr Jones reported our stòry#
/Mr Jones honestly reported our stòry#

as many as fifty-seven (89 per cent) judged them to be very different in meaning. Very few indeed, seven in fact out of sixty-four, were either in doubt or regarded them as very similar. The somewhat greater confidence in judging this pair to be very different in meaning reflects the greater semantic distinction between the disjunct and the manner adjunct. Of course, though the manner adjunct collocates with the verb *report*, it is also possible to interpret *honestly* as an intensifier. One informant obviously did so, since he replaced it by *really* as he had on the previous occasion when *honestly* was unambiguously an intensifier. What is more significant, as many as twelve informants moved the second *honestly* to the end of the sentence when they were asked to turn the verb into the present tense in the following sentence:

/hŏnestly# /Mr Jones honestly reported our stòry#

None of the informants had done so, however, when *honestly* was unambiguously an intensifier, juxtaposed to *believed*.

The greater distinction between the disjunct and the manner adjunct is also reflected in the results of the evaluation tests. Although in both cases a little under half of the informants rejected the sentence (and there would be stylistic grounds for doing so, anyway), seven of the informants (8 per cent) switched from considering the sentence as dubious to accepting it fully when *honestly* could be interpreted as a manner adjunct. Thus, twenty-nine informants (34 per cent) judged as 'perfectly natural and normal' the sentence:

/hŏnestly# /Mr Jones honestly reported our stòry#

Among other style disjuncts that have homonymous intensifiers, the most frequent are probably *literally* and *simply*. The intensifier *simply* tends to occur before the clausal negative particle, as in the following citation:

> His mother said: 'It is lovely to see you after so long, Martin, and most thoughtful of you to think of coming to make all the arrangements yourself, because, with so much on my shoulders at the moment, I *simply* can't find it in my heart to celebrate.'
>
> (6.3.202-2)

4.3.2 *Personally*

As style disjunct, *personally* tends to occur when the subject of the clause is *I*, e.g.:

> you /know if we're really going to set Stonehènge# on its fēet# ·
> /pĕrsonally# I'd /rather set human bèings on their feet#   (5b.16.47)

It can, however, co-occur with another Subject, e.g.:

> *Personally*, she's not my cup of tea.

The tie between the disjunct *personally* and the pronoun *I* will account for the fact that the vast majority of informants judged these two sentences, presented in the course of Battery I, to be very similar in meaning:

> / pĕrsonally# /I appròved of the idea#
> /I mysĕlf# ap/pròved of the idea#

Fifty-eight informants (90 per cent) considered them very similar, while only four (6 per cent) thought them very different. At first sight it is surprising that a higher percentages responded in this way to the above pair of sentences than to the pair in which *personally* itself was repeated in a similarity test in Battery II:

> /pĕrsonally# /I appròved of the idea#
> /I pĕrsonally# ap/pròved of the idea#

This time 124 informants, only 69 per cent, judged the two sentences to be very similar in meaning, while as many as forty-three (24 per cent) thought them very different.

The contrast in results of the two tests may be due to another possible interpretation of the last sentence, if informants had misperceived it, not hearing the tone unit boundary after *personally*. This interpretation does not seem open to the sentence with *myself*. /I *personally approved of the idea*# can be paraphrased by 'I approved of the idea in person'. This meaning is of course very different from the meaning of the disjunct. It may well be that many of the informants who believed these sentences to be very different understood it in that way.

There is evidence that at least three informants interpreted the sentence in this way in the analogous compliance test. Informants were required in the same Battery to turn the verb into the present in the sentence:

/pĕrsonally# /I pĕrsonally# ap/pròved of the idea#

Three informants moved the second *personally* to a position after the verb. When *personally* is in that position, the verb *approve* is likely to be interpreted as 'voice approval' rather than 'favour'.

In some contexts the distinction between the disjunct and the intensifier can be much sharper than the similarity test suggests. For example, in the next citation it is doubtful whether *personally* can be transposed before *I* without a clear distinction being perceived:

there are /some reciprocal sérvices# but /I pĕrsonally# have [ən]
/having /having had · travelled a little bít# · have /not received
one yèt#   (5b.16.50)

4.3.3. *Generally*

Two instances of *generally* as style disjunct appear in this passage:

The Joint Select Committee on Censorship of the Theatre . . .
was assembled to hear playwrights John Osborne and Benn
Levy . . .
Generally, the two writers were against any censorship.
Generally, the Committee was trying to point out that some sort
of stage censor might give them a better, more liberal, censorship
than just taking their chance with the normal laws of the land.
                                              (ST 4/12/66: 15, 1)

In this function *generally* can be replaced by *in general*.

Generally is more commonly a temporal adjunct expressing the notion of habitual action or state. It is then very similar in meaning to *usually* or *normally* (cf. pages 178ff.). In this function it differs from the style disjunct in several features. One is that it can be focused by clause negation, e.g.:

He doesn't *generally* write well, but he does write well occasionally.

Generally speaking may have a similar temporal function, e.g.:

Generally speaking, France announces Cabinet changes, and
so forth in this speech . . . (G 18/7/66: 9, 3)

Because *generally speaking* usually has this function, a writer wishing to convey the style disjunct function may feel it necessary to invert the order and place the participle first, e.g.:

Speaking generally, these crimes will no longer be tolerated in this city ... (G 12/6/66: 5, 4)[1]

4.4 Other form-classes

Some instances of other form-classes that function like style disjuncts are cited:

? non-
nuclear but you /knòw# *with ?res/pèct#* I /don't
rèally think# àny of us on this plátform# are
/cŏmpetent# to /jùdge#   (5b.1.20)

In short, she was mad, but happy.   (6.3.201-2)

/gìving# · what I can /only *in all còurtesy* call# his
/ill consìdered# and /ignorant opínions#   (5b.16.2)

To put it paradoxically, there is no such thing as a purely spiritual operation of the Spirit.   (8ab.2.145-1)

'This really upsets me, *to be honest*,' said Emma.   (6.2.92-3)

But what, if anything, can be done to get to the heart of the Fleet Street dilemma, which, *put crudely*, is how to stop the rich getting richer and the poor going bankrupt?
                                                             (ST 8/1/67: 11, 5)

Putting it at its lowest terms, the ability to pay someone a high fee to listen to one's problems for several hours a week,

---

1 The Middle English Dictionary edited by H. Kurath cites an early use of *generally* in a non-finite verb clause functioning like the style disjunct *generally*:

c. 1390 Chaucer CT. Mcp. H. 328: For litel speche ... Is no man shent, *to speke generally*.

The possibility of *generally* functioning as a style disjunct corresponding to *generally speaking* and the possibility of neutralisation between this function and the function of *generally* as a temporal adjunct will presumably account for the occurrence of forms like *normally speaking*, a temporal adjunct that can never function as a style disjunct. An example of *normally speaking* can be cited from a Survey text:

we /couldn't come by pláne# be/cause we'd sent this stuff by fréight# and it would ((have)) /cost much more than travelling – onesèlf that way# –
/nôrmally speaking# I /wouldn't go any other wày ((but by plane))
                                                             (S.1b.6a-2)

It is probable that other temporal adjuncts in this sub-class can be replaced by participial clauses formed from the participle *speaking* and the adjunct.

spread over many years, must be a deep source of satisfaction. (ST 9/10/66: 53, 3)

there /îs one thing# ə: · if /one may be serious again for one
móment# · al/though I · don't necessarily disagrée with
you# · ə: – ə (laugh) · ə and /that is thìs# –   (5b.16.69)

A few days ago, though, they fully discovered that the Labour
list was fully subscribed, but only a handful of Tories had
declared allegiance. Thirteen, *to be precise,* one MP says
slyly. (G 23/6/66: 10, 6)

A nation – *loosely speaking* (G 12/9/66: 9, 6 – headline)

Sometimes we have a series corresponding to the style disjunct. If,
for example, we take *frankly,* we find in the language:

style disjunct	– *frankly*
prepositional phrase	– *in (all) frankness*
to non-finite verb clause	– *to be frank, to speak frankly, to put it frankly*
ing non-finite verb clause	– *frankly speaking, putting it frankly*
ed non-finite verb clause	– *put frankly*
subordinate finite verb clause	– *if I may be frank, if I can put it frankly, if I can speak frankly*

Like *frankly* itself, these may contrast with adjuncts that are formally
identical, e.g. in the following sentence they are ambiguous, collocation with the verb making the adjunct function quite probable:

In all frankness, he disagrees with you.
To be frank, you need a great deal of courage.
Put frankly, it is not the thing to say.
If I may be frank, I'll tell you the whole story.[1]

Not every lexical base will necessarily present the full range just
illustrated. Thus, we have *in all fairness* but not *fairly, in short* but not
shortly, though *shortly* occurs as disjunct at an earlier period of English.[2]

---

[1] When the *if*-clause is functioning like a style disjunct, *then* cannot be inserted
in the superordinate clause, cf. page 84.

[2] Jespersen (1949, 84) exemplifies what he calls 'style-tertiaries' with the item
fairly: 'As a typical example may be given "she fairly screamed", which is =
"you may fairly say that she screamed".' On syntactic grounds we would not
class *fairly* among the style disjuncts, because, among other reasons, it cannot
occupy initial position. We may contrast:

In all fairness, she screamed.
To be fair, she screamed.

Table 8 lists the style disjuncts that seem to be the most frequent
in contemporary usage. The Table also displays correspondences with
similar function that are either prepositional phrases or clauses consisting of *to be* followed by an adjective. Most of the style disjuncts have
corresponding non-finite verb and finite verb clauses containing the
adjunct, so these have not been included in the Table.[1]

TABLE 8 *Style disjuncts and correspondences with similar function*

bluntly	—	to be blunt
briefly	in brief	to be brief
broadly	—	—
candidly	—	to be candid
confidentially	in confidence	—
crudely	—	to be crude
—	in (all) fairness [to . . .]	to be fair
flatly	—	—
frankly	in all frankness	to be frank
generally	in general	—
honestly	in all honesty	to be honest
literally	—	(?) to be literal
metaphorically	—	—
paradoxically	—	(?) to be paradoxical
personally	—	(?) to be personal
—	—	to be precise
relatively	—	—
seriously	in all seriousness	to be serious
simply	—	—
—	in short	—
specifically	—	to be specific
strictly	—	—
truly	in truth	—
truthfully	—	to be truthful

Style disjuncts are not entirely a closed class. I cite an unusual instance of a style disjunct to illustrate the possibility of adding new
members to this class:

where the prepositional phrase and the *to*-non-finite verb clause are functioning
like style disjuncts.
[1] Some of the adjuncts do not collocate with one or more of the verbs of speaking
that have been given in the correspondences, i.e. *speak, say, tell, put.* For example,
flatly, in the sense of 'bluntly', is a style disjunct, as in the sentence:
    Flatly, they have nothing to grumble about.
However, *flatly* does not collocate with the verb *speak.* We therefore do not have
the corresponding clause **flatly speaking,* although *put flatly* and *putting it flatly*
seem acceptable. Similarly, **if I may speak flatly* is unacceptable, while *if I may
put it flatly* seems acceptable.

Until now the matter has had its comic side. It is nice to think of Miss Jerry Allen searching the *Overland Journal* in the morning, and Mr Sherry turning the same yellow pages in the afternoon, each unaware of the other's ghostly presence, each a secret agent . . .

Soberly, one knows that in the academic profession the left hand often has no idea what the right hand is doing.

(New Statesman 11/11/66: 706, 2)

4.5 Semantic classification

For the semantic interpretation of style disjuncts a verb of speaking must be understood (cf. §**4.1**, pages 82ff.). Apart from a miscellaneous assortment, two semantic classes of style disjuncts can be distinguished: [1] those expressing that the speaker is making a rough generalisation: *broadly, crudely, generally, roughly, approximately*; and [2] those expressing that the speaker is being frank in what he is saying: *frankly, candidly, honestly, truthfully, bluntly, flatly*. Very often style disjuncts of the second class are used when the speaker is in fact not being frank. (See Feldman 1959 for a psycho-analytic treatment of instances of the use of some of these style disjuncts.)

Chapter 5

Attitudinal disjuncts

Disjuncts other than style disjuncts are termed ATTITUDINAL DISJUNCTS.[1] In general, they express the speaker's attitude to what he is saying, his evaluation of it, or shades of certainty or doubt about it. (cf. Chapter 8.)

5.1 Correspondences

Many, but not all, attitudinal disjuncts have correspondences. They can be grouped according to the correspondences they have. Disjuncts with the same types of correspondence are said to belong to a correspondence class.

5.1.1. Corresponding structures

[1] *that* CLAUSE *is* ADJECTIVE BASE – *it is* ADJECTIVE BASE (*that*) CLAUSE, e.g.: it's /*obviously* an inspired# /quěstion#   (6b.16.56)
→ *that* it's an inspired question *is obvious.*
→ *it is obvious* (*that*) it's an inspired question.

[2] *for* SUBJECT *to* NON-FINITE VERB CLAUSE *is* [or other appropriate tense form] ADJECTIVE BASE – *it is* [etc.] ADJECTIVE BASE *for* SUBJECT *to* NON-FINITE VERB CLAUSE, e.g.: At the top of the public's worries, is, *perhaps surprisingly*, Rhodesia. (G 4/7/66: 1, 7)
→ For Rhodesia to be at the top of the public's worries *is perhaps surprising.*
→ *It is perhaps surprising* for Rhodesia to be at the top of the public's worries.

[3] one is ⎫
    I am ⎬ADJECTIVE BASE (*that*) CLAUSE, e.g.:

At the moment, *thankfully*, it seems unlikely.   (G 4/7/66: 1, 7)

→ one is ⎫*thankful* (that) at the moment it seems unlikely.
   I am ⎭

---

[1] The designation 'attitudinal' is borrowed from Poldauf, 1959, 3.

[4] *It is* [or other appropriate tense form of the verb *be*] ADJECTIVE
BASE *of* SUBJECT *to* NON-FINITE VERB CLAUSE, e.g.: *Prudently*, they
left it out.   (G 17/6/66: 12, 2)
→ *It was prudent of* them to leave it out.

[5] SUBJECT *is* (or other appropriate tense and/or number form]
ADJECTIVE BASE *to* NON-FINITE VERB CLAUSE, e.g.: Mr Heath
rightly said the main danger of world war was now in the East.
                                                              (G 25/10/65: 2, 7)
→ *Mr Heath was right to* say the main danger of world war was
now in the East.

[6] *that* CLAUSE *is* PARTICIPLE BASE – *it is* PARTICIPLE BASE (*that*)
CLAUSE, e.g.: another *allegedly* states that Kennedy never wished
to make the trip to Dallas, . . .   (ST 16/10/66: 9, 3)
→ *that* another states that Kennedy never wished to make the
trip to Dallas *is alleged.*
→ *it is alleged that* another states that Kennedy never wished to
make the trip to Dallas.

5.1.2   Table

Table 9 sets out in the left-hand column correspondence classes
[A]–[J] with an instance from each class. Columns 1–6 denote the
corresponding structures listed in **§5.1.**1. When members of a class

TABLE 9 *Correspondence classes*

	1	2	3	4	5	6
[A] probably	+	−	−	−	−	
[B] certainly	+	−	+	−	?+	−
[C] surprisingly	+	+	−	−	−	−
[D] sadly	+	+	+	−	−	−
[E] happily	−	−	+	−	−	−
[F] fortunately	+	−	−	−	±	−
[G] characteristically	+	+	−	±	−	−
[H] rightly	−	+	−	±	±	−
[I] unusually	−	+	−	−	−	−
[J] allegedly	−	−	−	−	−	+

have a particular corresponding structure, this is indicated in the
appropriate cell by '+', while absence of a corresponding structure is
indicated by '−'. When a structure corresponds in certain environments, but not in others, this is indicated by '±'.[1]

---

[1] For some disjuncts ending in *–ically*, e.g. *tragically*, the adjective base form in
common use may end in *–ic*.

The possibility of correspondences [4] and [5] for classes [G] and [H] depends on two factors: (1) that the grammatical Subject is also the logical Subject, and (2) that the grammatical Subject is animate. For example, correspondence [5] is possible for *rightly* in only the first of the following sentences:

    Rightly, her uncle gave a present to Mary.

→ [5] *Her uncle was right to* give a present to Mary.

    Rightly, Mary was given a present by her uncle.

+> **Mary was right to* be given a present by her uncle.

The possibility of correspondence [5] is determined semantically for class [F]. It depends on whether the speaker's intention includes the grammatical Subject specifically in his attitudinal predication. For example, *fortunately* in the sentence

    Fortunately, her uncle gave a present to Mary.

might correspond to:

→ [5] *Her uncle was fortunate to* give a present to Mary.

On the other hand, it might well mean that Mary was fortunate or that the speaker was fortunate. Only the context of the sentence, linguistic or situational, would determine what the intention was, and whether it included any of the three persons suggested. We notice that for this class there is some doubt whether the grammatical Subject in the correspondence can be the logical Object, e.g.:

    Fortunately, Mary was given a present by her uncle.

→ [5] *?Mary was fortunate to* be given a present by her uncle.

An informant has queried the acceptability of this last sentence.

For class [B] these limitations do not apply. Thus, there may be the 'dummy' Subject *it* in the sentence:

$\left.\begin{array}{l}\textit{Surely}\\\textit{Certainly}\end{array}\right\}$ *it* has rained.

and yet we have:

It is $\left\{\begin{array}{l}\textit{sure}\\\textit{certain}\end{array}\right\}$ to have rained.

But there are some peculiarities with respect to tense, and these account for the '?+' in the cell for [5]. Let us take an example:

He is $\left\{\begin{array}{l}\text{sure}\\\text{certain}\end{array}\right\}$ to smoke a pipe.

In one interpretation this is semantically equivalent for some informants to:

$\left\{\begin{array}{l}\text{Surely}\\\text{Certainly}\end{array}\right\}$ he smokes a pipe.

On another interpretation it is semantically equivalent to:

$\begin{Bmatrix} \text{Surely} \\ \text{Certainly} \end{Bmatrix}$ he will smoke a pipe.

Let us compare the ambiguity in respect of time reference in

He is $\begin{Bmatrix} \text{sure} \\ \text{certain} \end{Bmatrix}$ to smoke a pipe.

and contrast it with the lack of ambiguity in:

He is $\begin{Bmatrix} \text{wise} \\ \text{right} \end{Bmatrix}$ to smoke a pipe.

However, there is no ambiguity when the non-finite verb group is marked for tense

He is $\begin{Bmatrix} \text{sure} \\ \text{certain} \end{Bmatrix}$ to have smoked a pipe.

He is $\begin{Bmatrix} \text{sure} \\ \text{certain} \end{Bmatrix}$ to be about to smoke a pipe.

which are equivalent to

Surely he has smoked a pipe.
Surely he is about to smoke a pipe.

5.1.3 Correspondence classes

The correspondence classes are set out below with a list of attitudinal disjuncts that belong to them. Some have been subdivided for reasons to be explained later in this section. The list is not intended to be exhaustive. In particular, correspondence class [C] is an open class. Disjuncts enclosed in square brackets have been supplied from recollection and have not been encountered in the material that has been examined. A number with question mark following a disjunct denotes doubt over whether the corresponding structure is acceptable or is fully equivalent semantically. Two disjuncts, *unsurprisingly* and *undoubtedly*, are followed by asterisks. These signify that the negative prefix must be replaced in the corresponding structure by the clausal negative particle *not*.

[A] – [1] clearly, evidently, manifestly ?1, obviously, patently ?1 plainly.
[2] arguably, conceivably, definitely, incontestably, [indis-, putably], indubitably ?1, possibly, presumably ?1, probably, unarguably, [undeniably], unquestionably.
[B] certainly ?5, surely ?1, ?5.
[C] – [1] [amazingly], [amusingly], [annoyingly], [astonishingly], [astoundingly], bewilderingly, comfortingly, disappointingly,

[disturbingly], embitteringly, [gratifyingly], interestingly, intriguingly, refreshingly, shamingly, (not) surprisingly, unsurprisingly*.

[2] appropriately, [aptly], bizarrely, [conveniently], curiously, crucially, [delightfully ?4], eerily, [funnily], illogically, (not) inappropriately, incomprehensibly, incredibly, inevitably ?2, ironically, mercifully ?2, miraculously, oddly, ominously, paradoxically, [puzzlingly], regrettably, relevantly, remarkably ?2, significantly, [staggeringly], [startlingly], strangely, [suitably], [suspiciously ?2], topically, [tragically], unaccountably, understandably.

[D]   sadly.

[E]   happily ?3, hopefully, thankfully, unhappily ?3.

[F]   fortunately, luckily, unfortunately, unluckily.

[G]   absurdly, characteristically, preposterously, splendidly, typically, uncharacteristically.

[H] – [1] correctly, incorrectly, rightly, unjustly, wrongly.

[2] [artfully] cleverly, cunningly, [foolishly], prudently, reasonably, sensibly, shrewdly, (not) unreasonably, [(not) unwisely], wisely.

[I]   conventionally, rarely, traditionally, (not) unusually.

[J] – (1) allegedly, admittedly, reportedly, reputedly, supposedly

[2] undoubtedly*.

5.1.3.1 *Should* in correspondences

Disjuncts in classes [C], [D], [F], and [G] differ from those in classes [A] and [B] with respect to a type [1] correspondence. They admit the special use of *should*, the use where *should* has both present and past time reference. 'In this use *should* is restricted to utterances that express surprise or some other kind of emotion.' (Palmer 1965, 131). We can contrast *surprisingly* from class [C1] with *certainly* from class [B]. With disjuncts from classes [A] and [B] *should* has the meaning *ought to* in the corresponding structure. Thus, for *surprisingly*:

Surprisingly, he ate a lot.
= *It is surprising that* he *should* have eaten a lot.
or *It was surprising that* he *should* eat a lot.

On the other hand, the equivalence does not hold if we substitute *certainly* for *surprisingly*:

Certainly, he ate a lot.
≠ *It is certain that* he *should* have eaten a lot.

This special use of *should* also obtains in correspondences for classes [E], [H], and [I]. For class [E] we have the equivalence:

Unhappily, he ate a lot.

$= \left.\begin{array}{l} I\ am \\ One\ is \end{array}\right\}$ *unhappy that* he *should* have eaten a lot.

(See, however, page 207, for a discussion of the accuracy of this equivalence.)

In class [H] the sentence

Mr Heath *rightly* said the main danger of world war was in the East.

does not have the type [1] correspondence:

*It was right that Mr Heath said ...

It will, however, allow this correspondence if *should* is used:

It was right that Mr Heath *should* say ...

Similarly, for class [I] there is a type [1] correspondence when *should* is used:

Traditionally they work hard.
= *It is traditional that* they *should* work hard.

On the other hand, for class [J] *should* in type [6] correspondence has the meaning *ought to* as it has for the type [1] correspondence of classes [A] and [B]:

Allegedly they work hard.
$\neq$ *It is alleged that* they *should* work hard.[1]

5.1.3.2 Anaphoric *it*

There is one respect in which the adjective base of disjuncts of [A2], e.g. *possibly*, and [B], e.g. *certainly*, differs from the adjective base of disjuncts of other classes that accept type [1] correspondence. [A2] and [B] will only allow the anaphoric use of *it* in the following construction:

It will be possible if he takes them.

It can here only refer back to some linguistic unit previously mentioned. On the other hand, in the following sentence where the adjective base of a disjunct from group [C] has been substituted for *possible*

It will be surprising if he takes them.

it is cataphoric, appositional to *if he takes them.* The cataphoric function of *it* in the second sentence is evident from our ability to formulate from this sentence the question and response:

What will be surprising? If he takes them.

---

[1] For the special use of *should* and the types of structure in which it appears, see Behre 1955 and Storms 1966, 267ff.

With the first sentence, however, the question

What will be possible?

can only be answered by the previous linguistic unit for which *it* is the pro-form.[1]

The ability of the base adjectives of groups [A1], [C], [D], [F], and [G] to predicate a conditional clause by means of the *It*-inversion structure may reflect some feature of modality that they possess. We have already seen that most of them admit the special use of *should* in the constituent clause, and this again may reflect their modal character.[2]

5.1.3.3   Classes [A1] and [A2]

Class [A] is unique in having type [1] correspondence only. [A1], e.g. *obviously*, differs from [A2], e.g. *possibly*, in allowing both of two features in the correspondence:

(1) Those in [A1] allow the addition of *to me* (or *to everybody*) after the adjective. Thus, for *obviously* of [A1] we may have

It is *obvious* $\left\{ \begin{array}{l} \text{to me} \\ \text{to everybody} \end{array} \right\}$ that it's an inspired question.

whereas we may not have for *possibly* of [A2]:

*It is *possible* $\left\{ \begin{array}{l} \text{to me} \\ \text{to everybody} \end{array} \right\}$ that it's an inspired question.

(2) those in [A1] allow *whether* in place of *that*, e.g.:

It is *obvious whether* it's an inspired question.

We may contrast this with an example containing *possibly*:

*It is *possible whether* it's an inspired question.

Some in [A2] may allow one or other of these features, but not both, e.g.:

It is *conceivable* $\left\{ \begin{array}{l} \text{to me} \\ \text{to everybody} \end{array} \right\}$ that it's an inspired question.

---

[1] *Inevitably* is like *possibly* in this respect. Semantically, it is close to members of group [A2], and there is a query whether the application of type [2] transformation is acceptable.

[2] Poutsma designates certain items as 'modal adverbs' or 'modal adverbial adjuncts' on the semantic grounds that like the modal auxiliaries they express 'the speaker's attitude with regard to the fulfilment of an action or state'. This semantic criterion would include all the members of group [A2] and possibly those of group [A1] as well. Curiously enough, his only example from these groups is *possibly*. He seems to be restricting the class of 'modal adverbs' to those that have modal auxiliaries that correspond semantically to them. (Poutsma 1928, 35; 1926, 163).

*It is *conceivable whether* it's an inspired question.

*It is *arguable* $\begin{Bmatrix} \text{to me} \\ \text{to everybody} \end{Bmatrix}$ that it's an inspired question.

It is *arguable whether* it's an inspired question.

5.1.3.4 Classes [A2] and [B]

Adjective bases of classes [A2], e.g. *probably*, and [B], e.g. *certainly*, do not readily allow future time reference in the predication of a clause. Contrast:

It will be $\begin{Bmatrix} \text{obvious} \\ \text{annoying} \\ *\text{probable} \\ *\text{certain} \end{Bmatrix}$ (to them) that he is taking it.

Adjectives from these two groups have no particular time reference when predicating a clause. If a past tense is used with these adjectives, it suggests a change in the time in which the speaker imagines himself, perhaps occasioned by narrative focus, but not introducing a substantial change in meaning. Thus, we may have

It was not annoying (to them) that he took it, but it will be if he does so again.

but not:

*It was not probable that he took it, but it will be if he does so again.

Certain is a special case since it is used with personal subjects.

He is certain to take it.

exists at the same time as

It is certain that he will take it.

The blend between the impersonal and personal use of *certain* may account for the acceptability of:

It was not certain to them that he took it but it soon will be.[1]

Nevertheless, the distinction between the anaphoric and cataphoric uses of *it* when an *if*-clause follows can be paralleled even here. Contrast

I will be certain if he takes it.

where the certainty refers back to something said previously, with

I will be happy if he takes it.

---

1 For a discussion of personal and impersonal adjectives and the gradience from impersonal to personal, see Bolinger 1961b, 377, 380.

where the happiness may refer forward to the action suggested in the *if*-clause. Apart from the adjective bases of groups [D], [E], and [F], this cataphoric reference that we have noted with *happy* will also apply with the *-ed* participle forms of group [C1], for example:

I will be annoyed if he takes it.

5.1.3.5   Classes [C1] and [C2]

Disjuncts of class [C1] are distinguished from those in [C2] by their *-ing* participle base. All the bases may function as adjectives, as we can see from their ability in suitable contexts to accept premodification by *very*. The verbal derivation of these bases allows also a correspondence of the form *It* VERBAL BASE *me* (etc.), as in the following example (where the premodifier is disregarded for the purpose of the correspondence):

> *More bewilderingly,* the proliferation of separate faculty colours in civic universities has brought so many clashes that even Sherlock Holmes would be hard pressed to sort the Manchesters from the Leeds from the Birminghams.   (G 25/4/66: 7, 2)

→ It bewilders me (etc.) that the proliferation . . .

5.1.3.6   Classes [D] and [E]

As far as I can determine, *sadly* is the only member of class [D]. The importance of this one-member class lies in its relation to class [E]. Class [E] may be best explained as arising from a process of serial relationship. This can be more easily seen in Table 10 where we extract information from Table 9 (page 95) and display in isolation classes [A] – [E] and parameters 1–3.

TABLE 10   *Types [1]–[3] correspondences for classes [A]–[E]*

	1	2	3
[A] probably	+	−	−
[B] certainly	+	−	+
[C] surprisingly	+	+	−
[D] sadly	+	+	+
[E] happily	−	−	+

The existence of *sadly*, with positive entries in columns for parameters 1, 2 and 3, as an attitudinal disjunct serves as a bridge between [E] and the other groups. We can support this suggested explanation for the existence of the small [E] group by pointing to the semantic properties shared by *sadly* and two of the common members of group [E], *happily* and *unhappily* (but cf. page 207).[1]

---

[1] For the theory of serial relationship, see Quirk 1965, 205ff.

5.1.3.7   Class [F]

Group [F] contains disjuncts that are very closely related semantically. As we have indicated above (page 96), the possibility of correspondence type [5] is dependent on the grammatical Subject also being the logical Subject. A further condition that would normally be required is that the grammatical Subject be animate. As a result of a failure to comply with these conditions, the following, for example, would not register a positive entry for column [5] in Table 9 (page 95):

> *Unfortunately*, because of the growth of authoritarianism to-gether with the inadequacy of the constitution itself, little protection has resulted. [group F]   (O 24/10/65: 10, 5)

> Manchester has been accused of exploitation and delusion (it has been alleged – *preposterously* – that he believed Ho Chi Minh to be responsible for the electricity failure which blacked out New York last winter). [group G]   (ST 16/11/66: 9, 3)

> And the maintenance of the policy is *rightly* held by the Government and by most of the nation to be one of the main conditions for Britain's economic recovery. [group H]   (G 19/5/66: 10, 2)

Possibility of correspondence [5] in the case of disjuncts of group [F] is dependent on the speaker's intention, on whether he wishes to restrict his evaluation to the Subject. It is not always possible to determine the speaker's intention, but sometimes the situational context or the verbal context may indicate an interpretation. In the next two quotations, for example, the writer's intention is conveyed by the verbal context. The first contains a disjunct, *unfortunately*, which seems to be restricted in its application to the Subject alone; in the second, *fortunately* seems to apply to the team as a whole, or perhaps even Britain.

> 'We have always been interested in hovercraft', says Mr D. R. Gripps, the Survey's equipment officer. '*Unfortunately* we are always short of money, so we couldn't afford to buy one on the off-chance that it would work.'   (O 24/10/65: 9, 5)

> So, with Hardisty also unable to show his usual speed or thrust, Britain's back division was crippled.
> *Fortunately*, all four three-quarters were on their toes.
> $$(G 24/10/65: 12, 7)$$

5.1.3.8   Classes [H1] and [H2]

Disjuncts in class [H] have a close relationship to the Subject, provided that it is the active Subject. If the Subject is active, it will usually be animate. However, they are primarily concerned with an evaluation of the Subject with respect to the action or state described in the clause. Consequently, they always admit of type [2] correspondence as well, where the adjective predicates the clause alone, e.g.:

Wisely, ⎱ he didn't say anything about it.
Rightly, ⎰

→ For him not to say anything about it *was wise.*

Affinity of the disjunct to the Subject seems to be closer for disjuncts of class [H2], e.g. *wisely,* than for those of class [H1] e.g. *rightly.* This intuition may receive support from the difference in the distribution of their adjectival base forms:

The action is wise.
→ It is a wise action.

The action is right.
→ It is a right action.

The man is wise.
→ He is a wise man.

The man is right.
→ *He is a right man.

Right (and other adjectives in the same semantic area, e.g. *wrong, correct, incorrect*) do not occur as attributive adjectives with the same meaning as they have as predicative adjectives, unless the noun is factive, like *action* above, cf. Bolinger 1967, 19. The fact that the adjective bases of disjuncts such as *wisely* may occur as attributive adjectives of animate Subjects suggests some closer affinity to animate Subjects of these adjectives and, perhaps as a consequence, of the disjuncts.[1]

---

[1] The disjuncts we have listed for [H1] correspond to a structure in which their base adjective predicates a *for to*-non-finite verb clause. The adjectives, like the disjuncts, convey a moral judgment:

This, *quite rightly,* has proved the sticking point so far as the British are concerned.   (G 19/12/66: 8, 2)

= *It was quite right for* this to have proved the sticking point . . .

Rightly would not be semantically equivalent to a structure in which *right* predicted a *that*-clause:

It is quite right that this has proved the sticking point . . .

Here *right* is synonymous with *true.* When they predicate a *that*-clause, the adjectives *correct, incorrect, right,* and *wrong* convey a judgment about the truth of a statement. There may be some exceptions to this generalisation. For example, if the Subject is animate, the adjective may be interpreted as conveying a moral judgment in certain contexts:

That she reprimands him frequently is right.

It is possible that this might be interpreted as 'is right of her'. On the other

5.1.3.9 Class [J]

Class [J] consists of disjuncts with an -*ed* participle base. These have a type [6] correspondence, analogous to type [1] except for the participle in place of an adjective. Those in [J1] have a further correspondence, analogous to type [5]:

SUBJECT *is* PARTICIPLE BASE *to* NON-FINITE VERB CLAUSE.

e.g.

Reportedly they have taken that job.

is semantically equivalent to

They are reported to have taken that job.

as well as to

It is reported that they have taken that job.

The exception is *undoubtedly*, which can only have a type [6] correspondence, allowance having to be made for a replacement of the negative prefix by the clausal negative particle.

Undoubtedly they have taken that job.

is semantically equivalent to

It is not doubted that they have taken that job.

but there is no corresponding

*They are not doubted to have taken that job.[1]

5.1.3.10 Disjuncts ending in -*ably* or -*ibly*

A number of disjuncts ending in -*ably* or -*ibly* correspond to structures of the form:

$$\left.\begin{array}{l} I \\ One \end{array}\right\} can \text{ VERB BASE}$$

---

hand, this interpretation seems much less likely when there is an *It*-inversion structure:

It is right that she reprimands him frequently.

There is no ambiguity, however, when *should* is in the *that*-clause:

It is right that she should reprimand him frequently.

Now the meaning of *right* is the same as in a *for to*-non-finite clause:

It is right for her to reprimand him frequently.

There is a more striking semantic difference between the predication of a *that*-clause and the predication of a *for to*-non-finite verb clause with the adjectives *possible* and *impossible*, cf. pages 149f.

[1] It is interesting that there is no form *doubtedly* in the present state of the language, though OED cites instances from the sixteenth and seventeenth centuries.

4*

These can be listed according to their correspondence classes:

[A2] arguably, conceivably, incontestably, indisputably, presumably, undeniably, unquestionably
[C2] incomprehensibly, understandably
[I]   undoubtedly[1]

Unaccountably will only have such a correspondence if *for the fact that* is inserted after the verb in the superordinate clause:

> *Unaccountably*, she neglected her youngest child.
> ≠ *One cannot account that* she neglected her youngest child.
> = *One cannot account for the fact* that she neglected her youngest child.

Unarguably likewise requires the insertion of *the fact that* with the substitution of an appropriate preposition:

> *Unarguably*, the actual cost of litigation is terrifying.
> (ST 12/6/66: 21, 5)
> ≠ *One cannot argue that* the actual cost of litigation is . . .
> = *One cannot argue against the fact that* the actual cost . . .

All the disjuncts ending in -*ably* that I have listed allow the insertion of *the fact that* in the corresponding structure. In the case of *arguably* a preposition would have to be introduced as well. In the only instance of *arguably* in our material, the appropriate preposition would be *for*:

> What's more, Sandys has recovered his command of the House; he *arguably* worsted Wilson on Tuesday; . . .   (G 23/2/67: 8, 6)
> = . . . *one can argue for the fact that* he worsted Wilson on Tuesday; . . .

In this context at least, *arguably* denotes that the content of the communication is to be considered as high on the scale of probability, and therefore the positive *argue for* appears in the corresponding structure. It is possible that some people use this disjunct to indicate low probability, and in that case the negative *argue against* would be appropriate.

Because of the time reference of *predictably* the verb in the corresponding structure must be in the past:

> *Predictably*, many letters recount the possession of a violin marked 'Stradivarius' . . .   (ST 21/8/66: 4, 4)
> = *One* $\left\{ \begin{array}{l} \text{was able to} \\ \text{could} \end{array} \right\}$ *predict (the fact) that* many letters would . . .

In the case of *preferably*, the suffix of the disjunct cannot be reflected in the corresponding structure:

---

[1] In the case of *undoubtedly* and other forms with a negative prefix, the prefix would have to be replaced by *not* in the corresponding structure.

Entries should *preferably* be upright . . . (O 24/10/65: 30, 3)
≠ *One can prefer that* entries should be upright.
= *One prefers that* entries should be upright.

Notice that with *preferably* there is no possibility of inserting *the fact that* in the corresponding structure:

One prefers the fact that entries should be upright.

The disjuncts ending in *-ably* that I have listed also correspond to clauses predicated by the verb in the passive voice, e.g.:

understandably, no patriot wants to fall into disrepute.

(G 22/1/66: 1, 8)
= that no patriot wants to fall into disrepute *can be understood*

This last, in turn, corresponds to the *It*-inversion structure:

= *It can be understood that* no patriot wants to fall into disrepute.

Such correspondences are possible for *predictably* if the verb is put in the past and for *preferably* if *can* is omitted. With *unaccountably* and *unarguably*, on the other hand, only the first of these correspondences is possible, and then only if the appropriate particle is added:

That she neglected her youngest child *cannot be accounted for.*
That the actual cost of litigation is terrifying *cannot be argued against.*

The *It*-inversion structure is not acceptable in these cases for stylistic reasons when a *that*-clause is preceded by a preposition:

It cannot be accounted for that she neglected her youngest child.
It cannot be argued against that the actual cost of litigation is terrifying.[1]

Regrettably differs in its correspondence from other disjuncts with a verb base ending in *-ably*. *Regrettably* means 'I/one must regret' and not 'I/one can regret', as the suffix *-ably* might suggest.

Regrettably, however, inevitably, there is far too much goading of star players by inferiors these days, . . . (G 22/11/66: 13, 1)

Apart from those we have listed, there are a number of disjuncts ending in *-ably* or *-ibly* which have no verb cognate to them in the

---

[1] With the *It*-inversion structure, the preposition appears to dominate the clause. The sentences are unacceptable by analogy with the syntactic unacceptability of the active forms of the sentences, in which the preposition is, in fact, dominating the clause:

* One cannot account *for* that she neglected her youngest child.
* One cannot argue *against* that the actual cost of litigation is terrifying.

language and some others that do not have verb bases that would allow a direct correspondence:

[A2] indubitably (one cannot doubt), possibly, probably
[C2] incredibly (one cannot credit), inevitably, remarkably, suitably
[H2] reasonably, sensibly, unreasonably
no correspondence: ostensibly

It will be observed, though the reason is not clear, that all the disjuncts assigned to correspondence class [A2] except for *definitely* end in *-ably* or *-ibly*.

5.1.4 Disjuncts with similar correspondences
Several attitudinal disjuncts have correspondences that are similar to those listed above for the correspondence classes (§**5.1.1**, pages 94f.):

(not) unexpectedly; ideally; predictably; preferably; maybe; likely (plus modifier)

5.1.4.1 (*Not*) *unexpectedly*
(*Not*) *unexpectedly* has the type [1] correspondence but requires a change of auxiliary to *would*:

Somewhat unexpectedly, his prose doesn't rise as readily to the florid possibilities of North Oxford.   (O 24/10/65: 26, 7)
→ *It was somewhat unexpected that* his prose wouldn't rise ...

or, if the negative prefix is replaced by clause negation and *somewhat* is omitted:

→ *It was not expected that* his prose wouldn't rise ...

5.1.4.2 *Ideally*
Ideally will admit two correspondences in certain contexts:

[i] *for* SUBJECT *to* NON-FINITE VERB CLAUSE *would be ideal* → *it would be ideal for* SUBJECT *to* NON-FINITE VERB CLAUSE
[ii] *It would be ideal if* SUBJECT $\begin{Bmatrix} \textit{were to } \text{NON-FINITE VERB CLAUSE} \\ \textit{would } \text{REST OF FINITE VERB CLAUSE} \end{Bmatrix}$

One such context is:

Ideally, every school should have its own welfare officer ...
                                                              (G 17/4/67: 3, 7)
→ *It would be ideal for* every school to have its own welfare officer
→ *It would be ideal if* every school $\begin{Bmatrix} \textit{were to } \text{have} \\ \textit{would } \text{have} \end{Bmatrix}$ ...

On the other hand, such correspondences are not available in the next citation:

Ideally, they would like to be consulted all along the line.

(G 5/8/66: 12, 2)

≠ *It would be ideal for* them to like to be consulted ...

≠ *It would be ideal if* they $\left\{ \begin{array}{l} \textit{were to like} \\ \textit{would like} \end{array} \right\}$ to be consulted ...[1]

Ideally speaking can replace the disjunct *ideally*.

5.1.4.3 Predictably

Predictably has a type [1] correspondence, but requires *would* in the second clause:

Predictably, these flirtations almost prove disastrous ...

(ST 3/7/66: 7, 2)

→ *It was predictable that* these flirtations would almost prove disastrous ...

5.1.4.4 Preferably

Preferably has types [1] and [2] correspondences, but for type [1] *should* or the subjunctive form of the verb is required:

Entries are *preferably* submitted in ink.

→ *It is preferable that* entries (*should*) be submitted in ink.

→ *It is preferable for* entries to be submitted in ink.

5.1.4.5 Maybe

Diachronically, *maybe* is either a shortened form of *It may be* or is a loan-translation based on the French *peut-être*. In any case, in Contemporary English it does not have the status of a verb group. We can see that this is so if we contrast it with *could be*. *Could be* can occur as a clipped version of *It could be* either as an independent sentence or as a superordinate clause, e.g.:

Does he smoke a pipe? *Could be.*

Could be he smokes a pipe.

However, it is unacceptable within the clause, at least in British English, e.g.:

*He *could be* smokes a pipe.

*He smokes a pipe, *could be*.

Contrast:

He *maybe* smokes a pipe.

He smokes a pipe, *maybe*.

---

[1] The presence of the verb group *would like* seems to preclude the correspondences.

The perception that *maybe* is not a verb group and is felt to be a single lexical item is reflected in written English in the traditional practice of writing it as a single word.

5.1.4.6 *Likely*

Likely as disjunct corresponds to *It is likely*. It functions as disjunct only when modified:

> *Quite likely* we are now at the very top of the investment boom.
> (O 24/10/65: 9, 2)

but not:

> **Likely* we are now at the very top of the investment boom.

When it is not modified, it may only function as Complement after an equative verb:

> the movement is not *likely* to be due to them; ...   (8a.1.103-4)

5.1.5   Other disjuncts

The remaining disjuncts do not admit the types of correspondences we have discussed. They can be divided into two groups:

[a] actually, apparently, assuredly, blessedly, decidedly, doubtless, factually, formally, indeed, justly, naturally, not unnaturally, nominally, ostensibly, outwardly, perhaps, potentially, really, seemingly, superficially.

[b] basically, essentially, fundamentally, officially, technically, theoretically.

Those in group [b] may be replaced by a clause with the participle *speaking*, e.g. *basically* by *basically speaking*. These are not, however, style disjuncts since they do not admit of the appropriate correspondences, cf. §4.1, pages 82f. Let us take *basically* as an illustration:

> *Basically*, play leadership is the technique of playground management. (ST 13/4/67: 57, 2)

It does not correspond to, e.g.

> *If I may speak basically [I would say (that)]* play leadership is ...

or

> *I am speaking basically when I say that* play leadership is ...

The lack of correspondences for some of the disjuncts in group [a], e.g. *apparently* and *naturally*, is referred to in the semantic classification of attitudinal disjuncts, Chapter 8.

5.2 Syntactic features

As with conjuncts (cf. §3.2, pages 37ff.), I shall first consider restrictions on the appearance of disjuncts in certain types of clause. Where relevant, differences between correspondence classes will be noted. I shall also take into account style disjuncts.

It must be emphasised that statements are being made about disjuncts and not about items. A particular item may also function as adjunct. I shall in this section note differences between disjuncts and homonymous adjuncts from time to time. (See also the discussion of individual disjuncts and their homonyms, pages 127ff.)

5.2.1 Appearance in clause types

[1] *Questions.* Most attitudinal disjuncts may not appear with questions, whether *yes-no* questions or *wh*-questions.[1]

Some contingency disjuncts in class [A1], namely *conceivably, possibly,* and *probably,* may more easily appear in a question, but not in the initial position that they may occupy in a declarative form of the clause.

*_Possibly_ will they leave early?

is certainly unacceptable, though

?Will they *possibly* leave early?

is only marginally unacceptable. (For the greater acceptability of these three disjuncts in questions, and the complicating factor of the existence of homonymous intensifiers for *possibly* and *conceivably,* see pages 148ff.) Two disjuncts in correspondence class [I], *conventionally* and *traditionally* are acceptable in non-initial position.

Of those outside the correspondence classes, disjuncts in group [b] (page 110) seem acceptable in non-initial position. Just within the borderline of acceptability are *maybe* and *perhaps.* (For the acceptability of *perhaps* in a question, cf. page 153.) The acceptability of style disjuncts in questions, even in initial position, has been mentioned previously (cf. page 84).

[2] *Indirect questions.* Most attitudinal disjuncts may not appear within indirect questions, whether introduced by *wh*-words or by *if,* e.g.:

---

1 See the reference by Katz and Postal (1964, 87–89) to sentence adverbials that do not occur in questions. The authors, who do not define the term 'sentence adverbial', see in this restriction a syntactic argument for postulating a Q morpheme in the underlying P-markers of polarity and *wh*-questions. The unacceptability of attitudinal disjuncts in questions has been tested experimentally, cf. pages 134f., 152f., 160f.

*He asked whether *disappointingly* they would leave early.
*He explained how *fortunately* they can leave early.[1]

The exceptions mentioned in [1] apply here too, apart from style disjuncts. Style disjuncts are unacceptable within indirect questions, e.g.:

*He asked whether *frankly* they would leave early.

[3] *Imperative and optative clauses.* Attitudinal disjuncts may not appear within imperative or optative clauses, e.g.

$$
\left.\begin{array}{l}
\text{*Certainly,} \\
\text{*Annoyingly,} \\
\text{*Foolishly,} \\
\text{*Admittedly,}
\end{array}\right\}
\left\{\begin{array}{l}
\text{do it at once, John.[2]} \\
\text{let's do it at once.}
\end{array}\right.
$$

We have noted previously the acceptability of style disjuncts in imperative and optative clauses, even in initial position (cf. page 85).

If an item that can function as attitudinal disjunct and as adjunct appears in final position in these two types of clause, it will be interpreted as adjunct, e.g.:

$$
\text{John} \left\{\begin{array}{l}
\text{do it at once} \\
\text{let's do it at once}
\end{array}\right.
\left\{\begin{array}{l}
\text{annoyingly.} \\
\text{amusingly.} \\
\text{correctly.} \\
\text{wisely.}
\end{array}\right.
$$

[4] *Subordinate non-finite verb clauses.* Disjuncts may not appear in certain types of subordinate non-finite verb clauses. Let us take the sentences:

$$
\begin{array}{l}
\text{He wanted them to read} \\
\text{He likes them reading}
\end{array}
\left\{\begin{array}{l}
\text{certainly} \\
\text{annoyingly.} \\
\text{foolishly.} \\
\text{admittedly.}
\end{array}\right.
$$

The items can only be interpreted as disjuncts if they relate to the superordinate clause and are equivalent to:

$$
\left.\begin{array}{l}
\text{Certainly,} \\
\text{Annoyingly,} \\
\text{Foolishly,} \\
\text{Admittedly,}
\end{array}\right\}
\left\{\begin{array}{l}
\text{he wanted them to read.} \\
\text{he likes them reading.}
\end{array}\right.
$$

---

[1] Katz and Postal (loc. cit.) argue that the presence of a Q morpheme will 'simplify the statement that questions are not embedded except in quotational contexts'. They might also have referred to the non-occurrence of their 'sentence adverbials' in indirect questions.
[2] Cf. Katz and Postal 1964, 77, who find a syntactic justification for their postulation of the occurrence of an I (imperative) morpheme in underlying P-markers

They may be attached to such clauses if the clauses are elliptical, e.g.:

He made them read and $\left\{\begin{array}{l}certainly\\annoyingly\\foolishly\\admittedly\end{array}\right\}$ write.
He wanted them to read and to write.
He saw them reading and writing.

He wanted them, $\left\{\begin{array}{l}probably\\certainly\\admittedly\\undoubtedly\end{array}\right\}$ to write.

In such instances the disjuncts are functioning in the ellipted super-ordinate finite verb clauses (cf. *hence*, page 40).

[5] *Clauses with equative verb 'be'*. Disjuncts may appear in clauses where the Verb is the equative verb *be*, e.g.:

They are out of town, $\left\{\begin{array}{l}certainly.\\annoyingly.\\foolishly.\\admittedly.\end{array}\right.$

In this feature disjuncts differ from homonymous adjuncts. For example, the manner adjunct *foolishly* in the sentence

They always behave *foolishly*.

could not appear in an equative clause.

Equative verbs require some complementation and this cannot be supplied by disjuncts. Consequently, disjuncts can only appear in a clause with an equative verb if the clause is elliptical and the complementation is implied from the previous context, e.g.:

Are they out of town? $\left\{\begin{array}{l}Certainly,\\Annoyingly,\\Foolishly,\\Admittedly,\end{array}\right\}$ they are.

Most disjuncts freely collocate with any verb, but there are some restrictions on disjuncts of class [H], which will be discussed later, cf. pages 154ff. In general, disjuncts, unlike their homonymous adjuncts, do not play a part in the subcategorisation of verbs (cf. page 41).

5.2.2 Function in the clause

Disjuncts (like conjuncts, cf. pages 41ff.) fail to satisfy the criteria listed in §2.1.2 (pages 18ff.) and displayed in Table 1 (page 23). I summarise

in the fact that imperatives do not co-occur with 'various kinds of sentence adverbials'.

the features applying to disjuncts that can be abstracted from that section and add others to them. Since for many disjuncts there are homonymous adjuncts, I shall point to features in which they differ.

[1] Disjuncts are acceptable in initial position in the clause. Adjuncts may also occur in that position, though it is probably unusual for them to do so outside literary narration. Thus, *frankly* and *amusingly* in the following sentence are ambiguous between disjunct and adjunct:

Frankly,
Amusingly, } he explained his position to me.

If we interpret them as adjuncts, we could paraphrase the sentence by *He was being frank* (or *amusing*) *when he explained his position to me*. If we interpret them as disjuncts, we could paraphrase the sentence by. *I am speaking frankly when I tell you that he explained his position to me* or *It is amusing that he explained his position to me*.

There seem, however, to be restrictions on the auxiliaries with which the adjuncts can collocate. For example, in the following sentences it seems that *frankly* and *amusingly* must be interpreted as disjuncts:

Frankly,   } he did explain his position to me.
Amusingly, } he has explained his position to me.

As has been pointed out (page 113), there are restrictions on the collocation of adjuncts with verbs. Thus, *frankly* and *amusingly* in the next sentence can only be interpreted as disjuncts because the adjuncts do not collocate with the verb *be*:

Frankly,
Amusingly, } he was their choice.

Similarly, *frankly* and *amusingly* must be disjuncts in the next example if *reminded* is interpreted as a perception rather than an action:

Frankly,
Amusingly, } he reminded me of my father.

[2] Disjuncts are acceptable in initial position even if the clause is negated. Thus, in the following example *frankly* and *amusingly* can only be interpreted as disjuncts:

Frankly,
Amusingly, } he did not explain his position to me.

[3] Disjuncts are acceptable in initial position even if they are in an independent tone unit and carry a rising, falling-rising, or level nuclear tone. It is probable that this feature also applies to manner adjuncts that occur in initial position, though it seems likely that if they carry a falling-rising nuclear tone they would be interpreted as homonymous disjuncts.

[4] Disjuncts cannot be the focus of clause interrogation, as demonstrated by their inability to be contrasted in alternative interrogation:

*Did they leave early *probably* or did they leave early *possibly?*

For most disjuncts this follows from their inability to appear within a question (cf. §5.2.1, page 111). But this negative feature applies even to those that can appear with a question, notably the style disjuncts, e.g.:

Frankly, did he speak to them about it?

On the other hand, the manner adjunct *frankly* can be focused:

Did he speak to them about it *frankly* or did he speak to them about it *deceitfully?*

We can apply a further test. If *frankly* is a manner adjunct in the sentence:

Did he speak to them about it *frankly or not?*

or not implies *or did he not speak to them about it frankly*. In other words, *frankly* is included in the negative clause implied in *not*. However, if *frankly* is the style disjunct, rather clumsily inserted in that position, *or not* will not include *frankly* in the implied clause:

Did he speak to them about it, *frankly, or not?*
= Did he speak to them about it, *frankly, or did he not speak to them about it?*

[5] Disjuncts cannot be the focus of clause negation, as demonstrated by their inability to be contrasted in alternative negation of the form:

*They didn't leave early *probably*, but they did leave early *possibly*.

We can apply a test analogous to the one suggested with clause negation. In the first of the following sentences, the manner adjunct *frankly* is implied in the negated clause, whereas the disjunct *frankly* in the second sentence is not:

[i] He spoke to them about it *frankly*, but she *did not.*
= He spoke to them about it *frankly*, but she *did not speak to them about it frankly.*
[ii] He spoke to them about it, *frankly*, but she *did not.*
= He spoke to them about it, *frankly*, but she *did not speak to them about it.*

Their inability to be the focus of clause negation accounts for their unacceptability immediately after the clausal negative particle. (Informant reactions to this position for some disjuncts are analysed on pages 136, 150ff., 157ff.)

Instances of disjuncts immediately following the clausal negative particle occasionally occur. In such cases, we would expect that in written English the disjunct would be separated from the rest of the clause by at least a pair of commas, though dashes or brackets are probably more common. In spoken English an independent tone unit and, probably, clearly perceptible pauses seem necessary. An instance in written English is cited:

'We do not, *naturally*, supply the foot-in-the-door, Flash Alf type' (ST 5/3/67: 5, 2)

The disjuncts themselves can be contrasted, as in the following citations:

HERBERT BOWDEN, Lord Plowden, Lord Bowden, Lord Snowdon. One of them, according to various half-deaf tipsters, was going to be the new chief of the ITA – *probably, but not certainly*, H. Bowden. (G 5/8/67: 6, 6)

Early witnesses and later observation indicate there were no civilians in the battle zone during the hours of combat and that the estimated 300 civilians now in Kuneitra returned to their homes, as the whole Druse population returned to its villages, after the ceasefire.
Possibly, but one can hope with reason not probably, there could have been 50 more civilian casualties in damaged private cars and isolated buildings along some major roads in West Jordan and the main Gaza road. (G 24/7/67: 6, 6)

We can invent an example with other types of disjunct:

Annoyingly, but not surprisingly, they left early.

[6] They cannot be the focus of clause comparison. Thus, these sentences are unacceptable:

*They left *more probably than he did*.
*They left *as probably as he did*.

In the following sentence, *frankly* is ambiguous between the disjunct and the adjunct:

Frankly, he explained the reasons for the escapade.

However, only the manner adjunct can be the focus of clause comparison:

He explained the reasons for the escapade *more frankly than she did*.

Disjuncts can be premodified by *more* or other comparatives, but the comparison does not refer to the following clause:

Face to face Dr Shaw has other criticisms, most of them about duplication. An Oxford doctor of medicine, for instance, has precisely the same gown as an Oxford doctor of civil law.

More bewilderingly, the proliferation of separate faculty colours in civic universities has brought so many clashes that even Sherlock Holmes would be hard pressed to sort the Manchesters from the Leeds from the Birminghams. (G 25/4/66: 7, 2)

Here, the comparison is with an implied disjunct *bewilderingly*, a disjunct related by implication to the previous sentence. In the next quotation, the comparison is fully explicit:

Obviously it may be true. *Equally obviously* it may be true that by creaming off all the brightest pupils in their 'catchment area' to a single school they have impoverished the intellectual life of the neighbouring grammar schools ...
(O 24/10/65: 33, 3)

Two disjuncts may be compared directly:

More amusingly than wisely, he often spoke to us in English.

Or a disjunct may be compared with its negation:

More amusingly than not, he often spoke to us in English.[1]

Some items are unlikely to function as disjuncts unless they are premodified by a comparative:

Officers of the national union were prepared yesterday for opposition on grounds of principle to this proposal, and possibly to another, from Central Middlesex, calling for compulsory medical examinations for Commonwealth immigrants on entering this country. In the first case the argument is likely to be religiously inspired. In the second it might be a protest against apparent racial prejudice.

Less contentiously, Ellesmere Port wants safety regulations extended to equipment at fairgrounds and amusement parks;

---

[1] In the following curious example of a disjunct premodified by *more*, there is Verb-Subject inversion:

No doubt some lover has found a rare plant hidden in the grass, and *more probably* have botanists found lovers.   (G 29/8/66: 10, 6)

It is possible that the comparative premodifier has influenced the inversion, since there exists the perfectly acceptable Verb-Subject inversion with *more often* and *more frequently*. There may indeed be a syntactic blend between these and *probably*, suggested by the previous mention of the word *rare*. Certainly, *more often* or *more frequently* would fit this context.

and Middlesbrough advocates more vigorous public warnings to young people about the risks of catching venereal diseases.

(G 18/5/66: 5, 5)[1]

[7] Disjuncts cannot be the focus of restrictives, e.g. *only, particularly*, or additives, e.g. *also, equally*, in respect of allowing Verb-Subject inversion when these precede them in initial position:

$$\begin{Bmatrix} *\text{Only} \\ *\text{Particularly} \\ *\text{Also} \\ *\text{Equally} \end{Bmatrix} \begin{Bmatrix} \text{certainly} \\ \text{annoyingly} \\ \text{foolishly} \\ \text{admittedly} \end{Bmatrix} \text{did they leave early.}$$

It would appear that they may not be the focus of restrictives under other conditions:

$$*\text{They left early} \begin{Bmatrix} \text{only} \\ \text{particularly} \end{Bmatrix} \begin{Bmatrix} \text{certainly} \\ \text{annoyingly} \\ \text{foolishly} \\ \text{admittedly} \end{Bmatrix}$$

They may, however, be the focus of additives, as in the quotation with *equally obviously*, page 117.

Several disjuncts that do not belong to correspondence classes can be the focus of restrictive *only* and will then allow Verb-Subject inversion when it precedes them in initial position:

$$\text{Only} \begin{Bmatrix} \text{nominally} \\ \text{officially} \\ \text{technically} \end{Bmatrix} \text{did discussions open today.}$$

It is possible to make these the focus of a cleft sentence when they are specified in this way:

$$\text{It was only} \begin{Bmatrix} \text{nominally} \\ \text{officially} \\ \text{technically} \end{Bmatrix} \text{that discussions opened today.}$$

Apparently also seems to have this feature, e.g.:

It should be noticed, however, that some longer groups are *only apparently* [*apparently* in italics in original] compounds of two or more types. (R. Quirk, 1965: *Use of English*, p. 187)

→ ?It is *only apparently* that some longer groups are compounds . . .

---

[1] Disjuncts cannot appear in the type of comparative construction open to some adjuncts, such as *usually*, in which the first clause is implied in the second elliptical clause, e.g.:

They left more readily than *usually*.
= They left more readily than *they usually did*.

For a recent discussion of comparative constructions, see Huddleston 1967, 91ff.

[8] Disjuncts do not allow Verb-Subject inversion when the clausal negative particle *not* precedes them in initial position. If we take the temporal adjunct *often* as an illustration, we see that it will permit such inversion when in initial position:

Not often did they leave early.

We may contrast the unacceptability of the disjunct *surprisingly* in this type of construction:

*Not surprisingly did they leave early.

Surprisingly, like many other disjuncts, may be item-negated though it cannot be the focus of clause negation. An instance of negated *surprisingly* appears in the next citation. The fact that *not* negates only *suprisingly* is emphasised by the graphic device of separating the group from the words on either side by spacing.

> He was *not surprisingly* arrogant and impatient with many enemies and the subject of several of Aubrey's scabrous anecdotes (which Miss Latham ignores). Yet he was loyal to his dependants and followers, and apparently of great charm.
>
> (TES 5/11/65: 990, 4)

Negation of the disjunct and of the clause may co-occur:

Not surprisingly, he was not arrogant and impatient on such occasions.

[9] Disjuncts cannot be the sole focus of a cleft sentence. Thus, the following sentences are unacceptable:

$$\text{*It was} \begin{cases} \text{certainly} \\ \text{annoyingly} \\ \text{foolishly} \\ \text{admittedly} \end{cases} \text{that they left early.}$$

Like the conjuncts (cf. page 42), most disjuncts may appear in the focal clause of a cleft sentence when another item is the focus. This seems to be most common for disjuncts of correspondence classes [A], [B], and [J], and those that are similar to them in meaning:

$$\text{It was} \begin{cases} \text{probably} \\ \text{certainly} \\ \text{admittedly} \\ \text{undoubtedly} \end{cases} \text{John who left early, and not Norman.}$$

Their function is different from that of restrictives and additives that focus the focal item:

$$\text{It was} \begin{cases} \text{only} \\ \text{particularly} \\ \text{also} \\ \text{equally} \end{cases} \text{John who left early.}$$

Whereas the transposition of the disjuncts to the beginning of the sentence would, in general, leave the meaning unaffected, provided the intonation pattern showed that the focus was on John, the transposition of the restrictives and additives would alter the meaning with varying degrees of seriousness.

This may be a convenient place to comment on a correlative structure which resembles the cleft sentence but is distinguished prosodically from it. In this type of structure the adjunct or disjunct is functioning within the superordinate clause. Let us take as an illustration the sentence:

It's *not* that he's young; it's *just* that he's inexperienced.

We can delete the *that* clause and substitute *that*, i.e.:

It's *not* that; it's *just* that.

In a cleft sentence, however, this would not be possible, e.g.:

It's *today* that we begin.
→ *It's *today* that.

The two structures are quite different. The cleft sentence is a 'rearrangement of a single source-sentence' (Lees 1963a, 375), while in the correlative structure the *that*-clause (or contact clause) is an immediate constituent of the sentence, an equative complement.

Some disjuncts, particularly those of classes [A] and [B], may function in a correlative structure, e.g.:

It's *not* that he's young; it's *surely* that he's inexperienced.
It's *possibly* that he's young; it's *probably* that he's inexperienced.

Only one part of a correlative structure may appear in the form we have set out. Instead of the last example we might have:

It's *not* that he's young; I *just* think he's inexperienced.
We *don't* object to his youth; it's *just* that he's inexperienced.

The contrast may be expressed by the negative in one part and zero in the other:

It's *not* that he's young; it's that he's inexperienced.

The negative may be combined with another item:

It's *not only* that he's young; it's *also* that he's inexperienced.

Items commonly appearing in these positions include *also, even, just, simply, merely, purely, only, rather, actually, really. Partly* may occur in both halves of the structure:

It's *partly* that he's young; it's *partly* that he's inexperienced.

[10] Disjuncts cannot serve as a response to an interrogative transformation of the clause introduced by *When, Where, How,* or *Why.* For example, for the sentence with the disjunct *foolishly*

Foolishly, he answered their questions.

we might ask

How did he answer their questions?

but the disjunct *foolishly* would not be an answer to this question. On the other hand, if we had the same sentence except that manner adjunct *foolishly* replaced the disjunct

He answered their questions *foolishly*.

we could ask our question and receive in reply the adjunct *foolishly*

How did he answer their questions? *Foolishly*.

As has been pointed out (page 25), disjuncts can serve as a response to a *yes-no* question, though they may need to be accompanied by *yes* or *no*. In the particular example we have been discussing, such a response would be ambiguous between disjunct and manner adjunct:

Did he answer their questions? Yes, *foolishly*.

[11] Disjuncts cannot be premodified by *How* to form either an interrogative transformation of the clause or an exclamatory transformation of the clause. Thus, for the sentence with the disjunct *foolishly*

Foolishly, he answered their questions.

we do not have the interrogative transformation

How foolishly did he answer their questions?

or the exclamatory transformation

How foolishly he answered their questions!

In contrast, for the sentence with the adjunct *foolishly*

He answered their questions *foolishly*.

we have both these transformations.

It is not clear, in any case, to what extent disjuncts are acceptable in exclamatory clauses. Colleagues have disagreed over the acceptability of sentences such as:

?How well he talks, *surprisingly*!
?How early he left, *annoyingly*!

Further evidence of informant reactions is needed.

[12] Most disjuncts do not 'specify' the tense of the verb to produce a designation of time relationship, cf. Crystal 1966, 1ff. Exceptions include disjuncts of class [I], and *potentially*, *preferably* and *ideally*. Unlike the other disjuncts, these restrict the time-references of certain tenses (cf. pages 173ff.).

5.2.3   Modification

Most disjuncts can be modified. Among attitudinal disjuncts in correspondence classes, those in class [J], e.g. *allegedly*, cannot be modified. *Presumably*, which has been tentatively placed in class [A2], also cannot be modified. Many disjuncts that are not in correspondence classes do not accept modification, e.g. *apparently*, *perhaps*, *really*, *potentially*, *basically*.

Likely is exceptional in that it has the function of disjunct only when modified, cf. page 110.

Disjuncts that accept modification vary in the modifiers they will allow.

[1] *very* can premodify disjuncts from most classes but none from [J] or [B], e.g. **very allegedly* or **very certainly*.

[2] *enough* is often used as a postmodifier of disjuncts from class [C]:

Yet, *paradoxically enough*, Americans really have not yet learned to live with genuine political dissent.   (G 8/11/65: 6, 2)

'Eh?' he wrote, and the Beatles weighed in, *understandably enough*, with 'Help!'   (O 24/10/65: 10, 6)

Intuitively, it seems particularly common as a postmodifier of disjuncts from group [C2] that evaluate the statement as odd, viz, *bizarrely*, *curiously*, *eerily*, *funnily*, *oddly*, when its meaning is not 'sufficiently'. *Oddly enough*, for example, can be paraphrased 'odd though it may seem'. These may, however, occur without *enough*, as evidence from newspapers demonstrates:

Curiously, all this stone-walling seems totally out of place.
(ST 3/7/66: 7, 2)

It's an open secret that a similar project for Kuwait has started rolling – though, *oddly*, our scout in Kuwait says that Ministers still deny it.   (G 8/9/66: 8, 6)

Ironsi has vanished from the face of the earth. It is almost, *eerily*, as though he had never existed.   (G 8/9/66: 8, 6)

Enough, like *very*, can postmodify disjuncts from most classes but none from [J]. From class [B] *surely enough* is acceptable, but not **certainly enough*. *Enough* is not acceptable for disjuncts with a negative prefix. Thus we may have *wisely enough*, but not **unwisely enough*.

[3] *not* may premodify disjuncts with a negative prefix:

> Mark Lane and a good many more Dallas addicts were en-
> raged by the treatment Lane got from Auntie on BBC-2's
> assassination talkathlon last January. (*Not unreasonably*; the
> programme's impartiality struck some curious notes.)
> (G 2/3/67: 8, 6)

> They look, and sound, like working models of the
> womb. *Not inappropriately* or, for that matter, perhaps, not
> so futuristically after all.   (ST 1/1/67: 39, 1)

Not may freely premodify the disjunct *surprisingly*:

> He added, *not surprisingly*, that they were well pleased with Walker's
> work for them.   (O 24/10/65: 19, 5)

It would not, however, be as freely acceptable as a premodifier of dis-
juncts of the same semantic class, e.g., *amazingly* or *astonishingly*.
Nevertheless, most disjuncts, except those of class [J] and several from
[A2], may be premodified by *not so*. We may contrast:

> *Not (so) surprisingly*, they were well pleased.
> ?*Not astonishingly*, they were well pleased.
> *Not so astonishingly*, they were well pleased.
> **Not (so) conceivably*, they were well pleased.

[4] *quite* may premodify most disjuncts, apart from those from
class [J]:

> Members *quite understandably* seek to use it for their own
> national interests, . . .   (G 17/6/66: 12, 2)

> At six, everybody had *quite rightly* gone home from the Persian
> Embassy.   (G 26/8/66: 8, 6)

For class [B] it may premodify *certainly*, but not *surely*. We thus have
the contrast:

> **certainly enough*   *surely enough*
> *quite certainly*   **quite surely*

[5] *rather* may premodify disjuncts from all classes apart from [A2],
[B], [H1], and [J]:

> there are one or two modish touches (Banquo is assassinated,
> *rather topically*, by *coloured* [ital. sic] men).   (ST 16/10/66: 3, 5)

> Suddenly, excitement arrived in the person of a young, rebellious
> Bavarian painter who *rather surprisingly* was invited to live
> with the family. (ST 8/1/67: 21, 2)

[6] the distribution of the premodifying comparatives *more, less, most*, is probably closely similar to that of *very*, cf. [1] above, page 122.[1]

While *too* may not premodify disjuncts, the intensifier *all too* premodifies most disjuncts that accept *very*. We may contrast the acceptability of *too obviously* when *obviously* is a manner adjunct

He won the game *too obviously*.

with the unacceptability of *too obviously* when *obviously* is a disjunct

Too obviously, he won the game.

On the other hand, *all too obviously* is acceptable for *obviously* in both functions:

He won the game *all too obviously*.
All too obviously, he won the game.

Other premodifiers of disjuncts also occur, e.g. *almost, altogether, somewhat*:

Finally, inevitably, and *altogether understandably*, there is the plea that all this can only do further harm abroad to the reputation of the Great Society. (G 2/4/67: 15, 2)

It was, *almost predictably* [no comma sic] a clear and luminous performance... (G 25/10/65: 7, 2)

Somewhat unexpectedly, his prose doesn't rise as readily to the florid possibilities of North Oxford. (O 24/10/65: 26, 7)

Disjuncts in classes [A], [B], and [J] may function in a dependent relationship to disjuncts in other classes:

Yet he feels, *probably correctly*, that to have other Arab troops in Jordan would mean the end of monarchy. (ST 11/12/66: 2, 7)

Perhaps inevitably its main function has become that of a Civil Service middleman between the service departments and the aircraft industry, ... (G 17/6/66: 12, 2)

Women are twice as likely as men to take this view and, *perhaps more surprisingly*, young people much more than old.
(G 25/10/65: 3, 3)

---

[1] The odd combination *more certainly* appears in the material that has been examined. *More certainly* is an intensifier and *more obviously* a manner adjunct.

If the selecting body were a group of MPs, holding open hearings in the different areas – with submissions and questioning of applicants on the record – justice might *more certainly* be done, and would anyway *more obviously* be seen to be done. (G 4/5/67: 16, 8)

Presumably the premodification is influenced by the parallelism between the two parts of this frequently-quoted dictum and the acceptable combination in *more obviously*.

5.2.4 Specification of range of disjunct

For most of the disjuncts in classes [C]-[I], a specification of the range of the disjunct can be added, usually in the form of a prepositional phrase introduced by *for*. Some citations will illustrate my meaning:

[a] *Fortunately for the Labour Party*, Mr Wilson, whatever the more naïve of the faithful may think, has not been taken in by his brave public stance. (O 14/11/65: 10, 2)

[b] When he [the father] took possession of his tomb, Ada moved first to Nottingham (D. H. Lawrence, perhaps *luckily for him*, was a mere infant at the time), then to London, and then on to what can only be called a husband-trawling-tour of Europe. (ST 8/1/67: 21, 6)

[c] *most embitteringly for some of us*, the speeches delivered in earlier debates by Labour front benchers look like providing splendid material. (G 8/11/65: 8, 5)

[d] *Sadly for General de Gaulle* his troubles do not end at the mouth of the St Lawrence River. (G 7/8/67: 6, 1)

[e] *Happily for the Arabs in the war zones*, and heartening for us all, the fact is the Third Arab-Israeli War, the Six Day War, scarcely touched the Arab civilian population. (G 24/7/67: 6, 4)

In each of these citations, the disjunct evaluates the statement. The evaluation, however, is not generalised. If we take the first citation as an example, we see that *fortunately for the Labour party* corresponds to *It is fortunate for the Labour Party* (*that*). We might have instead:

Fortunately for the Labour Party, but not for the Conservative Party, Mr Wilson . . .

Fortunately without *for the Labour Party* is unspecified in its range. It might mean *Fortunately for everybody* or perhaps merely *Fortunately for Mr Wilson*, and its probable range would be suggested by the linguistic or situational context (cf. page 103). In citation [a], however, it is not Mr. Wilson who is stated to be fortunate but the Labour Party. The disjunct with the specification of its range corresponds to *The Labour Party is fortunate* (*that*).

The range of some disjuncts cannot be specified by a prepositional phrase introduced by *for*, though other prepositional phrases may be employed. For example, the range of *understandably* in the next citation is specified by *from their point of view*:

Understandably enough from their point of view they do not want the tripartite system to continue inside the comprehensive school, . . . (TES 30/12/66: 1545, 1)

We cannot, I think, replace *from their point of view* by *for them* in this last sentence, just as this substitution would not be acceptable in the correspondence:

*It is understandable enough *for them* (that) they do not want ...

On the other hand, *from their point of view* is readily acceptable in the correspondence:

It is understandable enough *from their point of view* (that) they do not want ...

In particular, disjuncts from classes [A], [B], and [J], as well as many of those outside the correspondence classes, appear not to allow specification of their range by a prepositional phrase introduced by *for*, e.g.:

*Possibly
*Clearly   *for the Labour Party*, Mr Wilson ... has not been taken
*Allegedly   in ...
*Really

In the citations that have been given, the specifying preposition *for* is roughly equivalent to 'as far as ... is [or *are*]concerned'. Let us examine, however, the sentence:

Surprisingly for him, John failed the exam several times.

For him is now equivalent to 'in his case', and *for* can only specify a noun or pronoun that is co-referent with the Subject of the clause:

Surprisingly for him [i.e. John], John failed the exam several times.
**Surprisingly for his father*, John failed the exam several times.

The relationship between the range-specified disjunct and the clause may be explained by the paraphrase:

John surprises in that he failed the exam several times.

For him may be said to contain the active Subject of a clause formed from the base participle of the disjunct with the implied verb *be*, i.e. 'John is surprising'.

With other disjuncts in class [C1] that are not synonyms or near synonyms of *surprisingly*, *for* can specify others as well as the Subject:

Annoyingly for him [i.e. John], John failed the exam several times.
Annoyingly for his father, John failed the exam several times.

In this case the prepositional phrase contains the passive Subject, as may be shown by the paraphrases:

{It annoys him [i.e. John]}
{He [i.e. John] is annoyed} that he failed ...

{It annoys his father}
{His father is annoyed} that John failed ...

Him in *annoyingly for him* could also refer to someone other than the Subject.

In citation [e] (page 125) we have an interesting example of a contrast between disjunct and adjective:

Happily for the Arabs in the war zones, and *heartening* for us all, . . .

The disjunct *hearteningly* could replace *heartening* with little loss of force (cf. pages 213ff.). *Hearteningly* has the correspondence *it is heartening (that)*, while *heartening* is a clipped clause, elliptical for *it is heartening (that)*.[1]

Usually *for* specifies a personal noun. When an abstract noun is specified, the effect is to personify the concept:

Mr Thorne has used all the first-hand material available when he went to press and a great deal besides, so that he makes a new contribution to the subject. *Mercifully for history,* however, he is concerned with the truth as demonstrated by the evidence, rather than with startling his readers with smart novelties.

(ST 23/4/67: 52, 4)

5.3 Attitudinal disjuncts contrasted with adjuncts

In the previous section generalisations have been made about the syntactic features of disjuncts, with particular reference to attitudinal disjuncts belonging to correspondence classes. We shall now look at selected attitudinal disjuncts in considerable detail. Certain disjuncts require individual treatment to distinguish them from homonyms; others have been selected as typical of a class of disjuncts. We shall also wish to consider certain adjuncts that have affinities, syntactic or semantic, with items classed as disjuncts.

5.3.1 Disjuncts and intensifiers

Some attitudinal disjuncts express the speaker's conviction of the truth

---

[1] *Happily* in that citation is synonymous with *fortunately*. In the rather odd specification *thankfully for Frank* in the following citation there appears to be a 'blending' of *thankfully* with the acceptable form *happily for Frank*:

Cousins's momentous crusade against the prices and incomes policy seems set fair to start with a meek, mild acceptance of 3½ per cent, leaving the week-before-last's chief apostle of increased productivity trying to get his own unionists to practise what he preached. Will they co-operate? Again, *thankfully for Frank*, private portents are good. (G 14/7/66: 8, 6)

In the context it is clear that it is Frank that is thankful, and yet there is no correspondence:

* I am ⎫
* one is⎭ thankful for Frank that private portents are good.

See Quirk 1965, 215 for 'anacolutha' that involve 'blending' processes.

or reality of what he is stating, e.g. *certainly, definitely, actually, indeed,* and *undoubtedly.* When these are positioned next to an item (in the same tone unit, usually, in spoken English, or when not separated by punctuation in written English), certain of them appear to focus that particular item to such an extent that they are felt to be similar to intensifiers like *thoroughly, very,* or *completely.* A series of tests were conducted to determine the degree of similarity between certain attitudinal disjuncts in an independent tone unit in an initial position and the same items positioned before the verb. The disjuncts selected for this purpose were *surely, indeed, certainly, actually,* and *really.* The results of these tests, comprising compliance, evaluation, and similarity tests, are displayed in Tables 24–30, pages 244ff. The tables also show the results of tests conducted on certain other items for similar purposes.

The similarity tests (Tables 28–30) are particularly valuable in the discriminations they made. These tests show quite clearly that *actually* and *really* are felt to be much more different in meaning in the two positions than *certainly, indeed,* and *surely.* At the same time, this latter group is felt to be much more different in the two positions than are, for example, *nevertheless* and *suddenly.* Accordingly, we are justified in distinguishing for all five items between their effect in the two positions. Since the five differ between themselves in various ways, they are best discussed individually, although comparisons between them will need to be made.

5.3.1.1 *Surely*

Of the five, the similarity between the two instances of *surely* was felt to be the closest by the informants. This is most clearly demonstrated in the results of the similarity tests, where as many as 107 informants [60 per cent] judged the two sentences with *surely* 'very similar in meaning' as compared with the seventy-two [40 per cent] who made the same judgment in Battery II for the two sentences containing *indeed.* The two pairs of sentences were:

the /child surely apologises for his mistàkes#
/sùrely# the /child apologises for his mistàkes#

/some people indèed attempted it#
in/dĕed# /some people attèmpted it#[1]

The greater similarity between the two instances of *surely* is confirmed in the compliance test (Table 25), where informants were asked to make the verb past tense for the sentence:

/sùrely# the /child surely apologises for his mistàkes#

---

[1] It should be pointed out, however, that the result may be biased somewhat by the fact that in the sentence with intensifying *surely* the verb does not carry the nuclear tone.

Eighty-one informants [45 per cent] did not comply with the instruction, as compared with forty-nine [27 per cent] who failed to
comply when asked to make the verb present tense in the following
sentence:

in/dĕed# /some people indèed attempted it#

Moreover, more informants omitted one of the repeated items or
substituted another item in the sentence with repeated *surely* than in
the sentence with repeated *indeed*.

The greater unacceptability of the co-occurrence of the disjunct
surely and the intensifying *surely* is confirmed, but to a lesser extent,
in the evaluation tests (Table 27). In these tests, 145 informants [81 per
cent] rejected the sentence with the repeated *surely*, compared with 126
[70 per cent] who rejected the sentence with the repeated *indeed*.

Of the twelve instances of *surely* in the Survey corpus, we can con-
fidently assign seven to the class of disjunct, all of them in speech texts.
Surely is undoubtedly a disjunct when it occurs in a separate tone unit,
as it does in four of the instances, though in one instance it is preceded
by the conjunction *but*, from which it is separated by a pause:

/but · *sûrely*# · you /can · it is /necessary to thìnk# · as /well as
commùnicate#   (5b.2.32)

In one other instance it is separated from the following verb by both a
tone unit boundary and a pause:

but · /his choice *sûrely*# · /indicated ə mathemàtics# · for /logic
and rèasoning# · the /séa# · for /peace size expánsiveness# · and
/heraldry · *surely* was his rèst# · his /recreàtion#   (5b.2.8)

The second instance of *surely* has moved towards the intensifying
function. Two points about the above passage are worth noting: first,
surely carries a rising-falling tone in the first instance. Of the six instances in which *surely* bears a nuclear tone in the Survey material, four
are rising-falling tones. The paucity of material makes it difficult to
evaluate the significance of this number, but introspective evidence
seems to confirm the appropriateness of this intonation pattern for
the disjunct, which carries it in two-thirds of the Survey instances.

We have an example of the co-occurrence of disjunct and intensifying
surely in this next sentence:

−/but [ði:] the principle *surely* of · people paying · what they can
afford to páy# an /economic rēnt# is /*surely* rìght#   (5b.1.21)

The insertion of *surely* between the Nominal Group and its postmodifier
marks it as parenthetic and accordingly as the disjunct. On the other
hand, the second *surely* seems to be intensifying the adjective *right*, which
is functioning as Complement of the sentence.

5+S.E.A.U.

A distinction, however, must be made between the intensifying character of *surely* and *certainly*, on the one hand, and *really*, on the other. Intensifying *really* is closer to the premodifying function of *very* in pre-adjective position, as can be seen from its acceptability in the inverted structure:

Very
Really
*Surely
*Certainly } hot it was in Spain this summer.

Surely and *certainly* can focus more distinctly on the item or unit that is the focus of information when they precede it. Because they express conviction, this focus has an intensifying effect. And because *certainly* expresses conviction more strongly than *surely*, it has a stronger intensifying effect. *Surely* is a disjunct at the beginning of a clause even when it is not in an independent tone unit:

? nucleus type /surely that was his recreation not his ?thóught#   (5b.2.8)

Outside the conditions we have mentioned *surely* will be interpreted as having an intensifying effect, as in the following examples:

Now it will *surely* be objected that the fact that words [sic] 'is wise' occur in a remark do [sic] not guarantee that the remark is an assertion. (8b.1.149–3)

but ði: · /point about Burns *sùrely* ís# that we /celebrate hím#
                                                        (5b.1.33)

The difference in nuance between the disjunct *surely* (and this seems to apply, but to a lesser extent, when it has an intensifying effect) and other disjuncts expressing conviction (*certainly, definitely, incontestably, indeed, indisputably, indubitably, unarguably, undeniably, undoubtedly, unquestionably*) is that *surely* invites agreement from the person or persons addressed. It does not convey the forcefulness of the others since it appears to seek confirmation (cf. page 142).

Like the intensifying *certainly*, the intensifying *surely* is not acceptable in a question (cf. pages 134f.). In contrast, the prepositional phrase intensifiers *for certain* and *for sure* seem to be acceptable in questions, at least when the verb has a future time reference:

Will he be there *for sure*?
Will he be there *for certain*?
*Will he *surely* be there?
*Will he *certainly* be there?

In this respect, *surely* and *certainly* also contrast with *actually, really*, and *indeed*.

Again like the intensifying *certainly* (page 136), the intensifying *surely* does not come under the domain of clause negation. But in this respect they contrast only with *actually* and *really*, for *indeed* seems not to come under the domain of clause negation.

In some idiolects the disjunct *surely* may serve as a response, usually signifying agreement to a request. In other idiolects *sure* alone is used.

Surely also occurs as an adjunct in the fixed collocation *slowly but surely*, e.g.:

The troops advanced slowly but surely.

The phrase *slowly but surely* as a unit is to be considered a manner adjunct.

5.3.1.2 *Indeed*

As we have already shown (pages 128f.), informants felt that there was less similarity between the disjunct *indeed* and the intensifying *indeed* than there was between the two instances of *surely*. In the same Battery informants were asked to judge the similarity of meaning of two other sentences that were identical except that one contained the disjunct *indeed* and the other the intensifier *thoroughly*:

in/děed# /many soldiers hàted it#
/many soldiers thòroughly hated it#

The overall results of this test are similar to those for the test with the two instances of *indeed*, except that there were fewer queries and greater polarisation. Correlation of both these tests demonstrates, therefore, that on the whole informants considered the intensifying *indeed* to be very much the same as the intensifier *thoroughly*, which has no homonymous disjunct.

Of the twenty-one instances of *indeed* in the Survey corpus that can be classed unambiguously as disjuncts nineteen are at the beginning of their clause. In two of these instances the clause has zero Subject:

well /that brings us to ði: · sècond half of what I wanted to sáy#
· ə ə ə · be/cause ə · that is àlso typical# · of the /vìews of the
sentimentalists# on /thís# – /since it is not based on any kind of
factual evidence at áll# · /and indéed# /flìes# in the /fàce# of the
/very considerable body of factual evidence that exìsts#   (5b.51.10)

we /have to ask you what your · what yòur reasons are# since
/you · yourself admít# – and in/deed give · a rèason# for · ad/mitting
that the statistics are quite irrèlevant to thís#   (5b.51.49)

The separate tone unit for *indeed* (plus the preceding conjunction) in the first passage marks it as a disjunct. If the speaker had said /and indéed flìes# it would be interpreted as having an intensifying function. In the second passage *indeed* is interpreted as a disjunct because of its position at the beginning of the clause, though if it had carried the nuclear tone it would have been intensifying.

In written texts *indeed* is a disjunct when it is at the beginning of the clause, even if there are no commas, and elsewhere in the clause when it is enclosed in a pair of commas, e.g.:

> These compounds have, *indeed*, recently been shown by De Tar and Long (1958) to occur in the products of the decomposition of benzoyl peroxide in very dilute solution in benzene.
>
> (8a.4.39-2)

However, when it is at the beginning of a clause with zero Subject then there may be ambiguity between the two functions, since there is no indication whether the word is to be read as bearing the nuclear tone, e.g.:

> Originality is a striking quality that most sonnets till then had failed to give; 'others leaves' have been unsatisfactory and *indeed* appear so to ((us)) when compared to the force and '((. . . ishing))' quality of Sidney; . . .   (W6.1b-13)

Indeed differs from the other intensifiers in being postposited after items it is intensifying, usually in collocation with a preceding *very*, *so* or exclamatory *how*, e.g.:

> it de/pends · vêry much *indeed*# on the locáliti((es))#   (5b.16.63)

The disjunct *indeed* expresses conviction and at the same time denotes that there is a confirmation, corroboration or reinforcement of a previous statement. As a response utterance it may be used as an ironic expression of agreement or to express surprise or indignation.

5.3.1.3   *Certainly*

Another series of tests in Battery 1 was conducted to determine the similarity between the disjunct *certainly* and the intensifying *certainly*. The evaluation test produced a higher acceptability rating for the sentence with repeated *certainly* than for the sentence with repeated *indeed* in the same Battery (cf. Table 26, page 246). The greater acceptability of their co-occurrence suggests that informants felt the two instances of *certainly* to be less similar in meaning. This is confirmed to some extent by their explicit judgment in a similarity test in the same Battery on the pair of sentences:

> your /children cértainly dislíked me#
> /cĕrtainly# your /children dislíked me#

Fewer informants thought these very similar in meaning than did in the test on the pair with *indeed*, and slightly more thought they were very different (cf. Table 28, page 248).

The higher compliance rate for the sentence with *certainly* in two positions also reflects the relatively greater acceptability of their co-occurrence (cf. Table 24, page 244).[1]

In a further series of tests the disjunct *certainly* was tested for its similarity to the intensifier *entirely*. Informants were asked to replace *his workers* by *his worker* in the sentence:

/cĕrtainly# his /workers entírely distrùsted him#

The high non-compliance rate of 41 per cent, the highest for this type of test in Battery I (cf. Table 24, page 244) is probably to be accounted for by the fact that *entirely* does not collocate readily with *distrust* (cf. page 140). The evaluation test also shows that informants felt uncomfortable about this sentence, since a third rejected it or expressed doubts about it (cf. Table 26, page 246).

On the other hand, when informants were asked to judge the similarity of the pair of sentences

his /workers entírely distrùsted him#
/cĕrtainly# his /workers distrùsted him#

more thought the two sentences different in meaning than responded in that way to the pair with *certainly* in each sentence (cf. Table 28, page 248). The difference between the results of the similarity tests on *certainly/certainly* and *certainly/entirely* is considerably greater than the difference between the results of tests on *indeed/indeed* and *indeed/thoroughly*. A possible explanation is that, in these contexts at least, *entirely* conveys the notion of extent as well as intensification more clearly than *thoroughly*. Thus, one is more likely to interpret the sentence

his /workers entírely distrùsted him#

as 'his workers distrusted everything about him (or "everything he did")' than one would interpret

/many soldiers thòroughly hated it#

---

1 However, the non-compliance figures for the sentence with repeated *indeed* are probably inflated as a result of this test sentence being the first with a repeated item in Battery I. This particular test sentence was also given in Battery II, where the non-compliance rate was 27 per cent as contrasted with 37 per cent in Battery I. It is interesting that only one of the three groups that responded to Battery I was disturbed by the the first appearance of this type of test. The other two groups produced non-compliance rates of 26 and 28 per cent, very similar results to those for Battery II. The effects of the order in which tests are administered are being currently investigated under the auspices of the Survey of English Usage.

as 'many soldiers hated everything about it'. Consequently, there is a greater semantic difference between the two intensifiers *certainly* and *entirely* than there is between the two intensifiers *indeed* and *thoroughly*. *Certainly* is not acceptable within a question even in its intensifying function. The results of tests in this respect on *certainly* and on *strangely* make a good contrast. *Strangely* belongs to class [C2] and does not have an intensifying effect with respect to verbs (but cf. pages 189ff.).

In the course of Battery 1 informants were asked to make into a *yes-no* question these two sentences:

/stràngely# they refuse to pày#
/cèrtainly# the /car broke dòwn#

Sixty-six informants (78 per cent) failed to comply in the test with *strangely*, while as many as eighty (94 per cent) failed to comply when the test sentence contained *certainly*. At first sight this suggests that informants felt that *certainly* was more objectionable in a question. A more detailed analysis (cf. Tables 21 and 22, pages 241f.) shows that this was not the case.

The type of non-compliance manifested with *certainly* tended on the whole to be less drastic. More than half of the informants who failed to comply were satisfied to leave *certainly* in the sentence, merely transposing it, whereas less than one-fifth of those who did not comply in the sentence with *strangely* were content merely to move it elsewhere. Again, eleven more informants omitted or replaced *strangely* than felt it necessary to do the same with *certainly*. The relatively higher place of *certainly* on the scale of acceptability may be explained by its closeness in function to an intensifier when it is not in an independent tone unit. Indeed, three informants substituted intensifying *for certain*. The intensifying function that *certainly* frequently has may account for the differences in the transpositions. Thirty-three informants moved *certainly* to a pre-verb position, and only eight to the end of the clause. In contrast, only twelve moved *strangely* to a pre-verb position, and four of those marked it off from the verb by enclosing it in commas or dashes. We may suspect that some who moved *strangely* did so in a frantic attempt to re-interpret it as a manner adjunct. Thus, one informant produced the response 'Did they refuse to pay in a strange way?' Some informants evaded the problem by substituting an exclamatory 'Strange' or 'How strange'. One informant replaced *strangely* by *strange as it may seem*, a neat solution, since the parenthetic clause is acceptable, perhaps because it is longer and a weightier insertion within an interrogative clause is permissible. This explanation, if correct, may account for the reaction of one informant who added a modifier and responded with *strangely enough*. We may also mention that a number of informants sought a way out of their dilemma by resorting to clauses corresponding to the disjuncts. Thus, eight informants substituted a variant of 'Is it strange' for *strangely*, three replaced *certainly* by 'Is it certain' and three by 'Are you certain'.

The same informants were subsequently asked to evaluate the transformed sentences:

/strǎngely# /do they refuse to páy#
/cĕrtainly# /did the car break dówn#

Clearly, both sentences were generally considered unacceptable, only six informants (7 per cent) accepting the first and just one (1 per cent) the second (cf. Table 23, page 243). The results have to be read in conjunction with those for the compliance tests if we wish to know that this rejection was not merely disapproval on, for example, stylistic grounds, but because the sentences are not considered part of the language. Furthermore, the compliance tests demonstrate that these sentences were not rejected merely because *strangely* and *certainly* occupied initial position. This is evident if we consider similar tests on a sentence containing *suddenly* (cf. page 66). In the evaluation test, informants were asked to judge the acceptability of the sentence:

/sǔddenly# /did he open the dóor#

Two informants (2 per cent) accepted, seventy-six (89 per cent) rejected, and seven (8 per cent) queried, the sentence. The results are similar to those for the sentences with *strangely* and *certainly*. However, the sentence with *suddenly* is rejected because it is unacceptable in front of a question, as the compliance test demonstrates, but it becomes perfectly acceptable when positioned elsewhere in the clause. Virtually all those who did not comply with the instruction to make the sentence into a question when *suddenly* was at its head found an easy means of rectification by transposing *suddenly*. This easy way of solving the problem caused by the operation requirement was not, however, available when *strangely* or *certainly* were at the head of the question.

The constraint on the appearance of *certainly* within a question is grammatical and not semantic, since the virtually synonymous intensifier *definitely* seems perfectly acceptable within a question:

the /car definitely broke dòwn#
Did the car definitely break down?

We assume, though we have no experimental evidence for this as yet, that the intensifying *definitely* is more clearly distinguished from the disjunct *definitely* than the intensifying *certainly* is from the disjunct *certainly*.

I have referred above (page 130) to the difference between the intensifying function of *certainly* and *surely* on the one hand, and *really*, on the other. Intensifying *really*, *actually*, and *indeed* are different in that they are acceptable within questions. Furthermore, *really* and *actually* may come under the domain of clause negation. Tests were included in Batteries I and II to demonstrate the distinction between *certainly* and *really* in this last respect (cf. Tables 16–20, pages 236ff.).

Of the eighty-five informants in the experiment with Battery I who were asked to negate

he can /certainly drive a càr#

not even one responded with the target sentence

He can't certainly drive a car.

while in the evaluation test seventy-five (85 per cent) rejected the target sentence and only three (4 per cent) accepted it. On the other hand, of the 179 informants who were asked to negate in Battery II the sentence

I can /really believe what they sày#

139 (78 per cent) responded with the target sentence

I can't really believe what they say.

and in the evaluation test only one rejected it while 176 (98 per cent) accepted it.

We can account for the marked disparity in the results by the fact that the two functions of *certainly* (disjunct and intensifying) are closer than the corresponding functions of *really*. It is significant that none of the 139 informants who placed *really* immediately after the negative particle enclosed it in commas. Such punctuation would indicate that they were interpreting it as the disjunct. It is also significant that the two informants who introduced substitutions for *really* produced intensifying expressions that co-occur obligatorily with the negative and only occur as intensifiers after the verb:

I can't believe what they say *at all*.
I couldn't believe *a thing* they said.

In the compliance test, sixty-six informants (78 per cent) placed *certainly* before the auxiliary, i.e.

He certainly can't drive a car.

when they transposed it to avoid the unacceptable position after the negative particle. Twenty-three informants (13 per cent) transposed *really*, although the position immediately after the negative particle is perfectly acceptable for *really*. Another ten informants originally did so before altering the position of *really* to accord with the target sentence. These transpositions to the position before the negative particle suggest that *certainly* and *really* may intensify clause negation. Intensifiers related to disjuncts are available to intensify clause negation, whereas most other intensifiers cannot occupy positions before the negative particle. We may contrast:

{He doesn't really need it.
{He really doesn't need it.

{ He doesn't badly need it.
{*He badly doesn't need it.

{*I don't certainly agree with you.
{ I certainly don't agree with you.

{ I don't entirely agree with you.
{*I entirely don't agree with you.

Besides *certainly* and *really*, the emphatic intensifiers that are available to intensify clause negation include *definitely*, *actually*, *honestly*, and *simply*.[1]

The evidence in the Survey corpus suggests that there is in general a tendency for *certainly* and *really* to co-occur with clause negation. Of eighty-two instances of *really* as intensifier (in a few of these cases there is ambiguity between the intensifier and the disjunct) the clause is negative thirty-seven times. In sixteen instances, *really* immediately follows the negative particle, e.g.:

I /don't *rèally* think# /àny of us on this plátform# are
/cŏmpetent# to /jùdge# (5b.1.20)

when you /see things as òther things# · they are /not *rèally* other
things# (5b.2.34)

Really immediately precedes the auxiliary and negative particle in two instances:

I *really* don't know where we should be without you, Mr Percy.
(6.3.205–1)

yès# — /yēs# I ə I /wouldn't be surprìsed at thát# — I /*really*
wòuldn't# (S.1c.11–18)

There are no examples in the corpus of *really* between the auxiliary and the negative particle. A large proportion of the instances in the corpus of the intensifying *certainly* appear before negation. Of twenty

---

1 *Honestly* and *simply* are related to style disjuncts (cf. pages 85ff.). *Almost* and *nearly* are degree 'downtoners' that may precede clause negation. For 'downtoners' and intensifiers, see Stoffel 1901. For some other accounts of intensifiers, see Borst 1902, Spitzbardt 1965, Kirchner 1955 and the review on the last by Poldauf 1959, 1 ff.

5*

instances, nine occur before negation — five immediately preceding the negative particle, one before *never*, and the remaining three before the auxiliary.

Certainly and *really* collocate with a wide range of verbs. In tests intended to determine collocation that were included in Battery II informants were asked to complete the sentences:

the /man cērtainly
the /child rēally
I bādly
your /friend very mūch
they /all grēatly

In Battery III informants were asked to complete the sentences:

I en/tīrely
they /all ūtterly
we /all mūch
my /friend complētely

The collocates that appeared after *certainly* and *really* are set out below. 173 valid responses were registered for the test with the introductory words *the /man cērtainly* and 165 valid responses for the test with *the /child rēally*.

the /man cērtainly

PERSONAL ATTRIBUTES:

    (i) INTELLECTUAL: be a fool (6); not be a fool; be foolish; not be very bright; be very intelligent; be clever; not be very clever; be stupid; be crackers; be insane
        TOTAL: 15 (9 per cent)

    (ii) PHYSICAL: be drunk (2); not be good-looking; look attractive; look well; look ill; look peaky; look odd; look all right; look nice; look stupid; look tired; look like a tramp; have a bald head; dress well (2); be well-dressed; be unsteady on feet; be tall (2); be strong; smell; stink
        TOTAL: 23 (13 per cent)

    (iii) PSYCHOLOGICAL, MORAL, EMOTIVE, STATUS, ETC.: look happy; be guilty; be a fraud; be tricky; not be very adamant; be a bore; be a V.I.P.; be dignified; be weird; be brave; be honest; be sex-starved; be unfortunate; be good at football
        TOTAL: 14(8 per cent)
TOTAL 52 (30 per cent)

INTELLECTUAL STATE: know (22); not know (4); think; not understand; not believe
TOTAL: 29 (17 per cent)

LIKING AND DISLIKING: like (4); not like; dislike; love; hate (2)
TOTAL: 9 (5 per cent)

MOVEMENT: run (7); walk (2); go (4); not go (2); not come; not arrive; drive; dance; can-can; swim; fall; not be going to fall in; fall off; not get very far
TOTAL 25 (14 per cent)

OTHER VERBS OF ACTIVITY: eat (2); not eat; drink (3); smoke; snore; yell; speak; say; make point; lie; read; write; play; hit; fight (2); not kill; work (3); not work (2); wash face; never do the deed; do well (2); do job well; do it; not do it (2)
TOTAL: 33 (19 per cent)

MISCELLANEOUS: be here; be there; be; enjoy self; win; terrify; get own way; carry conviction; react predictably; miss opportunity; have a raw deal; lose money; fall for it; wear a hat; not stay; be surprised; astound; show self up; get what he deserved; have a lot to do; have lots to do; do; do not; deserve (2)
TOTAL: 25 (14 per cent)

the |child rēally

PERSONAL ATTRIBUTES:

  (i) INTELLECTUAL: be a genius; be clever (2); be intelligent (2); be a fool; be a simpleton; be stupid (2); be backward (2); be mad
    TOTAL: 12 (7 per cent)
  (ii) PHYSICAL: be good-looking; be pretty; be ugly; look well; look ill (4); be healthy; smell
    TOTAL: 10 (6 per cent)
  (iii) PSYCHOLOGICAL, MORAL, EMOTIVE, STATUS, ETC.: be mischievous; be a lively one; be naughty (6); be a nuisance (3); be annoying; be well-behaved (2); be better-behaved; be bad; be good (2); not be good; be spoilt (3); be immature; be a horror; be funny; be a comedian; be unhappy; be brave; be abnormal; be just like his mother; come from a rich family; go to a good school
    TOTAL: 32 (19)
TOTAL: 54 (33 per cent)

INTELLECTUAL STATE: know; not know (7); not understand (4); think hard; imagine; have no idea; believe (3)
TOTAL: 18 (11 per cent)

LIKING AND DISLIKING: love (16); hate (7); like (6); adore; lap it up
TOTAL: 31 (19 per cent)

CRYING: cry (6); not cry; scream; howl; yell
TOTAL: 10 (6 per cent)

VERBS OF ACTIVITY: do it; not do well; not work; eat (3); write; ask; not read; run away; go home; go to school; go to tea

TOTAL: 13 (8 per cent)

MISCELLANEOUS: need (5); want (4); be tired; be upset; be in a temper; not be allowed to do it (2); not try; try (2); care; not care (2); give of best; impress; not help it; enjoy (4); enjoy self; hurt self (2); stop eating; have a toothache; feel ill; grow (2); stay; lose way; fall out of; ought to be in bed

TOTAL: 39 (24 per cent)

It will be noticed from the above lists that the verb that appears most frequently is the verb *be*. Forty entries (23 per cent) are registered after *certainly* and forty-nine entries (30 per cent) after *really*. The verb *be* has a very light semantic load, and it therefore seemed justifiable to regard the following Complement as part of the collocate. In the other completion tests the verb *be* does not appear at all, since the degree intensifiers cannot precede it.

Intuitively, it would seem that *certainly* and *really* can collocate with any verb. However, two sets of collocates predominate among the responses. They are the set termed 'personal attributes' and the set of verbs of activity, from which two sub-sets can be isolated, verbs of movement and verbs of crying. Together, the verbs in these sets constitute over 60 per cent of the total responses for the test with *certainly* and nearly 47 per cent of the responses for the test with *really*. The absence of collocates of personal attribute in other tests may largely be accounted for by the fact that most of the collocates in this set are extended collocates containing the verb *be*, and the other intensifiers may not precede the verb *be*. As for the other set, we must simply say that in general verbs of activity do not collocate with the degree intensifiers.

The verbs that appear after *certainly* and *really* cover a wide semantic range. The verbs appearing after the degree intensifiers occupy a relatively restricted semantic range. For example, after *very much* 37 per cent of the verbs express the notion of liking or disliking and 30 per cent denote needing or wanting. With some degree intensifiers a particular verb appears with a very high frequency. Thus, after *entirely* the verb *agree* occurs in eighty-nine responses (82 per cent) and after *badly* the verb *need* occurs in 113 responses (65 per cent).

In the light of the previous suggestion that there is some tendency for *certainly* and *really* to co-occur with clause negation (cf. page 137), it is interesting that in the test with *certainly* the clause was negated in twenty-seven responses (16 per cent) and in the test with *really* it was negated in twenty-two responses (13 per cent).[1]

---

[1] For a full account of the completion tests, see Greenbaum 1969a.

The disjunct *certainly* expresses conviction and at the same time often suggests that the speaker or writer is restricting his conviction to what he is now saying, so that it may be paraphrased by 'this at least is certain', e.g.:

They played as well in this rubber as they have done for a long, long time. *Certainly*, Stilwell made up on Saturday for his disappointing showing against Barclay on Friday and Wooldridge carried out all his tasks resolutely. (G25/10/65: 12, 6)

Harris: Nevertheless, your Cabinet has had a hell of a year. P.M.: It has been a difficult year, *certainly*. (OM 24/10/65: 22, 2)

In the citations just given, the concessive force of *certainly* is related to what has been said before. It may also relate to what is about to be said, in which case *certainly* commutes with immobile *true*, a clipped form of the clause *it is true* (cf. page 215). The concessive nature of this expression of conviction is indicated by *but* in a succeeding clause, e.g.:

In the Bible and historical theology there is no Pneumatology apart from Christology. The person and work of the Holy Spirit is known only in relation to the Word made flesh. *Certainly*, mention is made of the Spirit in the Old Testament, just as there is mention of God apart from Jesus Christ. *But* the Old Testament does not stand alone. It is preparatory to the coming of Jesus Christ in whom it finds its fulfilment. (8ab.2.135-1)

When *certainly* is a response to a question, it usually expresses emphatic acquiescence. It is often used in granting permission following a request. In this latter use it can be replaced in some idiolects, with a slight difference in nuance, by *surely*. *Surely* urges the performance of the action for which permission is requested. For example, if the request is *May I help myself to a piece of cake?*, then the response *Certainly* is roughly equivalent to *Yes, you may* while *Surely* is nearer to *Yes, do*.

The response *Certainly* sometimes expresses concessive agreement, in which case *but* or a concessive conjunction or a concessive conjunct may be expected to follow it.[1]

5.3.1.4 *Actually*

The disjunct conveys explicitly the speaker's view that what he is saying is factually true. At the same time it suggests that what he is saying may be surprising to the person addressed. Typically, it relates to a statement that contradicts, or expresses reservations about, a previous statement, e.g.;

---

[1] *Certainly* with a concessive force should perhaps be classed with the conjuncts, since it is doubtful whether it could serve as a response to a *yes-no* question even if accompanied by *yes* or *no* (cf. page 25).

'I suppose you were called up.'

'Would have been.' Dinah stopped and lit a cigarette. She smokes, thought Madeleine, like a chimney. 'Being a widow with no home ties. *Actually*, I volunteered.' (6.1.21)

It picks out Mr Jayaprakash Narayan, the Indian Sarvodayah leader, as the man responsible for changing Mr Shastri's attitude.

Actually, besides Mr Narayan, those who met Mr Shastri last night included Mr B. P. Chalika, Chief Minister of Assam, and the Indian civil servants who have been conducting the peace talks in Nagaland. (O 24/10/65: 4, 6)

When *actually* occurs before the verb it has an intensifying effect unless it is separated by intonational or punctuational means from the verb. Broadly speaking, the intensifier can be paraphrased in two ways. Firstly, it is equivalent to 'in actual fact', e.g.:

The nerve-fibres in the nervous system of cyclostomes are not provided with myelin sheathes; in this they resemble the nerves of amphioxus. Conduction is slow in such non-medullated fibres, the only case *actually* investigated in cyclostomes being the lateral line nerve of *Bdellostoma* [ital. sic], found by Carlson to conduct at the low rate of 5 metres a second (frog about 50 m/sec., mammals up to 100 m/sec.). (8a.1.98-2)

Where the intensifier suggests that the statement may be surprising, it implies that it is surprising to the speaker as well. We may contrast:

He actually volunteered.

Actually, he volunteered.

The implication by this use of the intensifier *actually* that the speaker is surprised is highlighted by the similarity in meaning between sentences such as:

Did he *actually* volunteer?

Surely he didn't volunteer.

Both *actually* and *surely* express incredulity in these sentences. The effect of *surely*, which invites agreement, is rather like that of the tag question:

He didn't volunteer, *did he*?

In its other use, the intensifier *actually* has temporal significance, e.g.:

The word ['term'] is always to be understood in the second way, except when I am *actually* speaking of Quine's doctrines or using it in the context of the phrase 'singular term'.

(8b.1.154-1)

For *actually* to have this meaning, there probably needs to be another unit with temporal significance in the context. In this clause '*when* . . . *actually*' is equivalent to '*at the very time when* . . .'.

Actually may be interpreted as a disjunct when it occurs medially after the verb, e.g.:

I'm /very surprìsed *actually*# at /this · quotation of Rùssell's#

(5b.2.10)

It here interrupts between the verb and the particle with which it collocates, and is therefore taken as parenthetic. The intensifier may appear in front of the clause when there is Verb-Subject inversion, e.g.:

Actually doing that reckoning will be an executive committee of Lord Melchett, and Loeb, Rhoades' Clifford Michel, with Naess in the chair. (O 24/10/65: 7, 3)

We can contrast with this last example, the unacceptability of *surely* and *certainly* in this position in their intensifying function:

*Surely
*Certainly } doing that reckoning will be . . .

The intensifying *actually* can come within the domain of clause negation and interrogation. The ability of the intensifying *actually* to occur within a question accounts for the different results in the tests with the disjuncts *certainly* and *actually* (cf. Tables 21–3, pages 241ff.). When informants were asked in the course of Battery I to turn into a *yes-no* question the sentence

/ăctually# she /sat nèar him#

the majority found an easy solution of the problem, since by transposing *actually* they could retain the item in the question. When required to evaluate the transformed sentence:

/ăctually# /did she sit néar him#

nearly half the informants were prepared to accept the sentence as perfectly normal. It is interesting that in the compliance test one in-informant attempted to paraphrase *actually* by *Is it an actual fact*, using the adjective base of the disjunct. Another recast the sentence radically in seeking to convey an acceptable equivalent for *actually* within the question: he responded with 'Did she sit near him or not'.

The semantic distance between the intensifying *actually* and the disjunct *actually* is greater than for the other items we have been considering. It is nearer to the semantic distance between intensifying *really* and disjunct *really* (see below). In Battery II informants were asked to judge the degree of similarity between the following pair of sentences:

/some lectures are actually given before tèn#
/ăctually# /some lectures are given before tèn#

A hundred informants (56 per cent) thought the two sentences very different in meaning, while only forty (23 per cent) thought them very similar (cf. Table 29, page 249). Thus, less than a quarter of the informants judged these two sentences to be very similar in meaning.

5.3.1.5 *Really*

The disjunct *really* makes explicit the speaker's view that the statement being made is true. However, it is undoubtedly the most versatile of all the disjuncts and has the widest range of meaning. It is often difficult to distinguish between the disjunct and the intensifying functions of this item, though in a similarity test in Battery 1 a sharp difference between the two functions emerged.

Informants were asked to estimate the degree of similarity of meaning between the following pair of sentences:

/rĕally# the /students wòrk during the term#
the /students réally wòrk during the term#

Forty-seven informants (73 per cent) judged these two sentences to be very different in meaning and only twelve (19 per cent) thought they were very similar. The disjunct *really* (in the first sentence) may be paraphrased informally by 'it would be true to say that', while a reasonably accurate paraphrase of the second sentence would be 'the students work hard during the term' with *really* as intensifier of *work*. *Réally wòrk* is interpretable as 'work in the real (or true or full) sense of the word *work*'. Had the second sentence of the pair been given the intonation pattern:

the /students really work during the tèrm#

really would, presumably, have been ambiguous between the meaning just given for the intensifier and a meaning 'in reality' which is closer to that of the disjunct. This ambiguity when the intensifier does not bear the nuclear tone may be one of the factors accounting for the result of another similarity test given in the same Battery, a result that at first sight seems surprising.

Informants were asked to judge the similarity of meaning between the pair of sentences:

they were /really appalled by their lèader#
/frănkly# they were ap/palled by their lèader#

In this case only thirty-two informants (50 per cent) declared that the two sentences were very different in meaning, fifteen less than the number saying this for the two sentences with *really*, while as many as twenty-three (36 per cent) were prepared to consider the two sentences very similar in meaning. Since *really* does not bear the nuclear tone although in the same tone unit as the verb, it may be interpreted as 'in reality' and it could then be thought that the information content of the two sentences is not very different. For in many contexts *frankly* may in fact mean very little more than 'it would be true to say'. Even if *really* is interpreted as an intensifier, its effect is not so pronounced when it is intensifying the verb *appal* as when it is intensifying the verb *work*, since the verb *appal* intrinsically denotes intense feeling. *Frankly* itself is used as an intensifier in collocation with verbs denoting puzzlement or dismay, when the verbs are in the passive form.

In another test in the same Battery informants were asked to judge the similarity of meaning between the sentences:

your /children ábsolutely hòwl every night#
/rĕally# your /children hòwl every night#

Even fewer than before, twenty-four informants (38 per cent), judged these sentences to be very different in meaning. As before, the verb is intrinsically intensified, the intensive *howl* contrasting with the neutral *cry*. Accordingly, the omission of the intensifier *absolutely* does not affect the semantic content of the sentence for many informants. Equally, it seems that the addition of *really* in the second sentence of the pair does not essentially alter the semantic content, as we can see from another test, this time in Battery II.

Informants were asked to judge the similarity of meaning between the sentences:

/rĕally# your /children hòwl during the night#
your /children often hòwl during the night#

Ninety informants (50 per cent) considered these two sentences to be very different in meaning, a smaller percentage than for the pair of sentences each containing *really*. Presumably, once again, the omission of *really* was not felt to affect the semantic content radically. We must assume, moreover, that for many the presence or omission of *often* was not important semantically. There is, indeed, an ambiguity in the function of *often* in this sentence and in one sense of the word it can be omitted without radically affecting the semantic content of the sentence. In this sentence the use of the simple present tense of *howl* denotes that the action during the night happens repeatedly, which is semantically equivalent, roughly speaking, to the unambiguous function of *often* when it is in initial position. Thus

Often your children howl during the night.

may be informally paraphrased as

It often happens that your children howl during the night.

On the other hand, if *often* had been in the unambiguous position after the verb it would convey the added notion that the action happens repeatedly during the night. Thus, it would be perfectly acceptable to have both these contrasting sentences:

> Often your children howl occasionally during the night.
> Occasionally your children howl often during the night.

We can say that *often* in the first sentence of this last pair is related to the clause as a whole, while in the second sentence it is related to the verb and its complementation, whether by Complement or Adjunct. In the test sentence given to informants *often* appears immediately before the verb. In that position it is ambiguous between the two functions.[1]

We have referred at the beginning of this section to the wide range of meaning covered by the disjunct *really*. It is frequently difficult to pinpoint the various meanings, but we shall give a few illustrations.

[1] and /while I'm very ânxious# and /wîlling# – to a/wait the outcome of Mr Butler's reformative mêasures# – his /new detèntion centres# his ə · ʔə: /harder tràining# – of /young thugs and the remàinder# – /rêally# there /must bê ə:# – there /must be an · ènd# /sôme time# to /public pàtience in this matter#   (5b.51.42)

[2] I'm /sure he's a jolly decent chàp# but · /rêally# · /should he /is that the kind of man to have as a public ìdol# · of /téenagers# of /múms# at the · /sínk# and /anything èlse#
                                                                          (5b.1.3)

[3] /I think · you know · *really* [ði:] · you you /can't blame the individual in this cáse# this is a /problem of our modern prèss#
                                                                          (5b.1.6)

[4] 'It was an accident.' 'No,' said Treece. 'Oh, *really*,' said Emma. 'Must you make a crisis out of it?'   (6.2.96–2)

Really in [1] might be paraphrased by 'I really think', in [2] by 'I ask you for your real opinion' (in this case followed by a rhetorical question), and in [3] again by 'I really think' or 'it would be true to say'. In all three cases 'in reality' might be substituted for *really*, but with some loss of emotive force. In [4] *really* is a verbal gesture of impatience and indignation and cannot be replaced by *in reality*.

As a response utterance *really* may have the connotation suggested

---

[1] In a footnote, Bolinger (1967, 5) paraphrases an initial *occasionally* by 'It occasionally happened that', but the difference that he observes between 'Occasionally a sailor strolled by' and 'A sailor strolled by occasionally' does not exist in my idiolect. Both sentences allow both interpretations, namely, the same sailor strolled by now and then, and from time to time different sailors strolled by.

for [4], in which case it would normally bear a rising-falling nucleus. It may also, as a response utterance, connote surprise, in which case it would normally bear a falling-rising or rising nuclear tone. When it suggests surprise it may be paraphrased by 'Is that so?'. In both cases it could function as a response to a declarative clause.

The meaning of the intensifier is equally elusive, as the following quotations will illustrate:

[1] /if you've got · lòvely country# · /are you *rèally* happy# · to /have · a pretty grìm thing# /like a hòliday cámp# · /defàcing it#
(5b.16.64)

[2] /I · I'm quite frankly flûmmoxed# · /I didn't know we were still supporting the Krupp émpire# and · the /fellow who asked the question's a personal friend of míne# he's /*really* put me on the spòt# – /I quite honestly don't knôw#
(5b.1.39)

[3] How kind of you to tell me. I *really* don't know where we should be without you, Mr Percy.
(6.3.205-1)

[4] /what I *rĕally* think# is /thìs though#
(5b.2.4)

[5] /I'm not *really* wórried ((myself)) personally# if the /readership goes thróugh#
(S.1c.11-26)

Really in [1] appears to be intensifying the word *happy* and may be paraphrased by 'in the true sense of the word'. In [2] it is nearer in meaning to 'definitely'. We may notice the two other intensifiers in the context, *quite frankly* and *quite honestly*, which could be replaced by *really* with little loss of meaning. *Really* in [3] has a similar meaning, but in this case it can be replaced by *honestly*, which collocates with the auxiliaries *do* or *would* and *not know*. In [4] it can be more nearly paraphrased by *in actual fact* or *in reality*, and in this context *actually* will more readily commute with it. In [5] it may be paraphrased by 'very much', although again here it may mean 'in reality'.

Really is unambiguously the disjunct when it is in initial position and usually when it is in an independent tone unit. In the latter case it may still be an intensifier if its nucleus echoes another immediately preceding it, e.g.:

/these questions three and fŏur# /didn't make any dìfference#
/rèally# to the re/sult of the examinàtion#
(S.1c.11-68)

Here *really* is subject to clause negation. *Not really* and *really not* as responses to questions contain the intensifier *really* with ellipsis of the declarative transformation of the preceding interrogative clause (and, possibly, some adjustment of the personal pronouns). If, however, *really* were separated from *not* by intonation or punctuation it would be interpreted as the disjunct.

5.3.1.6 *Possibly*

Possibly is an intensifier when it collocates with *can* or *could* in certain environments.

One such environment is immediately following the negative particle in a declarative sentence, e.g.:

They $\left\{\begin{array}{l}\text{can't}\\\text{couldn't}\end{array}\right\}$ *possibly* leave early.

The logical affirmative of this sentence is:

They $\left\{\begin{array}{l}\text{can}\\\text{could}\end{array}\right\}$ *certainly* leave early.

Other auxiliaries do not collocate with *possibly* in this way. With auxiliaries other than *can* or *could*, *possibly* is normally unacceptable in the position immediately after the negative particle, e.g.:

*They won't *possibly* leave early.

Even in a negative sentence with *can* or *could* present, *possibly* is an intensifier only if it immediately follows the negative particle. If we take as our example the sentence *They can't possibly leave early*, with the intensifier *possibly*, we see the difference in meaning that results from the movement of *possibly* elsewhere in the sentence:

Possibly they can't leave early.
They *possibly* can't leave early.
They can *possibly* not leave early.
They can't leave early, *possibly*.

In these four sentences *possibly* corresponds to *it is possible (that)*.

An analogous environment is where the superordinate clause is negative and there is transferred negation, e.g.:

I didn't think they could *possibly* leave early.

A disjunct would be unacceptable within the subordinate clause if there is transferred negation, e.g.:

*I didn't think they could *probably* leave early.

Another environment is within an interrogative clause, even when the clause is affirmative, e.g.:

Can they *possibly* leave early?

Analogous environments are within indirect questions and in conditional clauses, e.g.:

I asked whether they could *possibly* leave early.
If they can *possibly* leave early, they will do so.

We may contrast:

*I asked whether they could *probably* leave early.
*If they can *probably* leave early, they will do so.

Finally, *possibly* can be an intensifier when a restrictive *only* appears earlier in the clause and is followed by Verb-Subject inversion:

Only on Saturdays can they *possibly* leave early.

Among the attitudinal disjuncts, *conceivably* is very like *possibly*, similarly moving to intensifying function in collocation with *can* or *could*. Thus there is, likewise, a distinction between

They can't *conceivably* leave early.

and the various forms of this sentence with *conceivably* in other positions. And *conceivably* can enter, in collocation with *can* and *could*, into the range of environments open to *possibly*.[1]

Perhaps because these intensifiers are acceptable in certain environments when in collocation with *can* or *could*, they are not entirely unacceptable when they are in the same environments but with other auxiliaries. When they co-occur in these environments with other auxiliaries they are understood as intensifiers, and not as disjuncts. We may illustrate this point with the sole example of a question containing *possibly* that occurs in the Survey corpus:

'Darling Mummy, how sweet of you. But how did you *possibly* afford it?' (6.3.212-2)

This question sounds somewhat odd. An informant was asked to paraphrase it and produced as his considered interpretation: 'But how did it happen that you could possibly afford it?' It will be noticed that *could* was supplied in the paraphrase, with the result that *possibly* has moved towards intensifying function. There is a motivation for using *did* in the context of the passage: *did* is marked for tense, whereas *could* (unless it occurs in a sequence of tenses in indirect speech) denotes a more tentative possibility.

This is a convenient point to mention that the disjunct *possibly* has only a type [1] correspondence, although the adjective *possible* may enter into a type [2] structure (cf. page 94). For example, the sentence

Possibly he smokes a pipe.

is semantically equivalent to

That he smokes a pipe is possible.

---

1 The range of environments open to the intensifiers *possibly* and *conceivably* in collocation with *can* or *could* is similar to the range available to intensifiers such as *at all* and *ever*, except that these are not restricted to collocation with particular auxiliaries.

and the corresponding *It*-inversion structure

It is possible that he smokes a pipe.

We can replace *possibly* and its type [1] correspondences by the auxiliary *may* in one of its senses

He *may* smoke a pipe.

If the progressive form is used here, *possibly* can be replaced by either *may* or *can*:

He $\left\{ \begin{array}{l} \text{may} \\ \text{can} \end{array} \right\}$ be smoking a pipe.

On the other hand, it is not semantically equivalent to structures where *possible* is predicative to a non-finite verb construction

To smoke a pipe is possible.
Smoking a pipe is possible.

or   For him to smoke a pipe is possible.

and the corresponding *It*-inversion structure

It is possible for him to smoke a pipe.

We can now substitute *can* and *be able to*, but not *may*:

He *can* smoke a pipe.
He *is able to* smoke a pipe.

There are analogous differences with the antonym *impossible*. We may contrast

That he smokes a pipe is impossible.

and the corresponding *It*-inversion structure

It is impossible that he smokes a pipe.

with

To smoke a pipe is impossible.
For him to smoke a pipe is impossible.
It is impossible for him to smoke a pipe.
Smoking a pipe is impossible.

In a compliance test in Battery I, informants were required to negate the sentence

he /will possibly become a tèacher#

Twenty-three informants (27 per cent) complied with the instruction, a minority but many more than did so for the analogous test sentences with *probably* and *certainly* in the same Battery (cf. Tables 16-17,

pages 236f.). Only four informants complied in the test with *probably*
and none at all in the test with *certainly*. The higher compliance for
possibly can perhaps be explained as due to the influence of occasions
when *possibly* immediately follows the negative particle, namely the
intensifier *possibly* in collocation with *can* or *could*. Thus, the negation
of the same sentence with *can* in place of *will* would result in an acceptable sentence:

> He can't possibly become a teacher.

It is, however, strange that no informants responded with *can't possibly*,
though two informants replaced *will* by *may*, which can sometimes be
substituted for *can*. It is puzzling that as many as eleven informants
substituted *probably* for *possibly*, although *probably* is even more unacceptable immediately following the negative particle than *possibly*, as
the analogous compliance test demonstrates. Indeed, all but one of the
eleven placed the negative particle after *probably*.[1] It may be that these
informants are attempting to negate *possibly* as well as the clause it is
related to. This can be more clearly demonstrated by substituting the
corresponding clauses:

> It's not that it's *possible* that he will become a teacher: it's rather that
> it's *probable* that he will become a teacher.

Possibly and *probably* are not antonyms, but they are at different positions in a gradience of polarity.

It is interesting that two informants responded with:

> It is impossible that he will become a teacher.

This is an attempt to produce the corresponding structure with a negation of the base adjective. However, both the adjective *impossible* and
the negation of *possible* in the corresponding clauses restrict the meaning
to the extreme end of the gradience. Thus, the response by another
informant:

> It is not likely that he will become a teacher.

is nearer semantically to a negation of *possibly* in the original sentence
than

> It is not possible that he will become a teacher.

or

> It is impossible that he will become a teacher.

---

[1] Since the test with *possibly* preceded that with *probably* and the word *probably*
did not appear in an earlier test sentence, it cannot be argued that the substitution of *probably* was caused by interference from memory of the previous occurrence of the word.

There is no disjunct *impossibly* corresponding to *it is impossible (that)* in this last sentence:

*Impossibly, he will become a teacher.

However, an interesting example of the use of *impossibly* occurs in the following citation:

> It is too easy to assume that they wish only for praise; though (since even dramatists are human) they wish to outrage their public and be admired by it at the same time, just as they *impossibly* wish to be ahead of their times and immediately understood. (ST 12/6/66: 10, 1)

It seems likely that *impossibly wish* is a conversion of *impossible wish* and should be paraphrased as 'have an impossible wish'. We may bring as contrast the manner adjunct *impossibly* in a sentence such as *They behaved impossibly.*

Of those who transposed *possibly*, nearly two-thirds placed it immediately before the negative particle. This was not the favoured position for transposed *certainly* or *probably* (cf. Table 17, page 237). It is not clear why there should be this difference.

The uncertainty in the minds of informants over the acceptability of *possibly* after the negative particle is indicated by the large percentage of hesitations over whether the problem should be evaded. Twenty-two informants (26 per cent) gave signs of this kind of hesitation in the test on *possibly* as compared with twelve (14 per cent) for *probably* and eight (10 per cent) for *certainly*. The uncertainty is also reflected in the larger number of queries in the evaluation test on the transformed sentence:

he /won't possibly become a tèacher#

(cf. Table 20, page 240).

In a compliance test in Battery II informants were required to turn this sentence with *possibly* into a *yes-no* question:

they will /possibly leave èarly#

Two informants replaced *will* by either *can* or *could* when making the interrogative transformation, thereby making the sentence perfectly acceptable. Two others replaced *will* by *may*, an auxiliary that has a semantic overlap with *can*, although one of the two also omitted *possibly*. As many as twelve informants substituted the corresponding clause and transformed that clause into a question:

Is it possible (that) they will leave early?

One other informant, while replacing *possibly* by its correspondence, introduced an interrogative superordinate clause:

Do you think it is possible that they will leave early?

Other substitutions imply a paraphrase of a conceptual interrogative transformation of *possibly*, though they do not contain its correspondence:

> Are they likely to leave early? [4 informants]
> Will they be likely to leave early?
> Is it likely that they will leave early?
> Will there be any possibility of their leaving early?
> Do you think they will leave early?

The compliance rate for *possibly* in a question is more like that for *perhaps* than for *probably* (cf. Table 21, page 241). It may be that the semantic similarity between *possibly* and *perhaps* has contributed to the higher acceptability of *possibly* (but cf. page 151).

Informants were subsequently asked to judge the acceptability of *possibly* in a question:

> /will they possibly leave éarly#

The somewhat higher acceptability of *possibly* within a question compared to that for the question with *probably* echoes the difference we have already noted in the compliance test (cf. Table 23, page 243). We may regard *perhaps* and *possibly* as on the borderline of acceptability with respect to their appearance in a question.[1]

5.3.2   Class [H] contrasted with other classes

Rightly and *wisely* are taken as typical of the two sub-classes [H1] and [H2]. They admit three correspondence types.

$$\left.\begin{matrix}\text{Rightly}\\\text{Wisely}\end{matrix}\right\} \text{ he tore it up.}$$

$$\rightarrow \begin{cases} \text{For him to tear it up was } \begin{cases}\text{right.}\\\text{wise.}\end{cases}\\ \text{It was } \begin{cases}\text{right}\\\text{wise}\end{cases} \text{ for him to tear it up.}\end{cases}$$

---

[1] The acceptability of *probably* in a question seems to decrease markedly when the verb has past time reference:

> * Did he probably stay late?

Past time reference does not seem, however, to affect the marginal acceptability of *perhaps* (more acceptable than *possibly* in my idiolect):

> ?Will he perhaps stay late?
> ?Did he perhaps stay late?

or of *possibly*:

> ?Will he possibly stay late?
> ?Did he possibly stay late?

$\rightarrow$ It was $\left\{ \begin{matrix} \text{right} \\ \text{wise} \end{matrix} \right\}$ of him to tear it up.

$\rightarrow$ He was $\left\{ \begin{matrix} \text{right} \\ \text{wise} \end{matrix} \right\}$ to tear it up.

The last two correspondences indicate that there is some specific relationship of the disjunct to the Subject. These correspondences are only possible if the Subject is active. For example, *rightly* does not admit these correspondences for the sentence:

> *Rightly*, the journalist was expelled.
> *It was right of the journalist to be expelled.
> *The journalist was right to be expelled.

This applies even when the verbal group is formally active but where there is a passive meaning:

> *Moreover, although the judiciary has *rightly* received the praise for the qualities I have referred to, it is very much open to question whether its method of training, its immurement within the walls of its own small Inns of Court and its organisation on an almost monastic footing is invariably right for the needs of a modern society.   (ST 12/6/66: 21, 8)

> *It was right of the judiciary to have received the praise . . . .
> *The judiciary was right to have received the praise . . .

Receive may mean 'accept into one's possession' or suggest merely that something has come into one's possession or consciousness. In the above passage, the verb phrase *has received the praise* is equivalent to 'has been given the praise' (cf. page 156).

5.3.2.1   Restricted environments

There are some restrictions on the environments in which disjuncts of class [H], such as *rightly* and *wisely*, may occur. The restrictions are not so much related to the particular verb in the clause as to the semantic implication in the clause. These disjuncts will co-occur with clauses where some decision by an animate being is implied. Thus, out of context these two sentences are deviant:

> *Wisely, Bob had a cold.
> *Wisely, the loaf weighed just over a pound.

The addition of suitable contextualisation can render them acceptable sentences:

> Wisely, Bob had a cold when he was supposed to be at the meeting.
> Wisely, the loaf weighed just over a pound, so the baker was not prosecuted.

We notice that now there has been added in the first sentence the implication that Bob pretended to have a cold. In the second sentence it is implied that the baker was careful to keep within the prescribed legal limit. Even such a deviant sentence as

*Wisely it was raining.

could be made acceptable if we imagine an account of a council of the gods where one god turns to the rain-god and says approvingly:

Wisely it was raining yesterday. The humans deserve to have their holiday spoilt.

Of course some sentences require greater contextualisation for their interpretation and acceptability. We may contrast:

Wisely, he had a drink.
*Wisely, he had a cold.

The involvement of a human agency is obvious in the first of these sentences, in which *had a drink* is roughly equivalent to *drank* (cf. Rensky 1964, 289ff. for this type of structure). There is therefore no need for further contextualisation.

Rightly and *wisely* differ a little in the types of environments into which they will normally enter. Table 11 displays the acceptability of these two in six types of clauses. Two other disjuncts, *fortunately* and *surprisingly*, are included for comparison, as well as the adjunct *reluctantly*. A '+' in a cell denotes that it is acceptable for the particular item to occupy initial position in a particular clause, a '−' denotes that it is unacceptable, and a '?' signifies doubt over the acceptability.

The six clauses are listed:

(1) – *it was raining*. The Subject of the clause is impersonal *it*.
(2) – *the man measures six foot*. The verb is a 'middle verb'; no human action is involved.
(3) – *the books sold easily last year*. The clause is of the 'process-orientated' type (cf. Halliday 1967, 47) where the verb is notionally equivalent to a passive form, i.e., in this case 'the books were sold easily last year'.

TABLE 11 *Restrictions on environments in which 'Rightly' and 'Wisely' may occur*

	1	2	3	4	5	6
fortunately, surprisingly	+	+	+	+	+	+
rightly	−	−	?	+	+	+
wisely	−	−	−	?	+	+
reluctantly	−	−	−	−	−	−

(4) – *he was very frightened*. The verb is of the emotive passive type (cf. Svartvik 1966, 135).

(5) – *the book costs only ten shillings*. The verb is a 'middle verb'; human action is implied, i.e., in this case the pricing.

(6) – *he was unimpressed*. The verbal group contains a morphologically passive compound (cf. Svartvik 1966, 137); in this case, some rational judgment by the Subject is implied.

At first sight, *reluctantly* appears to have one of the correspondences available to *rightly* and *wisely*:

$$\left.\begin{array}{l}\text{Rightly,}\\ \text{Wisely,}\end{array}\right\} \text{he tore it up.}$$

$$\rightarrow \text{He was} \left\{\begin{array}{l}\text{right}\\ \text{wise}\end{array}\right\} \text{to tear it up.}$$

Reluctantly he tore it up.

$\dashrightarrow$ He was reluctant to tear it up.

But in fact, as we have indicated, only the sentences with *rightly* and *wisely* are semantically equivalent to the sentences that follow. *He was reluctant to tear it up* does not necessarily imply that he tore it up, whereas *He was right (or wise) to tear it up* does necessarily imply that he tore it up. Thus, we may have

He was reluctant to tear it up, but nevertheless he did tear it up.

or He was reluctant to tear it up, and finally decided not to tear it up.

Whereas we may not have:

$$*\text{He was} \left\{\begin{array}{l}\text{right}\\ \text{wise}\end{array}\right\} \text{to tear it up, and finally decided not to tear it up.}$$

Rightly and *wisely* also differ in the possibility of their co-occurrence with certain 'receptive' verbs. In the following sentence *receive* is ambiguous. It may suggest that the judge accepted the bribe or it may only mean that the bribe was sent to him:

The judge received the bribe.

If the 'passive meaning' is obligatory or intended, then *wisely* cannot co-occur with *receive*; if, however, the 'active meaning' is intended, then it can. The following sentences illustrate the difference between *rightly* and *wisely* in respect of their co-occurrence with the verb *receive*:

Rightly, the judge received praise for his decision.

*Wisely the judge received praise for his decision.

Rightly, the judge received the bribe.

?Wisely, the judge received the bribe.

There is a class of 'receptive verbs', e.g. *deserve, merit, suffer, receive*, which include the 'receptive perception verbs', e.g., *taste, smell. Rightly* and its synonyms co-occur with these verbs (as indeed do most disjuncts), but *wisely* and its synonyms do not. *Wisely* co-occurs, for example, with *taste* in its active meaning, but not in its passive. Thus, the sentence

Wisely, he tasted the wine.

can only mean he deliberatively ascertained the taste of the wine. On the other hand, *rightly* can mean that he perceived the taste of the wine:

Rightly, he tasted the wine in the soup.

Once again, suitable contextualisation would allow *wisely* in this sentence too:

Wisely, he tasted the wine in the soup. He did not want to offend his hostess.

The implication now is that he pretended that he had perceived the taste of wine, and therefore human decision is involved.

5.3.2.2 Contrast with other disjuncts

It is instructive to contrast *rightly* and *wisely* with attitudinal disjuncts of other classes. In the course of Battery II tests were conducted involving the negation of a sentence with *wisely* and the interrogative transformation of a sentence with *rightly*. These will be contrasted with tests included in the same Battery that required the negation of a sentence with *fortunately* and the interrogative transformation of a sentence with *surprisingly*.

5.3.2.2.1 *Fortunately* and *wisely*

Informants were asked, in the course of Battery II, to negate the sentence:

I can /fortunately understand her mèssage#

Only nineteen informants (11 per cent) complied with the instruction (cf. Tables 16-19, pages 236ff.). Another four retained *fortunately* after the negative particle but failed to complete the sentence. 118 informants transposed either *fortunately* or a substituted *unfortunately*. Twenty of the thirty-seven transpositions of *fortunately* were to initial position, as were fifty-two of the seventy-one transpositions of *unfortunately*. The evidence suggests that initial position is the unmarked position for both *fortunately* and *unfortunately*.

111 informants (62 per cent) replaced *fortunately* by *unfortunately*. The substitution was not motivated by a desire to avoid the syntactic unacceptability of positioning *fortunately* immediately after the negative

particle, since most of the informants who substituted *unfortunately* (71 out of the 111) transposed it at the same time to some other position. It is clear that, like other disjuncts (cf. page 115), *unfortunately* is no more acceptable than *fortunately* in the position immediately after the negative particle. The motivation for the substitution appears to be semantic. It is more probable that the inability to understand a message is unfortunate than that it is fortunate (and the probability is even greater when the Subject is *I*), though one can imagine situations where it would be fortunate that somebody could not understand a message: for example, if the person or others would as a result be needlessly grieved or incur trouble.

Attitudinal disjuncts are more acceptable in the position immediately after the negative particle, if not fully acceptable, when they are separated from the rest of the sentence – intonationally in the case of speech and by punctuation in the case of writing. It is therefore understandable that a number of informants should insert commas when they left *fortunately* or *unfortunately* immediately after the negative particle. In fact, of the forty informants who placed *unfortunately* in that position, fourteen inserted commas, although three inserted the first comma only. In addition, five informants enclosed *fortunately* in a pair of commas.

When informants were asked to negate the sentence

She has /wisely refused your òffer#

the compliance rate was also very low. Only twenty-nine informants (16 per cent) complied with the instruction (cf. Tables, 16-19, pages 236ff). But there is a considerable difference between the realisations of the non-compliance in this test and in the test involving *fortunately* that we have just discussed. In the first place, far fewer replaced *wisely* by its antonym *unwisely* than replaced *fortunately* by its antonym *unfortunately*. We have explained the prevalence of the substitution of *unfortunately* on the grounds that the negation of the sentence with *fortunately* is semantically unacceptable. In this test, however, the negation of the sentence produces a semantically acceptable sentence

She has wisely not refused your offer.

though a number of informants felt that the double negation, i.e. the clausal negation by *not* and the lexical negation in *refused*, was redundant and therefore replaced *not refused* by *accepted*:

She has wisely accepted your offer.

Accepted is not necessarily the logical opposite of *refused*. Both these verbs express deliberate attitudes and there is, logically, a middle term denoting lack of expression of an attitude. Thus, we may have the sentence

She has neither accepted nor refused your offer.

or She hasn't yet accepted your offer, but she hasn't yet refused it either.

Accept and *refuse* are instances of what Jespersen (1917, 144) and Zimmer (1964, 21-2) have called 'contrary' terms. Other examples of pairs of verbs that are contrary terms and allow a middle term (though not necessarily expressed in an individual verb in English) are *like/dislike, agree/disagree, believe/disbelieve, trust/distrust, approve/disapprove, lower/ raise, open/close.* Instances of what Jespersen and Zimmer (loc. cit.) have called 'contradictory' terms, i.e. where there is an excluded middle, are also found among pairs of antonymous verbs, though probably less frequently. Examples include the pairs *live/die* and *stay/leave.*

Although, as we have seen, contrary terms allow an included middle, nevertheless the negation of one of the terms is usually felt to imply the other term when there is no explicit reference to show that this is not the case, as, for example, when a temporal adjunct is present:

She hasn't yet refused your offer.

It is therefore not unreasonable that sixteen of the informants (9 per cent) should prefer to use lexical negation, responding with the antonym *accepted*, rather than clausal negation, which is more difficult to understand when the verb has a negative meaning.

A somewhat smaller number of informants chose to negate the attitudinal disjunct rather than the clause by means of negative affixation and a similar number negated both the clause and the attitudinal disjunct. Only two of the twenty-six informants who substituted *unwisely* positioned it after the negative particle.

Another major difference between the results of this test and the test with *fortunately* relates to the positioning of the disjunct when it was transposed to evade the problem. Over three-quarters of those who transposed *wisely* placed it immediately before the negative particle and after the auxiliary, whereas most of those who transposed *fortunately* or *unfortunately* placed them in front of the Subject. This suggests that the position after the Subject (or after the auxiliary, if one is present), is the unmarked position for *wisely* and presumably for others in class [H].

Minority responses included one containing the negated form of one of the correspondences:

It was not wise of her to refuse your offer.

There is no indication that any of the informants interpreted *wisely* as a manner adjunct. The two informants who moved *wisely* to final position, the unmarked position for manner adjuncts, demonstrated their interpretation of it as a disjunct by placing a comma before it.

5.3.2.2.2   *Surprisingly* and *rightly*

Informants were asked to make this sentence a *yes-no* question:

/it's in the pàpers surprisingly#

More than three-quarters (137 informants or 77 per cent) failed to comply with the instruction (cf. Tables 21-2, pages 241f.). Nearly half (eighty-four informants or 47 per cent) omitted *surprisingly*.

Three informants replaced *surprisingly* by the corresponding equative plus adjective clause and transformed that into a question: *Is it surprising*, while four used nominal or verbal forms in the superordinate clause: *Is it a surprise that, Does it surprise you that*. Others substituted clauses that they tagged on to the end of the sentence: *surprise* (two informants), *I should not have thought it, I wonder, that's surprising, are you surprised*. Similar attempts to convey the notion of unexpectedness motivated the substitution of *by any chance* (two informants), *really, indeed* and *possibly*. One informant responded with *surprisingly enough*, presumably feeling that the longer group was a stage nearer acceptability (cf. page 134).

As many as twenty-two informants moved *surprisingly* to the middle of the question, placing it immediately after *is it*. Two possible explanations may be offered for this transposition. First, informants may have felt that the mid-position was somewhat more acceptable since *surprisingly* could then be rendered much more clearly as parenthetic. Indeed, one informant indicated that it was parenthetic by enclosing it within a pair of dashes, while four others enclosed it within a pair of commas. The other possible explanation is suggested by the response of one informant: *Is it surprisingly written up by the papers*. Mid-position may represent a desperate attempt to re-interpret *surprisingly* as a manner adjunct with some such word as *written* implied.

When informants were asked to turn into a *yes-no* question the sentence

he /rightly decided to make a will#

the compliance rate was much higher. Nearly half the informants (eighty-seven or 49 per cent) complied with the instruction (cf. Tables 21-2, pages 241f.).

Several informants replaced *rightly* by correspondences that were turned into questions:

Was he right to decide to make a will?
Was it right of him to decide whether to make a will?
Was he right in deciding to make a will?
   [twice, once with the mistaken addition of *not* before *in*]

Two other informants replaced *rightly* by a clause that paraphrased it:

Did he decide to make a will, as one should?
Did he decide, as he should have, to make a will?

The parenthetic clause is acceptable where the single word *rightly* would not be (cf. page 134).

Some of the informants apparently re-interpreted *rightly* as a manner adjunct. This can be clearly ascertained from two of the responses:

Did he decide rightly in making a will?
Did he decide rightly when he made a will?

We may assume that this re-interpretation is the motivation for the transposition of *rightly* by a number of informants:

Did he decide rightly to make a will?

The declarative form

He rightly decided to make a will.

contains an unambiguous attitudinal disjunct, whereas *rightly* when positioned after the verb is ambiguous:

He decided rightly to make a will.

On the other hand, the unacceptability of the attitudinal disjunct in an interrogative clause leaves *rightly* unambiguously a manner adjunct in the post-verb position within an interrogative clause:

Did he decide rightly to make a will?

It is perhaps the interpretation of *rightly* as a manner adjunct that led to the higher compliance rate for this test as contrasted with the test involving *surprisingly*. There is an even bigger contrast between the two evaluation tests. In the evaluation test involving *rightly* informants were confronted with the transformed sentence, in which *rightly* may still be interpreted as a manner adjunct. Such an interpretation is not easily available for the sentence with *surprisingly*, though we have seen an attempt at such an interpretation in the response sentence given by one informant: *Is it surprisingly written up by the papers.*

5.3.2.2.3 *Luckily*

In certain environments and in certain interpretations disjuncts of class [F] have two correspondences of the same type as those of class [H] e.g. *rightly* and *wisely*. *Luckily* in the sentence

Luckily she was in time.

corresponds to

It was lucky (that) she was in time.

6+S.E.A.U.

but it may also correspond to

She *was lucky* to be in time.

When this second correspondence applies, *luckily* and others like it in class [F] are nearer to disjuncts of class [H] in their relationship to the clause. There is some experimental evidence to show that informants felt a difference between *luckily* in a sentence for which the second correspondence was available and *luckily* in a sentence in which it was not available. Moreover, the difference seems to relate to the *luckily* in the position between Subject and Verb, the unmarked position for disjuncts of class [H].

In Battery II informants were asked to judge the similarity in meaning between the following sentences:

your /father luckily owns a càr#
/lŭckily# your /father owns a càr#

Eighty-eight informants (49 per cent) regarded these two sentences as very similar in meaning, but fifty-nine (33 per cent) considered them very different in meaning. I surmised that the third who considered the two sentences very different in meaning perceived the sentence *your /father luckily owns a càr#* as corresponding to 'your father is lucky to own a car' and the sentence */lŭckily# your /father owns a càr#* as corresponding to 'it is lucky (for you, us, them, etc.) that your father owns a car'.

Confirmation for this surmise can be brought from similarity tests included in Battery III. Informants were asked to judge the similarity in meaning between the following pair of sentences:

/lŭckily# the /game ends at sèven#
the /game luckily ends at sèven#

In contrast with the sentences in Battery II, the Subject of these sentences is inanimate. As a result, one of the correspondences that might have been perceived in Battery II was no longer possible. For the sentence *the /game luckily ends at sèven#* there was not available the correspondence *The game is lucky to end at seven*. We should therefore expect that a higher proportion of the informants would judge the two sentences to be very similar in meaning. Indeed, that was the case. This time 66 per cent (as compared with the previous 49 per cent) considered the sentences to be very similar, while only 19 per cent (as compared with the previous 33 per cent) considered them to be very different.

Further confirmation comes from another similarity test included in Battery III. Informants were asked to judge the similarity in meaning between the following pair of sentences:

sur/prĭsingly# your /father owns a càr#
your /father surprisingly owns a càr#

The pair of sentences are the same as the pair in Battery II except that *surprisingly* has been substituted for *luckily*. However, *surprisingly* belongs to correspondence class [C] and does not have correspondence [5]. Thus, the sentence *your /father surprisingly owns a càr#* does not have the correspondence **Your father is surprising to own a car*. Consequently, we should expect results in the similarity test like those for the sentences with *luckily* in Battery III rather than like those for the sentences with *luckily* in Battery II. Indeed, the results conformed to expectations. Seventy-two informants (62 per cent) judged the two sentences with *surprisingly* to be very similar in meaning, while only twenty (17 per cent) thought that they were very different (cf. Tables 29-30, pages 249f.). The tests show that if the Subject is animate many more informants perceive a difference in respect to disjuncts of the class of *luckily* according to whether the disjunct is positioned before the Subject or immediately after.

5.3.3 Disjuncts and aspectual adjuncts

A number of attitudinal disjuncts that do not belong to correspondence classes need to be differentiated from aspectual adjuncts. Three aspectual adjuncts occupy initial position in the following citation:

> *Morally, politically*, and *economically*, it is a matter of urgency that the British Government should act on more effective policies for trade and aid toward the developing nations.
>
> (O 24/10/65: 33, 8)

It is possible to show that *morally*, for example, is not a disjunct since it can be the focus of negation:

> → It isn't a matter of urgency *morally*, but it is a matter of urgency *politically*.

This test and the next test may be impossible to apply when the verb collocates with a manner adjunct, because the aspectual adjunct may be necessarily interpreted as a manner adjunct, e.g.:

> *Morally*, they didn't help them very much.
> They didn't help them very much *morally*.

Aspectual adjuncts can also be the focus of interrogation

> → Is it a matter of urgency *morally* or is it a matter of urgency *politically*?

Aspectual adjuncts ending in *-ly* can be replaced by a construction with the participle *speaking*, e.g. *morally* can be replaced by *morally speaking*. Here is an example of such a construction:

> The present Cabinet is in a pretty dilemma, *sartorially speaking*.
>
> (G 2/6/66: 8, 1)

In this example, *sartorially speaking* can be replaced by the aspectual adjunct *sartorially*. Despite the substitutability of a construction with *speaking*, *sartorially* is not considered a style disjunct. Indeed, because it may be the focus of negation and interrogation, it is not assigned to the class of disjunct at all. In any case, it does not correspond to a finite-verb clause with a verb of speaking. *Sartorially speaking* does not have such correspondences as *If I may speak sartorially* [*I would say* (*that*)], cf. pages 82f.

Not all aspectual adjuncts end in *-ly*. The suffix *-wise* may be added to nouns to produce a form that functions as aspectual adjunct. An example appears in the following citation:

> *Programme-wise*, the new thing last night was the serial of Thackeray's 'Vanity Fair', adapted by Rex Tucker and directed by David Giles, who directed much of the Forsyte Saga.
> (ST 3/12/67: 4, 4)

This derivational process for forming aspectual adjuncts seems to be highly productive in contemporary English, though the resultant forms appear to be informal in tone.

5.3.3.1 *Technically*, its synonyms and hononyms

Technically is a good illustration of an item that can be style disjunct, attitudinal disjunct, aspectual adjunct and manner adjunct. As attitudinal disjunct *technically* belongs to a group that includes *formally*, *officially*, and *nominally*. These are roughly synonymous with *theoretically* and antonymous to *really* or *actually* (cf. page 206). Some illustrations will clarify the distinction between these and their homonyms.

> *Formally* officials won't know who their new bosses are till May 2, though it's assumed that the Smith Square bush telegraph will drum out the odd committee chairman's name before then.   (G 18/4/67; 6, 6)

The context makes it clear that in reality officials will know who their new bosses are before that date. We may contrast with this function of *formally*

> Discussions open *formally* today in the two sides of industry about the policies to be followed from July 1 . . .   (G 19/1/67: 1, 7)

where nominalisation would produce

> The formal opening of discussions today . . .

Transposition of *formally* to initial position would change its function to that of disjunct:

> *Formally* discussions open today . . .

Again, we may contrast *officially* as disjunct

> *Officially*, of course, Dr Bazzaz resigned of his own accord, but it is almost certain that he only did so to forestall a less ceremonious departure in store for him if he tried to hold out.
>
> (G 8/8/66: 9, 1)

with the adjunct

> He has resigned *officially*.

As citations of *nominally* and *technically* as disjuncts we may quote:

> *Nominally* M. Mendès-France is standing as a United Socialist candidate. (G 23/1/67: 9, 7)

> When Mrs Kennedy asked me to write the book I promptly resigned from Wesleyan University in Middletown, Connecticut. That was on February 5, 1964. *Technically* I was jobless, a middle-aged, highly educated vagrant. (ST 26/3/67: 21, 4)

Technically in this function is very similar in meaning to *nominally*. The context indicates clearly that in fact the writer was not 'jobless'; he had the 'job' of writing the book.

There are two other functions of *technically*, both very clearly distinguishable from the function of the attitudinal disjunct exemplified in the last citation, which allow *technically* to be replaced by *technically speaking*. First, there is the style disjunct:

> A major issue in modern American verse has been to cut itself free from its British roots. *Technically*, that means getting rid of the iambic pentameter as the basis of rhythm and replacing it with a cadence modelled on colloquial American speech, where the length of line varies with the sense and the span of the speaker's breath. (O 24/10/65: 27, 2)

Here, *technically* can be replaced by *putting it technically* or *to be technical*, but not with *nominally*. Secondly, there is the aspectual adjunct:

> And beyond that, there is the fact that in every home in the developed world there is already a near-perfect facsimile reproducing device, in the ordinary fire-side television set. *Technically*, it is feasible today to transmit text and pictures, print it instantaneously inside the set, and drop it out through a slot below the screen. (ST 8/1/67: 11, 8)

We notice that in this function *technically* will not allow the replacements that we have mentioned. Perhaps the nearest paraphrase would be 'from a technical point of view'. A contrast would be possible in this context with, say, *politically*:

> It is not feasible *technically*, but it is feasible *politically*.

The aspectual adjunct *technically* is within the domain of clause negation in the next citation:

> Such a law is overdue. To tap a private telephone line is not *technically* a very difficult operation. (G 21/2/67: 6, 1)

It should be noted that the style disjunct, unlike the others, may be premodified by *very*:

> *Very technically*, that means getting rid of the iambic pentameter . . .
> **Very technically* I was jobless.
> **Very technically*, it is feasible today to transmit . . .[1]

An example of the manner adjunct *technically* would be:

> He always writes *very technically*.

5.3.3.2 Correspondences

Some of the attitudinal disjuncts that do not belong to correspondence classes have corresponding constructions with *speaking* or corresponding prepositional phrases. We have noted that *technically* in three functions (style disjunct, attitudinal disjunct, and aspectual adjunct) can be replaced by *technically speaking*. Unfortunately, we do not seem to be able to generalise. The different possibilities of some attitudinal disjuncts are set out below.

Some attitudinal disjuncts may be replaced by a participle construction with *speaking* but not others:

> basically = basically speaking
> essentially = essentially speaking
> officially = officially speaking
> technically = technically speaking
> nominally ≠ *nominally speaking
> superficially ?= superficially speaking
> ostensibly ≠ *ostensibly speaking
> outwardly ≠ *outwardly speaking

Some, but not others, may be replaced by a prepositional phrase in which the adjective base appears in the frame: *in a . . . sense*:

> basically ≠ in a basic sense
> essentially ?= in an essential sense
> officially = in an official sense
> technically = in a technical sense

---

1 It must be admitted that there is some ambiguity in the function of *technically* in the second citation, an ambiguity between the functions of style disjunct and aspectual adjunct, though it is unambiguously a style disjunct if premodified by *very*.

nominally ≠ in a nominal sense
superficially ≠ in a superficial sense
ostensibly ≠ *in an ostensible sense
outwardly ≠ *in an outward sense

Some of these disjuncts may be replaced by a prepositional phrase in which the adjective base appears in the frame: *from a . . . point of view*:

basically ≠ ?from a basic point of view
essentially ≠ ?from an essential point of view
officially = from an official point of view
technically ≠ from a technical point of view
nominally ≠ ?from a nominal point of view
superficially = from a superficial point of view
ostensibly ≠ *from an ostensible point of view
outwardly ≠ *from an outward point of view

Theoretically is like *officially* and *superficially* in allowing these replacements.

5.3.4 *Kindly* and other formulaic adjuncts

In certain restricted environments *kindly* is a 'formulaic' adjunct. Among other formulaic adjuncts are *cordially*, *graciously* and *humbly*. They conventionally appear in certain contexts. It is characteristic of formulaic adjuncts that they are restricted to the position before the verb. Thus, *kindly* in

He *kindly* spoke to the children.

is a formulaic adjunct, whereas *kindly* in

He spoke to the children *kindly*.

is a manner adjunct, which could serve as a response to the question

How did he speak to the children?

We may contrast *cordially* as a fomulaic adjunct in

You are *cordially* invited to the party.

with *cordially* as a manner adjunct:

You were invited to the party *cordially*.

Similarly, we may contrast *graciously* as a formulaic adjunct in

She *graciously* consented to our request.

with *graciously* as a manner adjunct in

She consented to our request *graciously*.

and *humbly* as a formulaic adjunct in

He *humbly* presents his apologies.

with *humbly* as a manner adjunct in

He presents his apologies *humbly*.

Unlike most attitudinal disjuncts, the formulaic adjuncts *kindly* and *graciously* can appear in a question, though only if the Subject is in the second person, e.g.:

Will you *kindly* close the door?
Will you *graciously* accept this bouquet?[1]

On the other hand, the formulaic adjuncts *cordially* and *humbly* cannot appear in questions. Thus, *cordially* and *humbly* in the following sentences would be interpreted as manner adjuncts:

Are you *cordially* invited?
Does he *humbly* present his apologies?

Kindly is unique among formulaic adjuncts in its ability to appear before an imperative, and even before a negative imperative, e.g.:

Kindly close the door.
Kindly don't say anything about it.

In such contexts it is less polite than *please*, and, indeed, is often used in contexts where the speaker is adopting a disrespectful attitude.

In a compliance test in Battery II informants were asked to make this sentence negative:

He has /*kindly* accepted our invitàtion#

The results of this test show unmistakeably that the target sentence

He /hasn't *kindly* accepted our invitàtion#

is unacceptable (cf. Tables 16-20, pages 236ff.) since 144 informants (80 per cent) did not comply with the instruction. This result was confirmed by the evaluation test, where only eighteen informants (10 per cent) accepted the form of the target sentence.

The formulaic adjunct does not normally appear in a negative declarative sentence. The exception is when the sentence is semantically a command, e.g.:

You will *kindly* not say anything about this.

The exception is not relevant to the test sentence. There was therefore no easy or obvious rectification of the problem with which in-

---

[1] If the third person is used they are interpreted as manner adjuncts, unless the third person is being used as a 'royal honorific' with second person reference.

formants were confronted when they were asked to negate the sentence containing the formulaic adjunct *kindly*. The dilemma of the informants when presented with this problem is reflected in the large number of omissions of *kindly* and in the wide scatter of responses. Indeed, the response sentence produced more often than any other was simply the target sentence with *kindly* omitted from it

He has not accepted our invitation.

but even so this was given only by thirty-five informants (20 per cent). Another eleven informants, while similarly omitting *kindly*, negated the verb lexically, replacing it by *refused* [7], *declined* [3], or *rejected* [1]. These informants did not negate the clause. Twenty-five informants placed *kindly* before the negative particle [14 per cent]. But the response:

He has *kindly* not accepted our invitation.

does not seem an improvement on the target sentence. Two others started to do the same, but apparently finding the result objectionable did not finish the sentence and omitted *our invitation*. Only one informant placed *kindly* before the auxiliary, but in doing so he introduced another change, a change of tense, substituting *did* for *has*.

Another group of twenty-one informants (12 per cent) retained *kindly*, but instead of negating the clause replaced *accepted* by its lexical negative *refused*:

He has *kindly* refused our invitation.

Variants on this response, which represent an evasion of the task to negate the sentence, were *kindly declined* (4) and *politely declined* (1).

The only other group of responses that emerges, though it is certainly not a homogeneous group, involved the replacement of *kindly* by its morphemic (and lexical) negative, *unkindly*. Fourteen informants [8 per cent] did this, and one other informant replaced *kindly* by another lexical negative, *churlishly*. Eight of the informants, including the one who substituted *churlishly*, also negated the verb lexically by replacing it with *refused*.

There is one interesting response in which *unkindly* approaches the attitudinal disjunct in its ability to appear in front of a negated clause. This is the only instance among the responses where *kindly* or its substitute appears in front of the clause apart from the obviously acceptable substitution of the disjunct *fortunately* in that position. In this instance, *kindly* has been replaced by the group *most unkindly* and the clause that follows has been negated:

?Most unkindly, he has not accepted our invitation.

It would appear that the premodification has caused the greater acceptability of this position, since

?Unkindly, he has not accepted our invitation.

6*

seems less acceptable, and, indeed, no informant produced this sentence
or one with *kindly* in front position.

A few informants reinterpreted *kindly* as a manner adjunct, transposing it to a position after the verb:

He has not accepted our invitation kindly. [2]
He has not accepted kindly our invitation. [1]

One informant, while reinterpreting *kindly* in a similar way, reformulated
the sentence:

He has refused our invitation, but kindly.

One other informant responded with a manner adjunct, but substituted
politely for *kindly* and at the same time negated the verb lexically by
replacing it with *declined*:

He has declined our invitation politely.

His motivation for this change, presumably, was to produce the more
collocable combination *decline politely*. For, while *kindly accept* is a likely
collocation, when *kindly* is a formulaic adjunct, *accept* and *kindly* are
not so readily collocable, when *kindly* is a manner adjunct.

Two responses are interesting because they echo the institutionalised
reply to an invitation:

'X' regrets that he is unable to accept your invitation.

The two replies

He has regretfully not accepted our invitation.
He has not been able to accept our invitation.

each contain components from the usual formula.

One other response might be mentioned, since it suggests that the
informant was reinterpreting *kindly*:

He was rather unkind and didn't accept our invitation.

In reformulating the sentence this informant has negated both *kindly*,
by lexical negation, and *accepted*, by clausal negation.

Apart from the responses that have already been mentioned (some of
which appear only once or twice), there are twenty-two other responses,
none of which occur more than twice.

Most of these are unfinished sentences (there are also two total
omissions) or involve wrong operations. The wide scatter of results
signifies the difficulty that informants had in coping with this operation.
Very few sought to interpret *kindly* as a manner adjunct, either because
the manner adjunct *kindly* does not freely collocate with *accept* or
because they perceived an obvious difference between the formulaic
adjunct and the manner adjunct.

5.3.5 Disjuncts and subject adjuncts

A distinction needs to be made between disjuncts and subject adjuncts, though an exhaustive account of the latter requires separate treatment. Some items that function as disjuncts or manner adjuncts function as subject adjuncts, particularly in initial position. Two examples of subject adjuncts appear in the following citation:

Painfully, resentfully, the miners have stood by their loyalty,
    and gone against their own conference. (ST 4/9/66: 8, 3)

In this context *painfully* and *resentfully* are not manner adjuncts corresponding to 'in a painful manner' and 'in a respectful manner' respectively. Their semantic interpretation can be conveyed more accurately by some such paraphrase of the sentence as 'To have stood by their loyalty and to have gone against their own conference was painful to the miners and they were resentful about it.' They are termed subject adjuncts because of their relationship to the Subject, as indicated by the paraphrase.

Unlike manner adjuncts, subject adjuncts cannot serve as the focus of clause interrogation, clause negation, or clause comparison (cf. pages 115ff.). Furthermore, subject adjuncts cannot serve as a response to the interrogative transformation of the clause introduced by *How*, nor can they accept premodification by *How* in an interrogative or exclamatory transformation of the clause (cf. page 121). In addition, it appears that subject adjuncts tend to occur in initial position or between Subject and Verb, whereas manner adjuncts tend to occur immediately after the Verb or, if present, the Complement. Finally, there appear to be differences between subject adjuncts and homonymous manner adjuncts with respect to the verbs with which they collocate. Thus, the manner adjunct *painfully* collocates with the verb *torment*, as in the following sentence:

The guards tormented him *painfully*.

On the other hand, it would be highly unusual for the subject adjunct *painfully* to collocate with the verb *torment*. Since it is unusual for the manner adjunct to occupy initial position, transposition of *painfully* to initial position in the above sentence produces an unacceptable sentence:

*Painfully, the guards tormented him.

In contrast, the subject adjunct *painfully* is acceptable in the sentence

Painfully, the miners have stood by their loyalty.

whereas the manner adjunct is unacceptable in collocation with the expression 'stand by one's loyalty',

*The miners have stood by their loyalty *painfully*.

Subject adjuncts differ from disjuncts in that they do not readily appear before a negated clause. *Reluctantly* is taken as an instance of a subject adjunct. In the course of Battery III informants were asked to evaluate the following sentence:

re/lŭctantly# they didn't insist on his resignàtion#

Only thirty-nine informants (33 per cent) accepted the sentence, while as many as forty-five (38 per cent) rejected it and a further thirty-three (28 per cent) were dubious about it. On the other hand, when the same informants were required to evaluate the following negated sentence, with *understandably* in initial position

under/stăndably# they /didn't open the lètter#

110 informants (94 per cent) accepted the sentence, while only two (2 per cent) rejected it and five (4 per cent) were in doubt about its acceptability.

Subject adjuncts resemble attitudinal disjuncts of class [H], such as *rightly* and *wisely*, in having a close relationship to the active Subject of the clause (cf. pages 103f., 153ff.). The relationship of subject adjuncts to the Subject is indicated, as has been said, by paraphrases. Thus, we may paraphrase the sentence

Miserably, he signed the death-warrant.

by 'He was miserable when he signed the death-warrant', and *miserably* is a subject adjunct. On the other hand, for the following sentence

He signed the death-warrant *miserably*.

an appropriate paraphrase would be 'He signed the death-warrant in a miserable manner', and in this sentence *miserably* is a manner adjunct. We can add to the sentence with the subject adjunct a manner adjunct, e.g.:

Miserably, he signed the death-warrant *clumsily*.

However, if we add an antonym of the manner adjunct *miserably*, the sentence becomes unacceptable, presumably because of the semantic overlap between subject adjunct *miserably* and manner adjunct *miserably*, e.g.:

*Miserably, he signed the death-warrant *cheerfully*.

In this respect, disjuncts such as *wisely* differ from subject adjuncts. Thus, the disjunct *wisely* co-occurs with the manner adjunct *foolishly* in the following sentence:

Wisely, he answered the soldiers' questions *foolishly* when he was captured.

Substitution of subject adjunct *proudly* and manner adjunct *humbly* would result in a completely unacceptable sentence:

Proudly, he answered the soldiers' questions *humbly* when he was captured.

Disjuncts such as *wisely* are related to the clause as well as the Subject, whereas subject adjuncts are related specifically to the Subject. The relationship of subject adjuncts to the Subject can be demonstrated syntactically as well as semantically. Two clauses linked by *but* may be contrasted by contrasts in Subject and manner adjunct, e.g.:

She waved *sadly*, but *he* waved *cheerfully*.

However, the two clauses cannot be linked by *but* if subject adjuncts are substituted for the manner adjuncts:

Sadly, she waved, but, *cheerfully*, *he* waved.

On the other hand, the two clauses can be linked by *but* with contrasting subject adjuncts if the Subject is the same for each clause and there are other contrasts between the two clauses, e.g.:

Sadly, she waved, but, *cheerfully*, *she* drove home.

In certain contexts there may be ambiguity over whether an item is disjunct or subject adjunct. For example, *sadly* in the following sentence may have either function:

Sadly, they sent in their resignation last week.

If *sadly* is interpreted as disjunct, the sentence may be paraphrased by 'It is sad that they sent in their resignation last week', and if it is interpreted as subject adjunct the sentence may be paraphrased by 'They were sad when they sent in their resignation last week'. The context will usually determine the more probable interpretation (cf. pages 186f.).

5.3.6 Temporal disjuncts and adjuncts

Attitudinal disjuncts in class [I] (*conventionally*, *rarely*, *traditionally*, *unusually*) and certain others (*unexpectedly*, *predictably*, *potentially*, *preferably*, *ideally*) have some temporal meaning. We shall consider how this temporal effect can be demonstrated for some of them (cf. Crystal 1966, 1ff) and we shall examine some temporal adjuncts to distinguish them from the disjuncts.

5.3.6.1 Temporal disjuncts

The sentence *The goalkeeper kicks well* is without time restriction. However, certain of the disjuncts that have been listed select habitual time reference and exclude instantaneous present time reference:

$$\left. \begin{array}{l} \text{Conventionally,} \\ \text{Rarely,} \\ \text{Traditionally,} \\ \text{Potentially,} \\ \text{Ideally,} \end{array} \right\} \text{the goalkeeper kicks well.}$$

If we substitute *predictably, unusually,* or *unexpectedly,* then the sentence is once again without time restriction and can refer to instantaneous present time:

$$\left. \begin{array}{l} \text{Predictably,} \\ \text{Unusually,} \\ \text{Unexpectedly,} \end{array} \right\} \text{the goalkeeper kicks well.}$$

Only *predictably, unusually,* and *unexpectedly* may be used where the linguistic context compels the interpretation that a specific perceivable event is taking place:

$$\left. \begin{array}{l} \text{Predictably,} \\ \text{(Not) unusually,} \\ \text{(Not) unexpectedly,} \end{array} \right\} \text{I'm enjoying this show.}$$

The other disjuncts with temporal significance may not occur in such a context:

$$\left. \begin{array}{l} \text{*Potentially,} \\ \text{*Preferably,} \\ \text{*Ideally,} \\ \text{*Conventionally,} \\ \text{*Traditionally,} \\ \text{*Rarely,} \end{array} \right\} \text{I'm enjoying this show.}$$

5.3.6.1.1 *Rarely*

Rarely is only a disjunct when it is in initial position and when the normal Subject-Verb order is followed. The disjunct occurs in the next citation:

> *Rarely, very rarely,* the master would admit defeat, . . .
> (TES 14/4/67: 1213, 2)

The adjunct *rarely* belongs to a group of negative adjuncts, the other members of which are *never, seldom, scarcely, hardly,* and (probably less frequently used in Contemporary English) *barely* and *little.*[1] Negative adjuncts have at least two features in common:

[1] they are followed by positive tag-questions:

---

1 See Klima 1964, 246ff. and particularly 261–70.

The master will $\left\{\begin{array}{l}\text{rarely}\\\text{seldom}\\\text{never}\end{array}\right\}$ admit defeat, will he?

Contrast the use of the negative tag-question with the disjunct *rarely*:

Rarely, the master will admit defeat, won't he?

[2] if they occur in initial position, Verb-Subject inversion is obligatory:

$\left.\begin{array}{l}\text{Rarely}\\\text{Seldom}\\\text{Never}\end{array}\right\}$ will he admit defeat.

For the disjunct, on the other hand, Subject-Verb order is obligatory.

5.3.6.1.2 *Unusually*

The disjunct *unusually* appears once in our material, without modifiers:

The predominantly Catholic population from here will form the core of the parish for which the Cathedral will – *unusually* – serve as a parish church. (G 15/6/67: 14, 2)

It is perhaps more usual for it to be premodified by *not*.

Although *unusually* seems to be the antonym of *usually*, only *unusually* is a disjunct. We shall be considering *usually* on pages 178ff. Here I shall only point out that *usually*, unlike *unusually*, specifies the tense of the verb:

Usually the team row well.

Usually has the effect here of restricting the time reference to the past. Furthermore, it is probably acceptable for *unusually* to co-occur with synonyms of *usually*:

?*Unusually*, the Cathedral will $\left\{\begin{array}{l}\text{normally}\\\text{generally}\end{array}\right\}$ serve as a parish church.

5.3.6.1.3 *Conventionally* and *traditionally*

In initial position, *conventionally* is unambiguously the disjunct, but ambiguity may arise in pre-verb position:

The wealthy *conventionally* send their sons to Eton.

Conventionally could be interpreted as the disjunct. The sentence would then be paraphrased by 'it is conventional for the wealthy to send their sons to Eton' or 'the convention is that the wealthy send their sons to Eton'. On the other hand, it could be taken as an adjunct, allowing the paraphrase 'the wealthy are conventional in sending their sons to Eton' or 'the wealthy are following convention in sending their sons to Eton'.

An example of the disjunct *conventionally* appears in the following citation:

> *Conventionally*, the Old Testament was divided into three sections, the Law, the Prophets and the Writings. (8ab.2.136-2)

This ambiguity in pre-verb position does not, however, apply to *traditionally*. Both instances of *traditionally* in the following citation are disjuncts:

> *Traditionally* second-hand car prices drop in the autumn and rise in the spring, but do not rely on getting £30 more by selling your £650 car next spring instead of now, . . .
>
> (OM 24/10/65: 39)

> The Smiths have *traditionally* favoured Eton, Cambridge and the City, but have never neglected politics. (OM 24/10/65: 40, 4)

This is not meant to imply that the disjunct *traditionally* has only one meaning. Two meanings have in fact been noticed. The first is exemplified in the next citation:

> France *traditionally* is a country of 100 cathedrals, 200 families, and 300 cheeses. (G 13/5/67: 6, 3)

This may be paraphrased by:

> There is a tradition that ⎱ France is . . .
> According to tradition ⎰

and not by:

> It is traditional for France to be . . .

The second meaning is exemplified in:

> The Smiths have *traditionally* favoured Eton . . .

This may be paraphrased by

> It has been traditional for the Smiths to favour Eton . . .
> By tradition the Smiths have favoured Eton . . .

and not by

> There is a tradition that ⎱ the Smiths have favoured Eton . . .
> According to tradition ⎰

The second paraphrase does not become appropriate even if the disjunct is transposed to initial position.

On the other hand, the sentence

> *Traditionally* second-hand car prices drop in the autumn . . .

allows both paraphrases

There is a tradition that second-hand car prices drop . . .
It is traditional for second-hand car prices to drop . . .

In one of the senses the disjunct evaluates the truth of the communication, so that it may then be contrasted with *actually*:

Traditionally second-hand car prices drop in the autumn, but
actually they don't drop till January.

In the other sense it may contrast with a temporal adjunct:

Traditionally second-hand car prices drop in the autumn, but *this
year* they dropped in the summer.

The manner adjuncts *conventionally* and *traditionally* seem to be
restricted to post-verb position:

Altogether, there are signs that Brittany this time may not
vote altogether *traditionally*.   (G 28/2/67: 9, 7)

Brittany this time may not vote altogether *conventionally*.

5.3.6.1.4 *Preferably*

The disjunct *preferably* tends to collocate with the auxiliaries *should*
and *ought to*:

Entries should *preferably* be upright . . .   (O 24/10/65: 30, 3)

It may co-occur with other auxiliaries, but in collocation with *may* or
might, *preferably* is not a disjunct and is immobile in its position before
the auxiliary:

You $\left\{ \begin{array}{l} \text{may} \\ \text{might} \end{array} \right\}$ preferably send it by hand.

This can be paraphrased by:

You $\left\{ \begin{array}{l} \text{may} \\ \text{might} \end{array} \right\}$ prefer to send it by hand.

It is probable that *preferably* in this function requires *you* as Subject.
It is doubtful if the substitution of *he* for *you*, for example, would
produce an acceptable sentence:

?*He$\left\{ \begin{array}{l} \text{may} \\ \text{might} \end{array} \right\}$ preferably send it by hand.

5.3.6.1.5 *Ideally*

Ideally tends to collocate with modal auxiliaries, particularly *should*,
ought to, and *would*:

Ideally, they *would* like to be consulted all along the line.

(G 5/8/66: 12, 2)

Ideally the scout *should* be aware of the event the moment it happens, or even before it happens.   (G 16/6/66: 8, 3)

In this case the metastable phase *could, ideally*, persist until conditions are changed so much that the free energy 'hump' YZX (fig. 3(a)) drops to nearly zero.   (8a.2.28-1)

5.3.6.1.6. *Predictably*

Predictably co-occurs with both present and past forms of the verb:

Predictably, though, he failed by 9343 votes to win Wycombe.
(STM 12/6/66: 12, 4)

Predictably, many letters recount the possession of a violin marked 'Stradivarius' but the likelihood of any being genuine is remote.
(ST 21/8/66: 4, 4)

It is unacceptable when the time reference is future:

Predictably, he will fail to win Wycombe.

5.3.6.2 Temporal adjuncts

Two temporal adjuncts have been selected to be contrasted with the temporal disjuncts. They are *usually* and *often*. Both select the habitual time reference of a verb in the simple present (cf. pages 173f.).

5.3.6.2.1 *Usually*

Usually is excluded from the class of disjuncts because of its failure to accept the second and third diagnostic criteria for members of this class (cf. page 24). It can be the focus of interrogation, as demonstrated by its ability to be contrasted with another focus in alternative interrogation:

Does he write well *usually* or does he write well *only occasionally*?

It can also be the focus of negation, as shown by its ability to be contrasted with another focus in alternative negation:

He doesn't write well *usually*, but he does write well *sometimes*.

Usually differs from attitudinal disjuncts in that it may appear, unlike them, in sentence forms other than the declarative. It may appear in the interrogative:

Does he write well usually?

or in the exclamatory form:

How well he usually writes!

It may even appear in the optative and imperative forms, though probably it is rare in such forms:

Let's usually write before breakfast.
Write usually before breakfast, John.

Like *usually* are *commonly, habitually, invariably, normally,* and *customarily*. They share the same correspondence type as those in class [I], e.g. *traditionally* and *unusually*, but they differ from them syntactically in the ways just described. *Rarely* has the same correspondence, but differs from *usually* and the others in its possession of negative features (cf. pages 174f.).

Similar to *usually* both semantically and with respect to syntactic potentialities are *generally, mostly* and *ordinarily*, but these do not have the same correspondences as *usually* and the others. Thus we have

It is usual for him to write well.

but not

*It is most for him to write well.
*It is ordinary for him to write well.
*It is general for him to write well.

For *generally* as style disjunct, see pages 89f.

5.3.6.2.2 *Often*

Often is like *usually* in that it can be the focus of negation and interrogation. However, it has a number of syntactic features that show it is more integrated within the clause than *usually*:

(i) *often* can be the focus of a cleft sentence:

It is *often* that they visit me.

(ii) it can be the focus of comparison:

They visit me more *often* than you do.

(iii) it can be premodified by *How* to constitute the opening of either an interrogative or an exclamatory transformation of the clause:

How often do they visit you?
How often they visit you!

(iv) it can be premodified by *so* in a construction that allows Verb-Subject inversion:

So often did they visit him, that he refused to see them any more.

(v) it can be an adjunct in certain types of non-finite verb clauses in which *usually* cannot function. For example, in

John wanted his son to read *often*.

often will be interpreted in written English as an adjunct in the non-finite verb clause and this will be the likely interpretation in spoken English unless the intonation pattern indicated that *often* was functioning in the superordinate clause. On the other hand, *usually* in

John wanted his son to read *usually*.

can only be functioning in the superordinate clause. The sentence is equivalent to

John *usually* wanted his son to read.

(vi) it can freely function in imperative and optative clauses:

Read *often*, my son.
Let us read *often*.

Frequently and *infrequently* share these syntactic features with *often*.

5.3.6.2.3 *Usually* and *often* in negative clauses

If there is another temporal adjunct present, then there may be a clear contrast between the positions before and after the negative particle for both temporal 'habit' adjuncts like *usually* and temporal 'frequency' adjuncts like *often*. In one case the adjunct is outside the domain of clause negation, while in the other it is within its domain. Thus, we can contrast

$\left.\begin{array}{l} \textit{Usually} \\ \textit{Often} \end{array}\right\}$ he doesn't speak for hours.

with

He doesn't $\left\{\begin{array}{l} \textit{usually} \\ \textit{often} \end{array}\right\}$ speak for hours.

The first sentence states the frequency of his taciturnity, while the second sentence states the infrequency of his volubility. For both *usually* and *often* a position after the negative particle will yield the same interpretation as the position before if there is intonation or punctuation separation, e.g.:

He doesn't speak for hours, $\left\{\begin{array}{l} \textit{usually.} \\ \textit{often.} \end{array}\right.$

This is true if there is intonation or punctuation separation when *usually* or *often* is immediately after the negative particle, though such a position is probably less likely when the adjunct is outside the domain of clause negation.[1]

---

[1] This generalisation is implied in the reference to adverbial frequency adjuncts in negative clauses made by Huddleston 1967, 96.

When another temporal adjunct is not present, then the contrast is clearer for *often* than for *usually*. With *usually* neutralisation takes place. A semantic contrast can be demonstrated between

> *Often* he doesn't speak.
> and   He doesn't *often* speak.

by the differing potentiality for the continuation of each sentence

> *Often* he doesn't speak, but *often* he does.
> *He doesn't *often* speak, but he does *often*.
> *Often* he doesn't speak, but *sometimes* he does.
> He doesn't *often* speak, but he does *sometimes*.

It is clear that in these sentences the position after the negative particle involves a negation of *often*, but not the position before the negative particle. On the other hand, we cannot demonstrate the same contrast for *usually*. Thus both these sentences are unacceptable

> *Usually* he doesn't speak, but *usually* he does.
> *He doesn't *usually* speak, but he does *usually*.

while both the following sentences, with the same contrasting temporal adjunct, are equally acceptable

> *Usually* he doesn't speak, but *sometimes* he does.
> He doesn't *usually* speak, but he does *sometimes*.

Informants were asked to negate sentences in which *usually* and *often* were placed between auxiliary and lexical verb. It was expected that they would be retained after the negative particle when the transformation was effected (cf. Tables 16-17, pages 236f.).

In Battery II informants were required to negate the sentence:

> he can /often explain what they mèan#

123 informants (69 per cent) complied fully with the instruction. Only twenty-six (15 per cent) transposed *often*, and a mere four (2 per cent) replaced it with another item. In the evaluation test the transformed sentence, with *often* immediately after the negative particle, was fully accepted by 162 informants (90 per cent).

The results were somewhat different for the test involving *usually*. In Battery I informants were asked to negate the sentence:

> he can /usually write wèll#

Fifty-one informants (60 per cent) complied fully with the instruction. As many as twenty-eight (33 per cent) transposed *usually*, most of them to positions before the negative particle. In the evaluation test the transformed sentence, with *usually* immediately after the negative particle, was accepted by only forty-four informants (52 per cent), and as many as twenty-four (28 per cent) considered it to be 'wholly unnatural and abnormal'.

The difference in the results of these two tests can be explained, in all probability, by the distinction in the function of *can* in the two sentences, a distinction which makes the negation of the first sentence a little odd.

He can *usually* write well.

with unstressed *can* is semantically similar to

He *usually* writes well.

whereas

He can *often* explain what they mean.

with unstressed *can* is semantically different from

He *often* explains what they mean.

If *usually* occurs after the negative particle when the auxiliary is *does*, the sentence seems to be perfectly acceptable:

He doesn't *usually* write well.

Indeed, it is probable that this last sentence is the logical negative of the sentence the informants were given, if *usually* is to be within the domain of the negation, when *can* has a 'characteristic' meaning (cf. F. R. Palmer 1965, 116). If *often* replaces *usually* in the target sentence of the test on *usually*, then the resultant sentence is still somewhat odd:

?He can't *often* write well.

On the other hand, if *usually* replaces *often* in the target sentence of the test on *often*, then the resultant sentence seems perfectly acceptable:

He can't *usually* explain what they mean.

It is clear that it is not the position after the negative particle that is unacceptable for *usually*. The unacceptability of *usually* in this particular construction has disturbed the possibility of a direct comparison of the acceptability of *usually* after the negative particle with the acceptability of attitudinal disjuncts in the same position. Even so, there is a far higher unacceptability for attitudinal disjuncts in this position (cf. Tables 16 and 20, pages 236, 240).

Chapter 6

Attitudinal disjuncts: position, punctuation, and intonation

6.1 Position, punctuation, and intonation as features for identification of attitudinal disjuncts

In an old film, recently relayed on the television screen, there is a scene in which the bridegroom, suspicious of his fiancée's behaviour the previous night, decides not to proceed with the wedding planned for that day. Deeply wounded, he complains bitterly to her former husband, and solemnly declares:

/I expect my wife to behàve# · /nàturally#

The other immediately retorts:

/I expect my wife to behave nàturally#

The grammatical punning in this exchange illustrates the way in which intonational means may distinguish the attitudinal disjunct *naturally*, equivalent to 'of course' (cf. pages 209f.), from the manner adjunct *naturally*, equivalent to 'in a natural manner', in a context where either disjunct or adjunct is possible.

The separation of *naturally* in an independent tone unit is not in itself sufficient to identify it as a disjunct. For example, *naturally* is ambiguous between disjunct and adjunct in the following sentence, even though it is in an independent tone unit:

/Bournvita helps you relàx# · /nàturally#

This sentence was uttered in a recent television advertisement. The advertiser is here punning on the two functions of *naturally*. The sentence can be interpreted both as 'Bournvita helps you relax, of course' and as 'Bournvita helps you relax; moreover, Bournvita helps you relax by natural means'. In the first interpretation *naturally* is the attitudinal disjunct, while in the second interpretation it is the manner

adjunct, sole linguistic unit in a 'supplementing' clause, a type of
elliptical clause for which the whole of the preceding or interrupted
clause constitutes the ellipsis. The relationship of the nuclear tones has
contributed to the ambiguity. As in the disconsolate bridegroom's
remark, *naturally* would be interpreted as disjunct in this sentence if
the nuclear tone were not to echo that of the previous verb. On the
other hand, if it were not in an independent tone unit, it would be
interpreted as adjunct.

The subtle distinctions that are possible in intonation are not always
paralleled in punctuation. In the written medium, *naturally* in the
advertiser's commendation would be ambiguous between the disjunct
and the supplementing clause:

Bournvita helps you relax, *naturally.*

The writer would have to move it to another position to make it clear
that he wanted it to be interpreted as a disjunct, and in this context
the initial position would be most suitable:

Naturally, Bournvita helps you relax.

In this position there is unlikely to be ambiguity, since homonyms of
the disjunct are unlikely to appear here. As a further consequence of this
lack of ambiguity, there would be no need for a comma after the word in
the written medium, and it would not need to be in a separate tone unit
in speech.

In the written form of the advertisement, *naturally* could not be
unambiguously a supplementing clause unless other linguistic units
were added, e.g.:

Bournvita helps you relax – and *naturally.*
Bournvita helps you relax – *naturally*, in fact.

There would not, however, be any ambiguity if the supplementing
clause were attached to a type of clause not open to a disjunct. Hence,
there is no doubt that *naturally* in the following headline is a supplementing clause. An article in a woman's magazine is seductively entitled:

HOW YOU
CAN
LOOK
PRETTIER –
NATURALLY   (*Woman* 2/7/66: 8, 1)

Since the disjunct cannot appear within an indirect question (cf. pages
111f.), *naturally* here is unambiguously an adjunct in a supplementing
clause.

The punctuation and intonation devices that we have been discussing
are available for the language user. He perhaps may not use them if the

context makes it obvious that a disjunct is intended. And for this purpose the context may be wider than the clause to which the disjunct refers. Within its clause the item may be ambiguous, but in the wider context it may lose its ambiguity. Once again, *naturally* will illustrate the contention:

> The Government urged caution yesterday on anyone who might be inclined to make too much of the TUC's votes on incomes policy.
> Ministers are *naturally* relieved that the votes did not go the other way. (G 8/9/66: 1, 1)

In certain cases homonyms of disjuncts may function as premodifiers. Again, if the context makes it clear that the item is a disjunct, it is not essential to separate it intonationally or by punctuation, e.g.:

> After the victories in Europe this season of Atilla, Aunt Edith, Super Sam, Polyfoto, Red Slipper and others there are *naturally* great hopes of Super Sam taking the prize at Laurel Park.
> (O 24/10/65: 18, 8)

Since commas may be used in written English to identify disjuncts in the middle of a clause (to distinguish them from homonyms), should the writer wish to suggest that the disjuncts themselves are parenthetic, he may prefer to enclose them in dashes or brackets:

> The impression given by this is that it has spent most of its time so far – *not unnaturally* – looking for a role.
> (TES 12/11/65: 1028, 2)
> He is (*rather splendidly*) defiant to the last; ...
> (ST 6/2/66: 45, 1)

Contrast the non-parenthetic appearance of *not unnaturally*:

> A few weeks before the coup, Nkrumah presented her with the Ford Thunderbird, purchased with public money, in which she was photographed (below). This flamboyant gesture seemed to earn her considerable dislike. Miss Marais was briefly imprisoned, forced *not unnaturally* to disgorge the Thunderbird, then deported to Uganda, despite her protests. (STM 5/3/67: 13, 1)

The possible interpretation of *not unnaturally* as an adjunct is prevented by knowledge of the wider context.

An adjunct in a supplementing clause may be separated merely by comma punctuation:

> 'He was only a very small one,' says Mr Marking, 'so I threw him back, *quickly*.' (ST 4/9/66: 9, 3)

Nor is the tea we are drinking today – 500 million pounds of it –
quite the tea we were drinking before the war. At least it isn't, *yet*,
instant tea.   (STM 9/7/67: 30, 3)

It may, however, be separated by brackets or dashes:

How they (*almost*) carried the bad news from Lagos to Port
Talbot: . . .   (G 2/8/66: 8, 6)

Greek tankers or no Greek tankers, if the flow of oil products
by road and rail from Mozambique and South Africa continues
Rhodesia will get by – *just*.[1]   (G 23/3/66: 10, 5)

In the preceding discussion, *naturally* has served to exemplify some
of the factors that may determine the position of disjuncts and intonation and punctuation features that accompany them. Disjuncts
vary in the restrictions on their placement and in their necessity for
intonation and punctuation marking. This variation is dependent on
whether homonyms exist and on the positional range of these homonyms.
Some disjuncts, e.g. *probably*, *inevitably*, and *admittedly*, are more
freely mobile than *naturally*, since these do not have homonymous
adjuncts. With others, e.g. *really* and *actually*, the range of their homonyms, the intensifiers *really* and *actually*, is much greater than that of
the adjunct *naturally*. As a consequence, the disjuncts may not appear
in positions available to the intensifiers without intonation or punctuation
marking (cf. pages 127ff.).

Let us now consider *sadly*, a disjunct which has a homonymous
adjunct appearing in initial position. The following four passages
contain examples of *sadly* in initial position in written English:

[1] Tea dripped steadily from the hem of her dress to the pave-
      ment; *sadly* he rubbed it in with his foot.   (6.2.96-2)
[2] Ghanaian history under Nkrumah: the postcard, one of the
      'Ancient History' series, claims that 'the science of medicine was
      originated by Africans in the empire of Ghana'. *Sadly* the gen-
      uinely impressive history of Ghanaian civilisation, one of the
      most attractive in Africa, was obscured by Nkrumahist bombast
      of this kind.   (STM 5/3/67: 8, 1)
[3] . . . Mai Zetterling's 'Night Games' was shown to the official
      jury and to the press – only. The police were on hand at the
      screening and in such circumstances officialdom looked very
      foolish. *Sadly*, Miss Zetterling says that she doesn't object to the
      film being cut on distribution.   (G 6/9/66: 7, 4)

---

[1] *Just* differs from the adjuncts in the previous citations in that it is away from its
normal position.

[4] A violent swinging show for the impending seventies. No comedian to warm the pizza-munching, pretty beat audience up;
just a continuum of strip cartoons, underground movies and
clips (erotic ones) from Antonioni's 'Blow-up' flashed on a
circular screen, with lukewarm jazz to boot. But there, *sadly*,
the bold new swinging stopped.   (G 28/3/67: 6, 6)

The presence or absence of commas does not distinguish the disjunct
from the adjunct in these four passages. From the context it is clear that
sadly in [1] is an adjunct, and the clause could be paraphrased by 'he
was sad when he rubbed it in with his foot'. It is equally clear that
sadly in [2] is a disjunct, corresponding to *it is sad* (*that*). Yet in both
cases there is no comma after *sadly*. In [3] and [4] *sadly* is separated from
the clause by commas. It is probably a disjunct in both passages, though
it is possible to interpret it in either as an adjunct.

In spoken English intonational features may be employed to distinguish the two functions of *sadly* in initial position if the sentence is
taken out of context. It would not, in that case, be necessary to turn
to the wider context to determine its function. Thus, *sadly* would be
an adjunct in

/sadly he rubbed it in with his fòot#

or in

/sàdly# he /rubbed it in with his fòot#

and

/sādly# he /rubbed it in with his fòot#

and perhaps in

/sádly# he /rubbed it in with his fòot#

while it would be taken as a disjunct in

/sădly# he /rubbed it in with his fòot#

Although intonational features could distinguish disjuncts from
homonymous adjuncts, it should be emphasised that they would not
necessarily be employed if the context indicated that a disjunct was
intended. And if the wider context suggested that the adjunct function
would be appropriate, then even if the item were given an independent
tone unit with a falling-rising nuclear tone, its function would remain
ambiguous between disjunct and adjunct.

Ambiguity between disjunct and adjunct may also arise when the
item is in pre-verb position, as with *happily* in the next citation:

But the most important object must be to get Jim Callaghan
out of the Treasury, where he is the impressive spokesman of

pure economic liberalism; he would be *happily* consoled with the
FO. (*New Statesman* 21/7/67: 80, 1)

In practice, ambiguities are usually resolved in the light of the wider
context, as we have suggested. Consider the function of *obviously* in
the next citation:

> Farmer-trainer Marsh called a vet who found both horses fit.
> Some Yarn went on to win the Fairlawne Hunters' 'Chase at
> Wye the same day – an odds-on favourite.
> Mr. Marsh said: 'Someone tried *obviously* to force the capsule
> into the horse's mouth, but he spat it out. The man must have
> panicked.' (8fa.2.13)

It is possible to understand *obviously* here as 'in an obvious manner',
but it is much more likely to mean in this context 'it is obvious'. Because
of the greater probability of the latter meaning, it is not absolutely
necessary to enclose the item within commas, which would have
swayed the balance to its interpretation as a disjunct. On the other hand,
if both interpretations are equally likely, then comma punctuation is
essential in order that the item should be taken as a disjunct. Commas
are thus essential in the next citation:

> Last week 'Miscellany' reported that the sex and morality
> report was selling like hot-cross buns. After yesterday's tortured
> debate and tortuous vote, it could go on to be the biggest selling
> (as well as hottest and crossest) bunfight of all time. Current
> sale: 48,000 in seven days. Fifteen thousand more, with yester-
> day's irresolute resolution appended, printing immediately. The
> book it has to beat, *clearly*, is 'Honest to God' ...
> (G 27/10/66: 8, 6)

It is, however, the context that indicates that *clearly* is a disjunct and
not an adjunct in a supplementing clause. In the next citation, *theoretically* must be a disjunct because the adjunct will not collocate with a
personal Object (i.e. active Object, here the grammatical Subject).
Hence the absence of commas around *theoretically* does not affect its
status:

> Although Prince Charles is to be treated *theoretically* as a
> schoolboy when he arrives in Australia on Monday to begin a
> term at the Geelong Grammar School's 'Timbertop' outpost in
> Victoria, the welcome will be scarcely informal. (G 29/1/66: 1, 2)

In the terminology of transformational-generative grammar, we may
perhaps say that the adjunct *theoretically* is in some way related to the
assignment of a feature of Object selection to the transitive verb *treat*, cf.
Chomsky 1965, 113-20. Compare:

Although the problem is to be treated *theoretically* . . .

where *theoretically* may be interpreted as an adjunct, an antonym to *practically*. In such a context the item must be transposed to ensure that it is taken as a disjunct:

Although *theoretically* the problem is to be treated . . .[1]

Many of the items that can function as disjuncts can also premodify other items. This premodifying function seems particularly open to those suggesting unexpectedness (cf. for disjuncts in this semantic subclass, pages 208f.). However, items from other disjunct semantic subclasses may also function as premodifiers. In a test given in Battery III, 117 informants were asked to judge the similarity of meaning of these two sentences:

the /book was unfortunately dìfficult#
un/fŏrtunately# the /book was dìfficult#

Twenty-nine informants (25 per cent) considered these sentences to be very similar in meaning, but as many as fifty-one (44 per cent) thought they were very different in meaning, while thirty-seven (32 per cent) were not sure or believed they were to be placed somewhere between the two extremes. Presumably, those who judged the sentences to be very different in meaning interpreted *unfortunately* in the first sentence as a premodifier of *difficult*. They may have understood the phrase *unfortunately difficult* to mean 'difficult to an unfortunate extent', with *unfortunately* having the force of an intensifier. The thirty-seven who were in some doubt evidently saw the ambiguity of *unfortunately* in that position.

The results of a test involving *surprisingly* were rather similar, except that there was a greater polarisation. Informants in the same Battery were asked to make a semantic judgment on the pair of sentences:

the /test was surprisingly èasy#
sur/prĭsingly# the /test was èasy#

---

[1] We can argue that we have two senses of the verb *treat*, although they are obviously related. Nevertheless, the verb in both senses will take a manner adjunct:

You must treat the problem *carefully*.
You must treat the Prince *carefully*.

They differ in the range of manner adjuncts that they will allow. We cannot have, for example:

* You must treat the problem *kindly*.
* You must treat the Prince *theoretically*.

Until more information is available about the ranges of manner adjuncts open to verbs, it is not possible to say how best to handle these restrictions on collocation.

This time thirty-nine informants (33 per cent) thought that the sentences were very similar in meaning, while fifty-five (47 per cent) thought them very different, and twenty-three (20 per cent) were in doubt. Those who noticed a difference between the two sentences presumably understood *surprisingly easy* in the first sentence as 'easy to a surprising degree'.

As a premodifier, *surprisingly* seems to lose some of the semantic force of 'surprise'. It appears to be moving towards the merely intensifying force of such premodifiers as 'terribly' and 'awfully'. This seems to be true of others in the same semantic sub-class, especially those with a participle *-ing* base, e.g. *amazingly, astonishingly*.

I give some instances of items that can function as disjuncts to the clause but here function as premodifiers. Their intensifying force will be noted.

But it is also true that most Americans are *curiously* uncertain about this war.   (O 24/10/65: 6, 7)

Their country is *unbelievably* beautiful, with a climate far cooler and kinder than Jakarta's.   (G 30/8/66: 9, 4)

The Charles Aznevour cult grows *strangely* slowly in Britain; in France he is No. 1.   (STP 19/12/65: 37, 2)

The production goes at all this *oddly* tamely.   (O 24/10/65: 24, 3)

But the third instalment of Sunday Night fell *woefully* short of the expectations raised by Peter Ustinov and John Berger.
(TES 12/11/65: 1020, 2)

For these items to be interpreted as disjuncts to the clause it would probably be necessary to separate them from the rest of the clause by dashes or brackets (cf. *rather splendidly* on page 185). In initial position comma separation would be sufficient. *Apparently* in the next example is a premodifier, but would be interpreted as a disjunct to the clause if followed by a comma:

It may be argued that the conflict over the gulf is not legal but political. But *apparently* insoluble political problems can sometimes be made more manageable by being reduced to legal terms, . . .[1]   (G 1/6/67: 8, 2)

When the premodifier is preceded by a deictic, however, it would seem impossible to change its function by means of punctuation or intonation:

---

[1] Of course, where *apparently* cannot be interpreted as a premodifier, then comma separation is optional:

Apparently the Madrid press, which is still carefully controlled by the Ministry for Information, had been given an inaccurate 'lead'.   (G 14/7/66: 1, 6)

Methadone *apparently* induces high tolerance to heroin.   (O 24/10/65: 12, 6)

Perhaps it would be prudent for judges, in their charge to the jury, to include a sentence or two to cover this *fortunately* rare contingency. (G. 28/2/67: 8, 6)

We have seen that items that function as disjuncts to the clause tend to have an intensifying force when they premodify adjectives or adverbs. Thus, *a curiously long letter* is interpreted as 'a letter that is long to a curious extent'. However, if an item that can function as either disjunct or adjunct premodifies a participle, it is normally interpreted as the adjunct. For example, *a curiously worded letter* is interpreted as a 'letter that is worded in a curious manner'. Two interpretations are possible if the item premodifies a participle that can be either verbal or adjectival (cf. Svartvik 1966, 134f.). For example, *his curiously disturbed friend* can be interpreted as either 'his friend who has been disturbed in a curious manner', in which case *disturbed* has retained its verbal force, or as 'his friend who is disturbed to a curious extent', in which case *disturbed* is adjectival and denotes a mental or emotional state.

From the evidence that we have displayed, it is clear that a disjunct cannot be identified merely by its position or by features of intonation or punctuation that accompany it. Where an item may be either a disjunct or an adjunct, the context will usually indicate the more probable semantic interpretation.

6.2 Positions of attitudinal disjuncts in the Survey corpus

Table 12 (page 192) sets out the positions of attitudinal disjuncts that occur in Survey texts. Only those that are unambiguously attitudinal disjuncts have been included in this table. Table 13 (page 193) states the positions of items that are ambiguous in function between attitudinal disjunct and intensifier (cf. pages 127ff.). Most of the symbols have been previously used to indicate the positions of conjuncts and are explained in §3.4, page 78. Some additional symbols are required for Tables 12 and 13:

Qm – the disjunct is within a question (in the only instance that occurs – *possibly* – the position is between the Subject and the lexical verb).
NFm – the disjunct is within a non-finite verb clause.

Table 12 demonstrates that attitudinal disjuncts in the Survey corpus appear more often in initial position than elsewhere in the clause. Just over half of those that are unambiguously attitudinal disjuncts occur in initial position. It will be recalled that a larger proportion of conjuncts, even if we only take into account mobile conjuncts, are in that position

TABLE 12 *Positions of attitudinal disjuncts in Survey corpus*

	F	VF	NF	M2	M3	M4	M5	M6	M7	M8	Qm	NFm	E	VE	NE	NGp	Total
SCIENCE (20,000)	17	5	3	8	1	3	8	3	5			2		1		2	56
PHILOSOPHY (5,000)	2			1	1	1			1								6
THEOLOGY (5,000)	7			1			2		2				2				12
NOVELS (20,000)	12	5	2	2	1	1	4			1			1	2	1		31
NEWSPAPERS (10,000)	2			2			1		2	2							10
STUDENT ESSAYS (5,000)	1	1							3								5
DISCUSSION (20,000)	35	12	1	3	3	2	4	1	2	1			6	2			72
CONVERSATION (10,000)	7	4		2	1	1	1		1				6	2			25
BBC NEWS (5,000)		1							1								2
Total	83	28	6	19	6	7	19	4	17	4	1	2	15	4	2	2	219

117   79   102   21

(cf. page 78, where it is reported that nearly twice as many mobile conjuncts are in initial position as appear elsewhere). If we include in our total the items that are ambiguously disjuncts (Table 13), the proportion of those in initial position falls to considerably less than the combined number in other positions. Even then, it is still very much higher than in any other single position. The position with the next largest number (if we take the ambiguous disjuncts into consideration) is M7, the position between an equative verb and the Complement.

TABLE 13 *Positions of query attitudinal disjuncts*

	VF	M1a	M3	M4	M5	M6	M7	M8	NFm	E	Total
SCIENCE						2	10				12
PHILOSOPHY		2		1	2		4			1	11
THEOLOGY						1	2				3
NOVELS	1	5	3		3	1	4				17
NEWSPAPERS					1	1					2
STUDENT ESSAYS							1				1
DISCUSSION	2	8	4	1	4		8	1	1	4	33
CONVERSATION		4	3		2	1	2			3	14
BBC NEWS							1				1
Total	3	19	10	2	12	6	32	1	1	8	94

83

Because of the small numbers involved, it is probably unwise to make any but the most tentative suggestions about the distribution of numbers of attitudinal disjuncts between the various texts. Table 14 is derived from the right-hand column of totals in Table 12. It displays more clearly the relative frequencies of attitudinal disjuncts in the text categories.

We notice from Table 14 the paucity of attitudinal disjuncts in news broadcasts as compared with discussion and conversation texts. This is to be expected, since BBC news broadcasts are intended to give the impression of being objective and impersonal. We would therefore expect that attitudinal disjuncts, which usually suggest a personal evaluation and comment, would be avoided. For written English, the highest number of attitudinal disjuncts is to be found in the scientific texts. By the nature of his training, the scientist tends to be cautious in the interpretation of his results and may prefer to express his assessments tentatively. It should be noted that of the 56 attitudinal disjuncts that occur in scientific texts (Table 12) 39 weaken the absolute character

TABLE 14 *Frequencies of attitudinal disjuncts in text categories*

Science	2·8	Student Essays	1
Philosophy	1·2	Discussion	3·6
Theology	2·4	Conversation	2·5
Novels	1·6	BBC News	0·4
Newspapers	1	TOTAL	2·2

[Frequencies are expressed in numbers per 1,000 words.]

of the writers' assertions: *apparently* 7, *presumably* 7, *perhaps* 7, *probably* 18.

As with conjuncts (cf. page 80), some attitudinal disjuncts seem to be restricted to particular varieties of English. For example, *happily*, *unhappily*, and *sadly* are likely to be found in the more formal varieties of written English, whereas *fortunately*, *unfortunately*, *luckily*, and *unluckily* appear to have a much wider range of distribution and are certainly appropriate in spoken English. *Maybe* is highly colloquial and casual, but *perhaps* seems suitable equally in spoken and written English, and in formal and informal varieties of both. A comprehensive plotting of the varieties of English in which individual attitudinal disjuncts are predictable awaits the analysis of a much larger corpus.

6.3 Information focus

Attitudinal disjuncts are not normally the major information point of the clause to which they are related.[1] However, the attitudinal disjuncts may help to focus the major information points in the clause, and this, to some extent at least, accounts for their placement in positions other than the initial position. Some citations will exemplify the point we are making:

[1] In the synagogue at Nazareth He *significantly* read from Isaiah: 'The Spirit of the Lord is upon me.'   (8ab.2.138-1)
[2] Immediately after seeing Mr Wilson last night Sir Alec Douglas-Home went to an upstairs committee room to face the Tory back-

---

[1] The exceptions are when all the other items in the clause have been stated previously. They are of course implied when the disjunct is the sole item in the clause, as in a response:

A they have a /grave pròblem on their hands#
B /òbviously#

They may, however, be present in the clause with the disjunct:

A they have a /grave pròblem on their hands#
B /obviously they have a grave problem on their hands#

benchers' 1922 Committee – and received *perhaps* his most
rousing ovation.   (8fa.2.5)
[3] These 'follicles of Langerhans' were, *appropriately enough*, first
seen by the discoverer of the islets in higher forms, . . .
                                                          (8a.1.90-1)
[4] Geach, *indeed*, is *required* (ital. sic) to say that 'smokes' stands
for something.   (8b.1.144-4)

In [1] what is significant is the reading from Isaiah. In this instance,
as in the subsequent citations, it would be possible to focus on this
part of the clause in a reading even if the disjunct were in initial position.
The reading would achieve this focusing by positioning the nuclear
tone on the item with the accompaniment of other prosodic features
such as stress or a jump in pitch. Placing the disjunct as near as possible
to the major information point helps to focus attention on it. This is
clearer in [2]. The doubt expressed by *perhaps* is whether or not this
was his most rousing ovation and not whether he received an ovation.
The placement of the disjunct helps to focus on this part of the clause.
Again, in [3] the focus is the first sight by the discoverer of the islets in
higher forms. Had the disjunct preceded the auxiliary the Subject
would have become a major information point. This is the case in [4]
where the Subject is focused by the disjunct. An additional major information point is graphically indicated by the italicising of *required*.
The placement of the disjunct in written English can be of importance
in providing a clue to the reading of the clause.

Since the disjunct is not normally the major information unit in the
clause, we would expect that in spoken English it would not normally
be the only item in the clause to carry the nuclear tone. Citations from
the Survey corpus illustrate the relation of the disjunct to the rest of the
clause with respect to the nuclear tone.

[1] The disjunct does not have the nucleus:
Mr /Fisher sāid# · it was /*probably* trúe# that /both countries
consider these [iə] aircraft to be outdàted#   (4c.1a-11)

[2] It is in a separate tone unit:
/I shouldn't have thought we've any power in the mátter#
/one way or the ôther# · /*sûrely*#   (5b.1.43)

[3] It is in a subordinate tone unit:
it's a de/báte [ap/párently#]# of the /rights and wrongs of the
Rènt Act#   (5b.16.10)

The subordinate tone unit, enclosed in square brackets in the citation,
has been ignored in the reduced system of notation used in this study
(cf. pages 10f.). It is defined in Crystal and Quirk 1964, 52: 'The primary
characteristic of the subordinate tone-unit is that its pitch contour, while

having a complete and independent shape within itself, falls broadly
within the total contour presented in the superordinate tone-unit.'

[4] It constitutes the 'tail' of the tone unit, i.e. the continuation of the
pitch movement started on a previous nuclear syllable:
I'm /very surprìsed ˙*actually*# at /this · quotation of Rússell's#

(5b.2.10)

As with the subordinate tone unit, the 'tail' has been ignored in the
reduced system of notation. It is indicated in this citation by a preceding raised dot, as in the fuller system of notation.

[5] It carries part of a complex nucleus:
it was /just like sùmmer *áctually*#   (S.1b.6a-13)

[6] It carries the nucleus but another item in the tone unit constitutes the 'tail':
/I think most of the women in this àudience# would /*próbably*
a˙gree# with /mé#   (5b.16.33)

[7] It alone carries the nuclear tone, but part of the clause is in another tone unit, with another nuclear tone marking the information
focus:
they're /all *appàrently*# /dead agáinst it#   (5b.16.32)

There are no instances in the Survey corpus where the disjunct is the
only item in the clause to bear the nuclear tone.

Chapter 7

Types of structure to which attitudinal disjuncts relate

To at least some of the attitudinal disjuncts, labels such as *sentence modifiers* and *sentence adverbs* have been applied (cf. page 2). If a distinction is made between sentence and clause, such terms may mislead, since they suggest that the items do not enter into a relationship with dependent constructions. Some examples can be given of the types of structure to which they are related.

[1a] 'non-restrictive' relative clause:
and soon he was rubbing an after-shave lotion, which *presumably* he had bought for the same eventuality, all over the legs and body of Tarquin, who had suddenly become more passive.
(6.3.209-3)

It is unlikely that the Field-Marshal will answer the points made by Mr Thompson whose sources, *disappointingly*, except for the Rommel Papers, are all British or American. (G 16/3/67: 10, 7)

The need is for it to be spelt out publicly in Washington, where, *unfortunately*, de Gaulle's words are not heeded.
(G 20/6/66: 8, 2)

[1b] 'restrictive' relative clause:
This means that the Government will have to bring in the compulsory powers which it has so far, *unaccountably*, neglected.
(ST 4/9/66: 10, 1)

[2] 'indirect question'
What *perhaps* struck home sharpest was the name of this instrument, ... (6.2.91-1)

What *apparently* sticks in the gullet of many is that Cadiz is politically a city of ill-repute, ... (G 20/6/66: 8, 6)

[3]   finite verb clause introduced by other subordinators:
/and ónce#/as · Màllalieu said# /quite rightly# we be/gan to see
Communists under every béd# – /we sold that pàss#   (5b.1.48)

It's an open secret that a similar project for Kuwait has started
rolling – though, *oddly*, our scout in Kuwait says that Ministers
still deny it.   (G 8/9/66: 8, 6)

no doubt she could have found work as a less qualified type of
nurse, but was so dashed by her failure that she *understandably*
didn't want to try.   (O 24/10/65: 30, 4)

In Britain itself the Prime Minister's decision to go was rap-
turously received though there were *admittedly* some senior
Conservatives who would privately have preferred a more
discreet probe into Mr Smith's intentions . . .
                                                (O 24/10/65: 3, 2)

As his germ-killer he chose carbolic acid – because, *bizarrely*,
he read in the newspapers that it had been successfully used to
'purify' sewage at Carlisle.[1]   (STM 19/2/67: 18, 2)

For the superconductive transition, type B (2), it is probable,
but not certain, that certain electronic states become empty
above the transition temperature, so that here also the theoretical
difficulty *probably* does not arise; . . .   (8a.3.31-4)

[4]   non-finite verb clause:
in addition she has an anal fin, *probably* used, as in salmon and
trout, to make a nest.   (8a.1.96-2)

The corresponding sharp, but not mathematically discontinuous,
changes predicted by theory for a large but finite assembly

---

[1] Within the context of this passage, *bizarrely* does not have its usual correspondence. We do not hold the meaning constant when we replace *bizarrely* by
it is bizarre that:

  As his germ-killer he chose carbolic acid – because *it is bizarre that* he read in
  the newspapers that . . .

This restriction seems to apply to disjuncts in clauses of cause, purpose, and result. With clauses of result, however, it is possible to set up correspondences for
several of the disjuncts that semantically express some degree of doubt about the
fulfilment of what is being communicated, e.g. *possibly, probably, maybe, quite
likely*. The next citation in the text contains a clause of result to which *probably* is
related.
  A similar difficulty in formally expressing correspondences applies to clauses
introduced by *whose*, and, for some disjuncts, to clauses introduced by a relative
pronoun that is preceded by a preposition:

  The predominantly Catholic population from here will form the core of the
  parish for which the Cathedral will – *unusually* – serve as a parish church.
                                                (G 15/5/67: 14, 2)

(containing *perhaps* 10^{22} molecules) are, from an experimental point of view, indistinguishable from those that would be expected for an 'infinite' assembly, . . .   (8a.3.23-1)

This is difficult to reconcile with the fact that the solvent radicals Ar˙ must be similar to R″ radicals of one type (C_6H_5˙), and so must, if they are formed, take part in the reaction in much the same way as R″, leading *inevitably* to the production of the symmetrical diaryl ArAr.   (8a.4.37-4)

The hush as he stood there, *seemingly* holding up the ceiling with the top of his hat, was packed to the brim with the many things a pilot had to cope with . . .   (6.4.54-3)

[5] non-finite verb clause introduced by a subordinator:

Though, *fortunately*, well looked after, she looked unhappy.

As *presumably* expected, he won the race.

Though, *unhappily*, selling very little, he kept his shop open till late at night.

[6] 'supplementing' clause, a type of elliptical clause for which the whole of the preceding or interrupted clause constitutes the ellipsis (cf. page 184):

The spinal cord is of a uniform transparent grey colour and is flattened dorso-ventrally, *apparently* to allow access of oxygen, . . .
                    (8a.1.98-3)

The yields are low, *probably* because of the violence of the reaction.   (8a.4.31-3)

I re/member my friend George Brówn# /talking to a miners · áudience# · in /Dérbyshire# *ad/mittedly* two or three years agó#   (5b.1.23)

He has remarked (*presumably* with humour) 'Please God let me die before this Ecumenical Council ends, so that I may die a Catholic.'   (O 24/10/65: 12, 5)

One must travel across the great land mass, *preferably* by bus or car.   (ST 16/7/67: 7, 3)

[7] 'appended' clause, a type of clause for which *part* of the preceding or interrupted clause constitutes the ellipsis, while the rest has the same function in that clause as part of the elliptical clause has in the ellipted clause:

it will do its authors little good in South Arabia, where the blows in the party contest are meant to hurt, and *perhaps* to kill.
                    (G 24/5/66: 10, 1)

The real angst for a wandering civil servant, judging by the table, must come when he decides to go, by hired vehicle, on a journey whose outward distance and, *surprisingly*, return distance also is 76 miles.   (G 1/7/67: 6, 6)

Mr Gilbert's address – mild on almost every topic except the use of aides and, *predictably*, teachers' pay – may cause the sparks to fly . . .   (ST 26/3/67: 3, 7)

But the success of his independent foreign policy will be judged by Britain – and *more importantly* – by the Russians – according to his ability to reinforce and sustain the wider agreement between the Russians and the Americans . . .

(G 20/6/66: 8, 1)

Without them, our conditions of life would swiftly become Spartan – and in the ensuing riots *perhaps* Hogarthian, too.

(G 20/6/66: 8, 2)

The logic of this is basically unsound, *perhaps* eccentric, but the situation discussed is mundane.   (W6.1a-9)

[8] within a prepositional phrase:
Papandreou – a man of the centre and an octogenarian – was voted into power at *perhaps* the most free elections the Greeks have ever taken part in.   (G 11/6/66: 8, 1)

Spenser may be read as a whole only unsatisfactorily except *perhaps* as a period piece.   (W6.1b-9)

For the sake of completeness we ought to mention that some attitudinal disjuncts may serve as response utterances. They include most of the disjuncts that express conviction or doubt to some degree, e.g. *apparently, definitely, presumably, perhaps*. Others will normally serve as response utterance only when associated with another linguistic unit, e.g. *yes* or *no*. A few instances of verbless clauses not subsumed under the types of structure we have just listed may be conveniently given here:

'Your brain is as good an instrument as mine. Better, *probably*.'
(6.1.20)

/Ted Leather ((sáys)) # /what right have we got to intervène#
/unfórtunately# /nòne#   (5b.1.44)

A some publisher or other – last year · about a year ago – asked me what I thought · about · a series – mm publishing early grammarians –
B /ôh# /Pèrrins *perhaps#*   (S.1b.6-15)

A /m · no Swedish (([mənə] money))

B *ap/parently* nôt#   (S.1b.6-64)

Although no instances occur in the material I have examined, it is possible to imagine many of the attitudinal disjuncts serving not only as utterances responding to preceding questions but also as utterances commenting on preceding declarative sentences. Two invented examples will be sufficient to illustrate this use:

[1] A They called in the police as soon as they suspected the maid of having taken the money.

   B *Very wisely.*

[2] A We lost every match this season.

   B *Surprisingly.*

7*

Chapter 8

Semantic classification of attitudinal disjuncts

In this chapter I shall classify attitudinal disjuncts semantically and relate the classification to that by correspondence classes (cf. §5.1, pages 94ff.). The items included in this chapter do not constitute an exhaustive list of attitudinal disjuncts. It would not be possible to list all attitudinal disjuncts, since they are not a closed class. They include, however, all those in the material I have examined as well as some others I have recalled from my experience of the language.

8.1 Semantic set [1]

These attitudinal disjuncts express an opinion on the truth-value of what is being said. They can be subdivided into two sub-sets:

[1a] those that express shades of doubt or certainty about what is being said.

[1b] those that state in what sense the speaker judges it to be true or false.

8.1.1 Semantic sub-set [1a]

Sub-set [1a] can be further subdivided into two sub-sets:

[1a(i)] those that merely express shades of doubt or certainty about what is being said

[1a(ii)] those that in addition refer to the observation or perception of a state of affairs.

8.1.1.1 Semantic sub-set [1a(i)]

We further distinguish between those that express conviction and those that express some degree of doubt. The attitudinal disjuncts are displayed below according to this distinction, together with an indication of the correspondence class, if any, to which they belong.

those that express conviction:
[A2] definitely, incontestably, indisputably, indubitably, unarguably, undeniably, unquestionably
[B]   certainly, surely
[J1] admittedly
[J2] undoubtedly
[others] assuredly, decidedly, indeed
those that express some degree of doubt:
[A2] arguably, conceivably, possibly, presumably, probably
[J1] allegedly, reportedly, reputedly, supposedly
[others] doubtless, quite (etc.) likely, maybe, perhaps

Among those expressing conviction, *certainly* and *admittedly* have concessive force (cf. page 141 for *certainly*). They imply a reluctant acceptance by the speaker that what is being said is true. *Admittedly* suggests in addition some reluctance to mention the acceptance. On the other hand, *surely* expresses the speaker's conviction while inviting agreement from the person or persons addressed (cf. page 130). It implies desire for corroboration and anticipation of some opposition. We may paraphrase it informally by 'I am sure about what I am saying. Wouldn't you agree with me about it?' The others expressing conviction assume conviction on the part of both the speaker and his audience. It should be mentioned that *assuredly* and *decidedly* are of course not equivalent to what might seem to be their correspondences, *it is assured* (*that*) and *it is decided* (*that*) respectively, but are closer semantically to *surely* and *undoubtedly*.

Those expressing some degree of doubt can be roughly ordered according to the degree of doubt expressed, with *doubtless, presumably, likely,* and *probably* at one end implying least doubt and *conceivably* at the other implying most doubt. Several imply that other people may be convinced of the truth of what is being said, e.g. *conceivably* and *arguably*. Some, e.g. *allegedly* and *reportedly*, imply in addition that what is being said has been stated previously by others. *Doubtless* implies some doubt, despite the suffix -*less*, which usually has a negative import. It is roughly synonymous with *presumably* and not with *undoubtedly* or 'without doubt'.

Corresponding structures cannot be easily perceived for the disjuncts *indeed* and *perhaps* in present-day English, though there are of course structures that use the same stem as the latter, e.g. 'it may *happen* (that)'.[1]

---

1 This is also true for some of the archaic forms that are synonyms of *perhaps*: *haply, mayhap, perchance,* and *peradventure*. We lack, however, a synchronically recognisable link between the surface forms. Such a link is presumably 'deeply' perceivable. This might apply to *indeed* as well, where the substitutability in many cases of *in fact* would lead us to perceive *indeed* as equivalent to *it is a fact* (*that*).

8.1.1.2   Semantic sub-set [1a(ii)]

Among those referring to the observation or perception of a state of
affairs, we can distinguish between those that express conviction and
those that express some degree of doubt.

Those that express conviction
   [A1] clearly, evidently, manifestly, obviously, patently, plainly

Those that express some degree of doubt
   apparently, seemingly

Evidently seems to express a lesser degree of conviction than the others
with which it has been placed.

The disjunct *seemingly* looks as if it were related to a participle
seeming. In present-day English, however, *seeming* is not used predica-
tively, so that there is no **It is seeming*. The O.E.D. cites this use of
seeming for an earlier stage of the language, its latest quotation in the
sense we are discussing dating from the first half of the fifteenth century.
For the purposes of this synchronic study, the only structures that correspond to *seemingly* are 'it seems' or 'it would seem'.

Apparently is interesting, since colleagues who have been consulted
disagree on its possible correspondences. A citation will help to clarify
the point at issue:

   it's a de/bate *appárently#* of the /rights and wrongs of the Rènt Act#
                                                                   (5b.16.10)

Apparently denotes some doubt about what is being said and it is
therefore not semantically equivalent to *it is clear (that)*:

   It is clear (that) it's a debate of the rights and wrongs of the Rent
   Act.

The question is whether *it is apparent (that)* can have any meaning
apart from *it is clear (that)*. If not, then *apparently* does not correspond
to *it is apparent (that)*. In my own idiolect *apparently* is closer in
meaning to *it would appear (that)* or *it would seem (that)* or even, at least
in this context, *so far as this is apparent*. For some colleagues, however,
it is apparent (that) can be equivalent to *it appears (that)* or *it seems (that)*.
For these *apparently* corresponds to *it is apparent (that)*.[1]

---

1 O.E.D. (in a volume completed 1888) cites an instance under its entry for
apparently from as late as the mid-19th century in which it is undoubtedly
synonymous with *it is apparent (that)*:

   2 ... 1853 H. Rogers *Ecl. Faith* 138 the malady, which is but too apparent,
      is also as *apparently* without a remedy.

O.E.D. does not mark as obsolete this use of *apparently* as a synonym of *clearly*.
In the particular citation there may be a playful shift of meaning to allow for the
parallelism between *too apparent* and *as apparently*.

There is some doubt over the acceptability of *it is patent (that)*:

From Galsworthy's best work life has *patently* not escaped.
                                                    (ST 8/1/67: 22, 4)
?*It is patent (that)* from Galsworthy's best work life has not escaped.

The acceptability of this structure is raised when *patent* is premodified:

It is quite *patent (that)* from Galsworthy's best work life has not escaped.

Similar doubts exist over the acceptability of *it is manifest (that)*, though in this case premodification of the adjective seems to lower acceptability.

Normally, the perception of a state of affairs that the disjuncts in this sub-set convey is a mental perception. We may compare the common use of *see* in expressions like 'I *see* now what you mean'. It does, however, seem that in some contexts these disjuncts may denote visual perception as well. In a test in Battery III informants were asked to judge the similarity in meaning of the pair of sentences:

the /students obviously understood the lècture#
/ŏbviously# the /students understood the lècture#

Fifty-seven informants (49 per cent) thought that the two sentences were very similar in meaning, but twenty-nine (25 per cent) thought them very different. As many as thirty-one (26 per cent) thought them 'somewhere between' these extremes. It is possible that in the first sentence *obviously* meant for many informants something like 'It could be visibly seen (that)'. This may have been the effect for these students of its placement near the verb.

Three of the disjuncts in this semantic sub-set have homonymous manner adjuncts, viz., *clearly, obviously, plainly*. None of the other disjuncts of group [A] have homonymous manner adjuncts. We need to differentiate between *clearly* and *plainly* as attitudinal disjuncts and as style disjuncts. Normally, these two are attitudinal disjuncts belonging to the correspondence class [A1] and the semantic sub-set [1a(ii)], but it is possible for them to be used in certain contexts to refer to the way in which the speaker makes his statement. The style disjunct function of these two items seems more likely when they are premodified by *more*. *More clearly* and *more plainly* may have as correspondences either *it is more clear that* and *it is more plain that* or *speaking more clearly* and *speaking more plainly*. Style disjunctives that correspond to these would include *clearly speaking, to be (quite) clear, to make myself (quite) clear, if I may make myself (quite) clear*, and *putting it clearly*, and the same constructions with the appropriate substitution of *plain* or *plainly*. It does not seem possible for *obviously* to function as a style disjunct, perhaps because its use as a manner adjunct is infrequent and therefore it would not be readily available for use in the construction *speaking obviously*. On the other hand, the adjective base enters into the style disjunctive *to be (rather) obvious*.

8.1.2 Semantic sub-set [1b]

The disjuncts in sub-set [1b] state in what sense the speaker judges what he says to be true or false. With the possible exception of (*only*) *apparently*, none belong to correspondence classes.

Most of the disjuncts in this sub-set can be contrasted with *actually*, *really* and *factually*:

(only) apparently, formally, nominally, officially, ostensibly, outwardly, superficially, technically, theoretically.

Potentially is somewhat similar in that it implies that the assertion it qualifies is not really true. It differs from the others, however, in its implication that it might become true. *Ideally* likewise implies a contrast with reality, but in addition makes a value judgment.

Three disjuncts that belong to this sub-set constitute a group of their own: *basically*, *essentially*, and *fundamentally*. These assert that what is being said is true in principle, despite minor qualifications that might be made.

For some colleagues *apparently* can, with certain intonation patterns, have a meaning similar to *only apparently*. For others, including myself, *apparently* is always distinct from *only apparently*, which is roughly equivalent to *ostensibly*.

8.2 Semantic set [2]

Most of the attitudinal disjuncts that have not been included in set [1] convey a judgment about what is being said.

8.2.1 Semantic sub-set [2a]

Disjuncts in sub-set [2a] express the judgment that what is being said is fortunate or unfortunate:

[C2] tragically
[D] sadly
[E] happily, unhappily
[F] fortunately, luckily, unfortunately, unluckily
[others] blessedly

Ominously [C2] presumably belongs here, with its implication of impending adversity. An instance of *blessedly*, a synonym of *fortunately*, appears in the following citation:

Some men got by in less, and by 1951 language-teaching methods had been so streamlined that 10 weeks proved enough for most of the Italians. But the crash course *was* [ital. sic] concentrated. *Blessedly*, our immigrants of the 1960s do not generally need the physical rehabilitation that for ex-inmates of the concentration camps was a condition of survival.

(G 8/11/65: 4, 2)

Blessedly does not belong to any of our correspondence classes, but it may be perceived as corresponding to *it is a blessing* (*that*).

Happily and *unhappily* have been assigned to correspondence class [E] on the grounds that they correspond to:

I am ⎱ happy ⎱ (that)
One is ⎰ unhappy ⎰

However, this assignment is misleading if it suggests they always admit such a correspondence type. *Happily* and *unhappily* are synonyms of *fortunately* and *unfortunately*, respectively. In many contexts it would be far-fetched to suggest that there is any involvement by the speaker which would make it reasonable to ascribe the happiness or unhappiness to him personally. We illustrate this point in the next citation:

Last Wednesday the Committee of the Marylebone Cricket Club took the bold step of asking members for a 50 per cent increase on their present annual subscription of £6. It proved, *unhappily*, to be too bold, because, despite concise representations to 200 members gathered to hear the reasons why, the matter was referred back for further consideration.　(O 24/10/65: 20, 8)

Both *I am unhappy* and *one is unhappy* are inappropriate correspondences in this context. An appropriate correspondence here would be *I am unhappy to say*; the emotive force of *unhappy* is weakened in this expression, the opposite of the conventional *I am happy to say*. It may well be that it would be better to see the structures with *to say* as the regular correspondences to *happily* and *unhappily* since they have wider applicability. In the passage cited next, written by a lawyer, *I am unhappy* is a possible correspondence, but *I am unhappy to say* also corresponds to *unhappily*:

But, it would be an injustice to lawyers as a whole to regard the need for change as a reflection on them. The cost of litigation is, *unhappily*, not caused for the enrichment of lawyers.[1]

(ST 12/6/66: 23, 5)

---

[1] It is interesting that, although unable to predicate a clause, *happy* and *unhappy* are synonymous with *fortunate* and *unfortunate* in certain restricted contexts, e.g.

He was in the *happy* position of owning a house with a large garden.

The results of the child's experiments with chemicals were not always *happy*.

8.2.2   Semantic sub-set [2b]

Disjuncts in sub-set [2b] state that the content of the communication causes satisfaction or the reverse:

[C1] comfortingly, gratifyingly, refreshingly; annoyingly, disappointingly, disturbingly, embitteringly, shamingly
[C2] delightfully; regrettably

Since we have set as a requirement for membership of this sub-class that the disjuncts should be causative, it is not surprising that all of these may be related to verb forms. Those from [C1] are, of course, *-ing* participle forms with the addition of the *-ly* suffix. The relationship between *delightfully* and *regrettably* and the respective verb forms *delight* and *regret* is not so direct, since it is mediated by the adjective forms *delightful* and *regrettable*.

8.2.3   Semantic sub-set [2c]

Disjuncts in the sub-set [2c] convey the attitude that the content of the communication is in some measure strange or unexpected:

[C1] amazingly, astonishingly, astoundingly, bewilderingly, intriguingly, puzzlingly, staggeringly, startlingly, surprisingly
[C2] bizarrely, curiously, eerily, funnily, illogically, inappropriately, incredibly, ironically, miraculously, oddly, paradoxically, remarkably, strangely, suspiciously, unaccountably
[G] absurdly, preposterously, uncharacteristically
[I] unexpectedly, unusually

At an earlier stage of the language *happily* in the sense of *fortunately* could function as an adjunct. The O.E.D. cites this usage in *Henry VIII* and in a work translated into English a century and a half later:

1613 SHAKS. *Hen. VIII*, v. ii. 9, I am glad I came this way so *happily*.
1756–7 tr. *Keysler's Trav.* (1760) II. 421 How *happily* several members of the Arcadian academy have succeeded.

There is no clear citation in the O.E.D. for the use of an adjunct *unhappily* as an antonym to *happily* in the sense given in the above citations.

Luckily, unluckily, happily, unhappily, and *unfortunately* (and, more dubiously, *fortunately*) may be used as adjuncts in the sense of 'appropriately' or 'aptly', though the verbs with which they collocate in this function are probably very few indeed:

He worded his last letter very { unfortunately. / unhappily. / unluckily. / ?fortunately. / happily. / luckily.

Happily and unhappily also function as adjuncts with quite a different meaning:

They lived *happily* ever after.
He paid the bill *unhappily*.

A more refined classification would group these disjuncts into those that say that the content of the communication is surprising, e.g. *amazingly*, and those that say it is peculiar, e.g. *bizarrely*. It is noteworthy that most of the disjuncts in this sub-class have correspondences with both the structure involving predication of a *that*-clause and the structure involving predication of a *for to*-non-finite clause.

8.2.4   Semantic sub-set [2d]

Disjuncts in sub-set [2d] convey that what is being said is in some measure expected or appropriate:

[C1] unsurprisingly
[C2] appropriately, aptly, inevitably, suitably, understandably
[G]   characteristically, typically
[others] naturally, predictably, not unnaturally.

Naturally is equivalent to 'as might have been expected' or 'of course'. It does not correspond to *it is natural (that)* or *it is natural for* (plus non-finite verb clause).

Not unnaturally is a form of litotes for *naturally*, and can be paraphrased in the same way:

By continuing to use the railways while refusing to pay for their upkeep Zambia has tried to have the best of both worlds, and *not unnaturally* the railways board has had to enforce payment. (G 24/5/66: 10, 1)

Not unnaturally does not correspond to:

It is not unnatural (that) the railways board has had to . . .
It is not unnatural for the railways board to have had to . . .

However, *unnaturally* without modifiers or with any modifiers apart from *not* has correspondences of those types:

Unnaturally
Quite unnaturally } these children { hate their parents.
                                   { don't love their parents.

These disjuncts are semantically equivalent to:

It is { unnatural
       { quite unnatural } that these children . . .

It is { unnatural
       { quite unnatural } for these children { to hate . . .
                                              { not to love . . .

Notice that the disjunct *naturally* is not an antonym of the disjunct *unnaturally*. Contrast:

Naturally
Quite naturally } these children { love their parents.
                                 { don't hate their parents.

Naturally has here the usual meaning of the disjunct, i.e. 'of course' or 'as might have been expected'. Although *naturally* exists in English as a disjunct, the disjunct *unnaturally* exists in its own right, and cannot be derived from *naturally* by the addition of a negative prefix. We may compare the more obvious absence of unprefixed forms corresponding to *unexpectedly* and *undoubtedly*. Present-day English does not possess the items **expectedly* or **doubtedly* (cf. page 105). On the other hand, the disjunct *not unnaturally* is best explained as owing its existence to the occurrence of a disjunct *naturally* rather than as a negation of the disjunct *unnaturally*. In its meaning as an understatement for *naturally*, the *not* is obligatory.

8.2.5   Semantic sub-set [2e]

Disjuncts in sub-set [2e] pass judgment on the rightness of the action described:

> [H1] correctly, incorrectly, rightly, unjustly, wrongly
> [others] justly

The disjunct *justly* is a synonym of *rightly*.
In the sentence

> *Justly*, they thought he would escape

justly does not correspond to

> *It was just for* them to think . . .
> *It was just of* them to think . . .
> They *were just to* think . . .

It is, however, semantically equivalent to these structures if *right* is substituted for *just*, e.g.:

> They were right to think . . .

No instances of either *justly* or *unjustly* occur in the material I have examined. I illustrate their use from citations taken from Jacobson (1964, 217). Both are taken from books published in the early 1940s. The citation for *justly* comes from *Hemlock and After* (page 50), a novel by Angus Wilson, and the citation for *unjustly* from *A Short History of English Literature* (page 213) by B. Ifor Evans.

> He had no illusions about his abilities, but believed, *justly*, that he would make as good a target as anyone else for the King's enemies to shoot at.

> His style has an elegance that depends on balance, and is *unjustly* remembered by the few more ponderous phrases that are sometimes quoted against him.

8.2.6 Semantic sub-set [2f]

Disjuncts in this sub-set pass a judgment on the wisdom of the action described or the skill with which it has been performed:

> [H2] artfully, cleverly, cunningly, foolishly, prudently, reasonably, sensibly, shrewdly, unreasonably, unwisely, wisely

This is the only example of a complete one-to-one relation between semantic sub-set and correspondence class.

The remaining attitudinal disjuncts fall into much smaller semantic sub-sets or else are isolated semantically from the others in our material. Three of them – *hopefully* [E], *ideally*, and *preferably* – express the speaker's desire that the content of the communication should be realised. Another three – *conventionally*, *rarely*, *traditionally* (all belonging to class [I]) – comment on the rarity or the reverse of what is contained in the communication. The rest are merely listed:

> [C1] amusingly, interestingly
> [C2] conveniently, crucially, mercifully, relevantly, significantly, topically
> [E] thankfully
> [G] splendidly

Of this list, *mercifully*, *thankfully*, and *splendidly* can be associated with some members of sub-set [2b], e.g. *delightfully*, and with some members of sub-class [2a], e.g. *luckily*, in a grouping which expresses a favourable appreciation of the consequences of what has been communicated.

8.3 Semantic sets and correspondence classes

We are now in a position to venture some generalisations about the correlation of correspondence classes with semantic sets. Semantically, attitudinal disjuncts can be assigned to two major groupings:

> [1] those that convey an attitude towards the truth-value of what is being said, e.g. *clearly, certainly, outwardly*.
> [2] those that convey any other attitudes towards what is being said, e.g. *tragically, delightfully, oddly, rightly*.

A considerable number of disjuncts do not belong to any of the correspondence classes. These include disjuncts that must be assigned to grouping [1], e.g. *seemingly, decidedly, perhaps, ostensibly, outwardly, superficially*, while others must be considered as within grouping [2], e.g. *blessedly, justly, naturally*. Several disjuncts, though not belonging to a correspondence class, have corresponding structures, viz. *ideally, unexpectedly, predictably, preferably, maybe, likely*. If we leave aside the disjuncts that have no correspondences, we may in general point to one feature in possible corresponding structures, the presence or absence of which would distinguish disjuncts in one of the major groupings from those in the other. Those disjuncts that convey an attitude towards the truth-value of the content of the communication do not allow the special use of *should* (cf. pages 89f) in a type [1] correspondence, while the others do. We can contrast:

> *Clearly*, he is behaving badly.
> ≠ *It is clear that* he *should* be behaving badly.
> *Interestingly*, he is behaving badly.
> = *It is interesting that* he *should* be behaving badly.

This test also applies to some of the disjuncts that have correspondences but are not members of the correspondence classes. We can contrast:

> *Maybe* entries are submitted in ink.
> ≠ *It may be that* entries *should* be submitted in ink.
> *Preferably* entries are submitted in ink.
> = *It is preferable that* entries *should* be submitted in ink.

Semantically, of course, *maybe* belongs to the first of our major groupings, while *preferably* belongs to the other. There are three exceptions – *unexpectedly*, *ideally*, and *predictably*. These ought to be in our second grouping, but they require *would* in the constituent clause of their corresponding structures. (See page 108, where *were to* is given as an alternative to *would* for *ideally*.)

If we now turn to the sub-sets of set [1], the disjuncts that express an opinion on the truth-value of what is being said, we find that the semantic distinction between the first two sub-sets [1a(i)] and [1a(ii)] (pages 202ff), represented by *probably* and *obviously* respectively, is paralleled by differences between the distribution of their adjective bases (cf. pages 99ff). However, there are a number of disjuncts in these two sub-sets that do not have adjective bases, e.g. *seemingly*, *indeed*, *perhaps*, *reportedly*. As for the third sub-set, [1b], (page 206), none of the disjuncts (e.g. *nominally*, *ostensibly*, *outwardly*) have correspondences, with the possible exception of *(only) apparently*.

Of the second major grouping, most items in sub-set [2e], e.g. *rightly* (page 210), and sub-set [2f], e.g. *wisely* (page 211), belong to the same correspondence class. The semantic difference between the two sub-sets is paralleled by a difference between the distribution of the adjective bases of the disjuncts (cf. page 104). Otherwise the division into semantic sub-sets for this second major grouping does not tally with the correspondence classes. And, as I have pointed out above, there are a few disjuncts in this grouping that have no correspondences.

Chapter 9

Attitudinal disjuncts and other form-classes

Some instances of other form-classes function very similarly to attitudinal disjuncts. I examine examples of these in this chapter as well as some instances of correspondences where the syntactic relationship to the clause may be different.

9.1 Adjectives

In its relationship to the clause an adjective in initial position may be semantically equivalent to an attitudinal disjunct with the same adjective as base (cf. page 127). This applies, in particular, to most of the adjective bases of attitudinal disjuncts that appear in the corresponding frame:

It is ADJECTIVE BASE (*that*) CLAUSE.

The adjective base can appear in front of the clause with the omission of *it is*, e.g.:

Strange, it was she, Dinah, who had dreamed always of living in the country, ... (6.1.17-3)

Arthur Brackman, formerly a reporter on the 'New York Herald Tribune', is 61, though he hardly looks it, greying, quite heavily lined face – *not surprising* since he has been in newspapers over 35 years and runs a photographic agency with branches in many countries. (G 15/3/66: 10, 6)

These adjectives can be analysed syntactically as superordinate clauses to which the related clauses are subordinated. If we analyse them in that way, then they are elliptical verbless clauses, with zero *It is*. They differ from disjuncts in that they are immobile, and in that the zero elements (including the optional *that*) can be supplied. Moreover, they allow an indirect question to follow. Contrast:

> *Strange* how she always dreamed of living in the country.
> *Strangely how she always dreamed of living in the country.

This potentiality indicates most strongly that the clause is dependent on *strange*, since an indirect question would normally be a subordinate clause, unless it was being used as a heading or title (cf. page 184).[1]

Another analysis would relate the adjective to a clause with zero *What is*:

> *What is* ADJECTIVE, CLAUSE

e.g.:   *Strange*, it was she, Dinah, who dreamed . . .
        What is strange, it was she, Dinah, who dreamed . . .

This clause can be seen, in turn, to correspond to a clause in equative relationship with the following clause:

> *What is* ADJECTIVE *is* (*that*) CLAUSE

Our example would then give us the corresponding clause:

> *What is strange is* (*that*) it was she, Dinah, who dreamed . . .

In this analysis, *what* is a 'clausal relative' obligatory for a 'relative clause' in initial position, corresponding to *which*, a 'clausal relative' obligatory for a 'relative clause' in final position:

> It was she, Dinah, who dreamed . . ., *which is strange*.

If we analyse the adjective in this way, it would be an elliptical verbless clause (with zero *What is*) subordinate to the following clause. This analysis has the advantage of bringing the adjective close to the subordinate status of the disjunct.[2]

---

[1] It is worth mentioning here that there are several other circumstances in which an attitudinal disjunct is not possible though predication of the clause by the adjective base is possible or, of course, the rearrangement of this predication in the *It*-inversion structure:
  (1) where indications of tense or modality are required:
      That we have a grave problem on our hands *may have been obvious*.
      It may have been obvious that we have a grave problem on our hands.
  (2) where the 'evaluation' itself is questioned:
      Is it obvious that we have a grave problem on our hands?
  (3) when some modifiers are required:
      It is suddenly obvious that we have a grave problem on our hands.
[2] We notice that in our two citations on page 213, only *strange* can be replaced by a *what*-clause, *what is strange*. *Not surprising* can only be replaced by *which is not surprising*. It is subordinate to the previous clause, while the following *since*-clause is in turn subordinate to *not surprising*.

We have shown that one adjective, *likely*, can function as a disjunct when modified (cf. page 110). As a disjunct, it is of course mobile. *True*, although probably still generally positioned before the clause, seems to be on the way to the status of a disjunct since it appears to be becoming acceptable in final position and could occur parenthetically within the clause. However, it differs from *likely* in that it can only occur within the clause parenthetically. Contrast:

They have *quite likely* reached the top of the mountain by now.
They have (*true*) reached the top of the mountain by now.

Adjective Groups with the comparatives *more* or *most* may also be semantically equivalent to attitudinal disjuncts that have the same adjective bases and are similarly modified, e.g.

Altogether the shares put on 1*s* 3*d* to 14*s* 6d and are now a hefty 61 per cent above the year's low. *More remarkable still*, the 'A' have completely outpaced the Ordinary shares, only 39 per cent up. (O 14/11/65: 8, 2)

Behind the scenes, his was the most powerful voice in Afrikaner commerce and industry. *In many ways most important of all*, he dominated the secret and powerful Broederbond society ...
(G 7/9/66: 8, 3)

The director, Mr J. B. Ward-Perkins, has himself taken part. *Even more important*, he and successive deputy directors and librarians have put their knowledge at the disposal of the organizers.
(TES 12/11/65: 1035, 5)

In the above passages *more remarkable*, *most important*, and *more important* can be replaced, without changing the meaning, by the attitudinal disjuncts *more remarkably*, *most importantly*, and *more importantly* respectively. The adjective groups can be analysed as elliptical clauses with either zero *It is* or zero *What is* (cf. page 60 for *better* and *worse*).

9.2 Nominal group

The nominal group *no doubt* functions as a disjunct, e.g.:

It was *no doubt* clever of him, ...   (G 23/2/67: 16, 6)

It is semantically closer to *doubtless* (cf. page 203) and lacks the conviction of *there is no doubt*, which might be thought to correspond to it.
    On the other hand, *no wonder* is restricted to initial position, as in the following citation:

No wonder General Suharto was cautious.   (G 23/2/67: 8, 2)

If we replace *no doubt* by *no wonder* in the earlier citation, the sentence becomes unacceptable:

   *It was *no wonder* clever of him.

No wonder is like a number of nominal groups or nouns in initial position that can be analysed as superordinate clauses to which the related clauses are subordinated. They are elliptical clauses with zero *It is*, and sometimes the article is also ellipted, e.g.:

   Pity he didn't buy it.
   A wonder he doesn't complain.
   A good job they were insured.

9.3 Finite verb clauses

Finite verb clauses introduced by the relatives *what* and *which* may be disjunctive (cf. page 214). An instance appears in the material examined:

   Governors have gone on courses to learn about social casework and *what is most significant of all*, among the ordinary discipline staff there has been a dramatic shift towards desiring to take an active part in counselling.   (O 24/10/65: 11, 5)

What is most significant can be replaced by *most significant* and *most significantly* with no perceptible effect on meaning. *What is most significant* and *most significantly* are both subordinate to the related clause, whereas *most significant* may be interpreted as an elliptical clause and, like *it is most significant*, as superordinate (cf. pages 213f.).

We also notice the correspondence relationship between attitudinal disjuncts and non-restrictive relative clauses of the form '*which is* ADJECTIVE', when the adjective is identical to the adjective base of the disjunct and *which* refers to the whole preceding superordinate clause, e.g.:

   He is very happy, *surprisingly*.
   He is very happy, *which is surprising*.

This type of correspondence does not appear to be available for attitudinal disjuncts that judge the truth-value of what is being said, e.g.:

   He is very happy, *certainly*.
   *He is very happy, *which is certain*.

although it is available if the disjunct is also concerned with the perception of what is being said, e.g.:

   He is very happy, *obviously*.
   He is very happy, *which is obvious*.

9.4 Non-finite verb clause

To be sure is the only instance of a non-finite verb clause in the material examined that functions like an attitudinal disjunct:

> This, so far as the public record goes (and the public record keeps changing), is the Constitution worked out in HMS Tiger, which would leave the whites in control of Rhodesia for the foreseeable future and a withdrawal of the pledge not to grant independence before majority rule had been achieved. *To be sure,* Mr Wilson has promised to consult the Commonwealth first about the latter part of the deal, but he may calculate that with every month that passes the African section of the Commonwealth, preoccupied with internal crises, carries less weight.
>
> (G 13/7/67: 6, 1)

The difference in nuance between *to be sure* and *surely* is that *surely* adds to the expression of firm conviction an invitation to agreement on the part of the person or persons addressed (cf. page 130). *To be sure* has a concessive force similar to *certainly* (cf. page 141).

9.5 Prepositional phrases

Some prepositional phrases that function like attitudinal disjuncts incorporate an abstract noun that has the same stem as a disjunct. Many of them take the form *to* plus nominal in the possessive plus abstract noun, e.g. *to my bewilderment, to our (great) happiness*. These correspond to range-specified disjuncts, e.g. *to my bewilderment* corresponds to *bewilderingly for me* (but cf. *surprisingly* and its synonyms, page 126).

Some illustrations of such prepositional phrases are given:

> *To Pätsch's astonishment,* the Minister of the Interior assured the Bundestag that secrecy of telephone and mail was strictly observed. (O 24/10/65: 4, 1)

> Week by week, we cleared the office, keeping only those few products which were definitely hopeful. But *much to our dismay,* week by week the council's very conscientious officers searched around for objects to fill it up again. (G 16/5/67: 6, 5)

> *To the surprise of hardened administrators* almost all have chosen to teach in primary schools and nearly half have opted for infants. (TES 5/11/65: 973, 4)

As an illustration of the difference between adjunctive and disjunctive functions of prepositional phrases, let us contrast:

> *To my relief,* the soldiers came in time.
> The soldiers came in time *to my relief.*

The first sentence may be paraphrased by 'It was a relief to me that the soldiers came in time', whereas the second sentence corresponds to 'The soldiers came in time to relieve me'. We notice that the prepositional phrase in the second sentence can be the focus of interrogation, negation, cleft sentence, and clause comparison. It may be focused by restrictives, additives and *not* in initial position, and will then make Verb-Subject inversion obligatory:

> Only ⎫
> Also ⎬ to my relief did the soldiers come.
> Not ⎭

These are features that we have noted do not apply to attitudinal disjuncts (cf. pages 113ff.).

In some cases the nouns derive from verb stems or have cognate verbs, so that the prepositional phrase corresponds to a clause, e.g. *to my bewilderment* has the correspondence *it bewilders me* (*that*) and *I am bewildered* (*that*). Examples of such correspondences are set out in Table 15). The pronominal forms for third person plural (*they*, *their*, *them*) are used to illustrate the correspondences.

Annoyingly in Table 15 exemplifies the pattern for correspondence class [C1].[1] Otherwise, the information from Table 15 does not lend itself to generalisation.

A number of prepositional phrases parallel to disjuncts of classes [E] and [F] contain abstract nouns that have no related verbs, e.g. *to my (great) happiness, to my good fortune, to my misfortune*.

I give a number of examples of other prepositional phrases that function like attitudinal disjuncts:

> *In all likelihood*, however, the custom that seems likeliest to survive is that which marked Harlow's (and everybody else's) weekend festivity. (G 29/8/66: 3, 1)

> Since it seems that what America does today Britain does tomorrow, we had better be ready for the 'psychedelic evangelics' – ready, *for preference*, with a rational response.
>   (ST 31/7/66: 33, 4)

> North Vietnamese leaders have frequently been accused of overestimating the effectiveness of opposition in the United States to the American in the war in Vietnam – and *with justice*, if we may believe the accounts of visitors to Hanoi like Mr James Cameron. (G 23/4/66: 8, 1)

---

[1] *Refreshingly*, which belongs to class [C1], is an exception. There is no *to their refreshment* to correspond to *refreshingly for them*. The probable reason is that *refreshment* usually has a concrete meaning.

TABLE 15 *Disjunctive prepositional phrases and their correspondences*

disjunct	prep. phrase	active animate	passive animate	cataphoric IT
			subject of *finite-verb clause*	
refreshingly	—	—	—	—
regrettably	to their regret	they regret (that)	—	—
—	to their joy	they rejoice (that)	—	—
annoyingly	to their annoyance	—	they are annoyed (that)	it annoys them (that)
—	to their relief	—	they are relieved (that)	it relieves them (that)
—	to their grief	they grieve (that)	they are grieved (that)	it grieves them (that)
delightfully	to their delight	they delight (that)	they are delighted (that)	it delights them (that)

> *Without doubt*, his successor, John Denison, will carry on the good
> work.   (G 8/11/65: 7, 6)

These correspond respectively to the attitudinal disjuncts *very likely*,
preferably, *justly*, and *undoubtedly*. Others have no corresponding disjuncts, e.g.:

> No undergraduate bookmaker is laying much in the way of odds
> as to who might win. *On the face of things* the Conservatives
> proliferate, but there is no guarantee that Mr Iain Macleod will
> follow into office colleagues like Lord Butler and Mr Quintin
> Hogg.   (G 8/11/65: 4, 8)

> *On paper* Super Sam was a good contender. *In the event* he was a
> bad last.   (O 14/11/65: 18, 3)

> *Of course*, nobody believes the decline of the Labour Party in
> Smethwick is entirely due to the immigrant problem.   (8fa.1-10)

> This corresponds to tracing out the curve from P to C and then
> back to P, so that C is *in fact* a 'natural end' to the curve.
>
> (8a.3.30-3)

Chapter 10

Correspondences and transformations

My investigation of correspondence classes has been influenced by transformational-generative grammar, in which a central place is given to the concept of transformational rules (cf. Chomsky 1965, 128ff.). Since, however, I have not attempted to present my observations within the framework of this theory of grammar, I have preferred to coin a new term, *correspondence*, rather than adopt the term *transformation* with the specific sense it has acquired in the theory. This chapter illustrates some of the problems that need to be taken into account if one wishes to describe the material in the terms of transformational-generative grammar.

10.1 Productivity of transformational processes

From the evidence to be presented in this chapter it is clear that if transformational rules are formulated to account for disjuncts it will also be necessary to account for many exceptions. The type of rule that can be applied approximates to the semi-productive rule about which Bendix writes: 'The latter [generative] type of rule can in theory be applied automatically whereas the semi-productive rule requires additional knowledge of the morphological relation between a given B-noun and its counterpart before it can be applied' (Bendix 1966, 57 note 10). In general, the correspondences in this study are instances of *quasi-transformations*, in the sense that this term has been used by Harris (1957, 330ff.). Individual morphemes have to be specified to satisfy the condition for a transformational relationship.

10.1.1 Correspondence type [1]
Let us first consider the relationship of attitudinal disjuncts to correspondence type [1] (cf. page 94) as resulting from a transformation,

disregarding whether another correspondence type applies too. The transformational rule can be informally expressed by the following notation:

$$\left.\begin{array}{l} \textit{that}^\frown S^\frown \textit{is}^\frown \text{adjective} \\ \textit{it is}^\frown \text{adjective}^\frown (\textit{that})\ S \end{array}\right\} \rightarrow \text{adjective} + \textit{ly}^\frown S$$

The rule would account, for example, for the derivation of the attitudinal disjunct *obviously* in the sentence *Obviously he didn't write* from *is obvious* and *it is obvious (that)*.[1]

However, this transformational rule does not have general validity. Failure to produce an attitudinal disjunct by means of this transformation can, to some extent, be classified:

(i) the functional position has been pre-empted by a style disjunct, e.g.:

$$It's\ \left\{\begin{array}{l} \textit{serious} \\ \textit{confidential} \end{array}\right\}\ (\textit{that})\ \text{he hasn't a job.}$$

does not produce a semantically equivalent:

$$\left.\begin{array}{l} \textit{Seriously,} \\ \textit{Confidentially,} \end{array}\right\}\ \text{he hasn't a job.}$$

Seriously and *confidentially* can only be style disjuncts here, equivalent to *seriously speaking* and *confidentially speaking*. This is mentioned as a possible explanation. If it accounts for the failure of the transformational process to apply in these cases, then we must assume that there is a 'disjunct slot' in the structure of the sentence. When it is occupied by a style disjunct it is not available to an attitudinal disjunct and *vice versa*. However, ambiguity between style disjunct and attitudinal disjunct can occur when the disjunct is premodified by a comparative. For example, *more seriously*, though probably not *more confidentially*, can function as an attitudinal disjunct:

He hasn't any money. *More seriously*, he hasn't a job.

More seriously may be ambiguous between style disjunct and attitudinal disjunct, as in the following example though sufficient context may resolve the ambiguity:

More seriously Bernstein takes a more heavyweight view of the finale than the Danish conductor Tuxen who directs the existing Decca version of the symphony.   (G 8/11/65: 7, 4)

(Cf. also *more clearly* and *more plainly*, pages 205f.)

(ii) the functional position has been pre-empted by a conjunct:

It's incidental (that) he hasn't a job.

---

[1] For the purpose of this discussion, the relationship between the two forms *It is obvious (that) he didn't write* and *That he didn't write is obvious* can be ignored.

does not produce a semantically equivalent:

Incidentally, he hasn't a job.

If this explanation and that advanced in (iii) account for the failure of the transformational processes to apply, then the 'functional slot' admits more than just disjuncts (cf. *incidentally* as conjunct, pages 54f.).

(iii) the functional position has been pre-empted by the initiator
    well (cf. page 27)

It's good (*that*) he hasn't a job.

does not produce a semantically equivalent:

Well, he hasn't a job.

(iv) there is no *-ly* form corresponding to the adjective, or it is rare,
    e.g.

It's lovely (*that*) he hasn't lost his job.

where the attested form *lovelily* is not in common use, and in any case does not seem acceptable as attitudinal disjunct.

We might conveniently mention here *likely* which has no corresponding form *likelily*. Of course, *likely* itself functions as an attitudinal disjunct, but only when premodified.

Other cases where the previous explanations do not apply include:

$$\text{It's} \begin{Bmatrix} bad \\ nice \\ false \\ hard \\ sufficient \end{Bmatrix} (that) \text{ he hasn't a job.}$$

which do not produce corresponding disjuncts:

$$\begin{rcases} *Badly, \\ *Nicely, \\ *Falsely, \\ *Hardly, \\ *Sufficiently, \end{rcases} \text{ he hasn't a job.}$$

10.1.2   Correspondence type [3]

Let us now consider the relationship of the disjuncts to correspondence type [3] (cf. page 94) as resulting from a transformation. We again disregard whether another correspondence type will apply as well. The transformational rule can be expressed:

$$\begin{rcases} one\ is \\ I\ am \end{rcases} {}^{\frown}\text{adjective}^{\frown}(that)\ S \rightarrow \text{adjective} + ly^{\frown}S$$

This rule would account, for example, for the derivation of the attitudinal disjunct *thankfully* in the sentence *Thankfully, he didn't do it*
from *I am thankful* or *one is thankful* (*that*).

Adjectives that are semantically close to the adjective bases of attitudinal disjuncts in correspondence classes [B], [D], and [E] (cf. pages
97f.) have been selected to demonstrate the very restricted applicability
of this rule.

$$\begin{matrix} One\ is \\ I\ am \end{matrix} \left\{ \begin{matrix} glad \\ grateful \\ confident \end{matrix} \right\} (that)\ he\ hasn't\ lost\ it.$$

do not produce:

$$\left. \begin{matrix} *Gladly \\ *Gratefully \\ *Confidently, \end{matrix} \right\} he\ hasn't\ lost\ it.$$

It might be argued that the existence of homonymous adjuncts for
these three items, adjuncts that may occur in initial position if only
in an affirmative form of the clause, has inhibited the production of
disjuncts. However, to take but one example, *sadly* can function both as
a disjunct and as an adjunct in initial position (cf. pages 186f.). In one
of the Survey texts the adjunct *sadly* appears in initial position:

Tea dripped steadily from the hem of her dress to the pavement;
sadly he rubbed it in with his foot. (6.2.96-2)

It may be convenient to refer at this point to correspondence classes
[H], e.g. *rightly*, and [I], e.g. *unusually*. Neither correspondence type
[1] nor correspondence type [3] applies to disjuncts in these two classes.
However, type [2] applies (cf. page 94). If we formulate a transformational-generative rule to account for the relationship of disjuncts to
correspondence type [2] it would also account for items like *usually* and
commonly that we have expressly excluded from the class of disjuncts
(cf. pages 178ff.).

If, however, we consider the potentiality for allowing more than one
correspondence type, it is interesting to note that there do not appear
to be any other items with the same correspondence potentialities as
members of class [H]. In addition to type [2], this class often allows
types [4] and [5] in certain circumstances (cf. pages 95f.). It will be
recalled that class [H] is a relatively closed class, consisting of two
semantic sub-sets of attitudinal disjuncts (cf. pages 210f.).

10.1.3   Correspondences for class [J]

Most of the disjuncts in correspondence class [J] have two correspondences, although only one is available to *undoubtedly* (cf. page 105). The
transformational rule that will include *undoubtedly* can be expressed:

$$\left. \begin{matrix} that \frown S \frown is \frown V\ ed \\ it\ is \frown V\ ed \frown (that)\ S \end{matrix} \right\} \rightarrow V\ ed + ly \frown S$$

This rule would account, for example, for the derivation of *reportedly* in the sentence *Reportedly, he has left London* from *It is reported (that)* or the matrix sentence *is reported*. However, there are many participles semantically similar to the participle bases of disjuncts of correspondence class [J] that can appear in the constructions on the left-hand side of the rule yet do not have derived attitudinal disjuncts. For example, there are participles that may appear in both constructions, though I illustrate them with the first only:

That they have taken the job *is* $\begin{cases} \textit{implied.} \\ \textit{announced.} \\ \textit{not questioned.} \\ \textit{acknowledged.} \\ \textit{rumoured.} \end{cases}$

However, there are no derived disjuncts:

$\left. \begin{array}{l} *\textit{Impliedly,} \\ *\textit{Announcedly,} \\ *\textit{Unquestionedly,} \\ *\textit{Acknowledgedly,} \\ *\textit{Rumouredly,} \end{array} \right\}$ they have taken the job.

There are some participles that seem acceptable only in the second construction:

It is $\begin{cases} \textit{judged} \\ \textit{said} \\ \textit{argued} \end{cases}$ (*that*) they have taken the job.

With these too there are no derived disjuncts:

$\left. \begin{array}{l} *\textit{Judgedly,} \\ *\textit{Saidly,} \\ *\textit{Arguedly,} \end{array} \right\}$ they have taken the job.[1]

10.1.4 Style disjuncts
In §4.1 (pages 82f.) we have set out various correspondences to style disjuncts. If we consider these correspondences as source sentences and

---

[1] It might be argued that the production of *unquestionedly* and *arguedly* has been inhibited by the existence in the language of the disjuncts *unquestionably* and *arguably*, which occupy a semantic and syntactic gap in the language. But we have in English two analogous co-existing disjuncts, *undoubtedly* and *indubitably*. We set out the difference, from a transformational point of view:

   it is indubitable (that) → indubitably : it is not doubted (that) → undoubtedly
   it is unquestionable (that) → unquestionably : it is not questioned (that) → *unquestionedly
   it is arguable (that) → arguably : it is argued (that) *arguedly.

formulate a rule for generating style disjuncts from them, we shall find that it will include many items that are unacceptable as style disjuncts.

There are no disjuncts *concisely, convincingly, honourably, humorously, unflatteringly*, although these formal items will fit into transformational frames as adjuncts in the same way as *briefly* or *honestly*, which do occur as style disjuncts:

$$\text{I would say} \atop \text{I tell you} \left\{ \begin{array}{l} \text{concisely} \\ \text{convincingly} \\ \text{honourably} \\ \text{humorously} \\ \text{unflatteringly} \end{array} \right\} \text{(that)} \ldots$$

or:

$$\text{If I may speak} \atop \text{If I may put it} \left\{ \begin{array}{l} \text{concisely} \\ \text{convincingly} \\ \text{honourably} \\ \text{humorously} \\ \text{unflatteringly} \end{array} \right\} \text{I would say (that)} \ldots$$

Indeed their adjective bases would occur in the additional type of potential source sentence:

$$\text{If I may be} \left\{ \begin{array}{l} \text{concise} \\ \text{convincing} \\ \text{honourable} \\ \text{humorous} \\ \text{unflattering} \end{array} \right\} \text{I would say (that)} \ldots$$

Furthermore, they will all serve as adjuncts in non-finite verb clauses that function as style disjuncts:

$$\text{To put it} \atop \text{Putting it} \left\{ \begin{array}{l} \text{concisely} \\ \text{convincingly} \\ \text{honourably} \\ \text{humorously} \\ \text{unflatteringly} \end{array} \right\}$$

With *clearly* and *plainly* we have the reverse of what we noticed for *seriously* and *confidentially* (cf. page 222). *Clearly* and *plainly* are attitudinal disjuncts, not style disjuncts. Nevertheless, there exists in the language the potential source sentence:

$$\textit{If I may speak} \left\{ \begin{array}{l} \textit{clearly} \\ \textit{plainly} \end{array} \right\} \textit{I would say (that} \ldots$$

and we have non-finite verb clauses with the same morpheme that function like style disjuncts: *clearly speaking, plainly speaking*, and *to be (quite) clear, to be (quite) plain*. Further, *more clearly* and *more plainly* may be style disjuncts rather than attitudinal disjuncts (cf. page 205).[1]

10.1.5 Extreme cases of unproductivity

Some extreme cases of unproductivity have been listed in §5.1.4 (pages 108ff.), e.g. *predictably* and *preferably*.

10.1.6 A productive sub-class: [C1]

Sub-class [C1] is exceptional. It seems that all participles ending in *-ing* that enter the frame *it is* participle *(that)* have a corresponding attitudinal disjunct. Some of these disjuncts have been listed on pages 97f. Many more can easily be added to that list and will function acceptably as disjuncts, even if they are not very common in usage:

$$\left.\begin{array}{l}\text{Demoralisingly}\\\text{Horrifyingly}\\\text{Maddeningly}\\\text{Shatteringly}\\\text{Terrifyingly}\end{array}\right\}\text{he hasn't taken that job.}$$

We can therefore formulate a transformational-generative rule, expressed informally as:

$$\left.\begin{array}{l}\text{that}\frown\text{S}\frown\text{is}\frown\text{V ing}\\\text{it is}\frown\text{V ing}\frown\text{(that) S}\end{array}\right\}\rightarrow\text{V ing}+\text{ly}\frown\text{S}$$

10.2 Difference and sameness in transformational history

(1) Some attitudinal disjuncts cannot be derived from a transformation to account for their relationship to sentences, but nevertheless they have the same function as those to which a derivation can be assigned. We may cite as an example *decidedly*. This disjunct is roughly synonymous with *undoubtedly* and possesses the same syntactic features. But whereas we might derive *undoubtedly* from some underlying structure with, for example *it is not doubted (that)*, it does not seem possible to provide such a derivation for *decidedly*. In some cases the lack of an underlying structure of this form in a synchronic analysis

---

1 *Truly* is exceptional in having as correspondences both *it is true (that)* and correspondences available to style disjuncts. They are both semantically equivalent to the disjunct. *Truly* has been assigned to the sub-class of style disjuncts because it may appear in front of a question, e.g.:

'I think that's a shameful plea,' said Treece. 'I really do. *Truly*, what do we live for?' (6.2.107–1)

None of the attitudinal disjuncts with a type (1) correspondence appears before a question, whereas this position is acceptable for style disjuncts (page 84). In the above citation, *truly* corresponds to *tell me truly* and not to *it is true (that)*.

can be explained as the result of a semantic shift that would be registered in a diachronic analysis. This may be true of *assuredly, decidedly*
and *apparently*, for example (cf. pages 203, 204, 206).

(2) On the other hand, there are some attitudinal disjuncts to which
we can assign different transformational derivations, but which nevertheless have the same syntactic features. A striking example would be
the three synonyms *sadly, unhappily* and *unfortunately*, which belong
to correspondence classes [D], [E], and [F] respectively (cf. pages
98, 102, 206f.).

(3) There are cases where we could assign more than one derivation
and there are no compelling reasons for preferring a particular one.
The point is best exemplified by the several possible correspondences
for style disjuncts. In addition, different derivations would seem to
be needed for style disjuncts in declarative sentences and for their
two interpretations in interrogative sentences (cf. §4.1, pages 82f.).

(4) There are items that could be said to be derived from an underlying structure of the same form but which differ syntactically. Thus,
usually and *normally* may be derived in the same way as *unusually*
and *traditionally*. But because of differences in their syntactic features
we have assigned *usually* and *normally* to the status of adjuncts, while
we have classed *unusually* and *traditionally* among the disjuncts (cf.
pages 173ff.).

(5) The potentialities for modification of attitudinal disjuncts may
differ, although the disjuncts may be said to have the same transformational history. Some examples will clarify what is meant.

Quite certainly is acceptable, but not *quite surely*:

$$\left.\begin{array}{l}\textit{Quite certainly}\\ \textit{*Quite surely}\end{array}\right\} \text{he has acted hastily.}$$

Nevertheless, in the possible source sentence both of the base adjectives
allow premodification by *quite*:

$$\begin{array}{l}\textit{One is}\\ \textit{I am}\end{array}\left\{\begin{array}{l}\textit{quite certain}\\ \textit{quite sure}\end{array}\right\} \textit{(that)} \text{ he has acted hastily.}$$

Again, *not* can freely premodify *surprisingly* when it is in initial position,
but is less acceptable as premodifier of *astonishingly*:

$$\left.\begin{array}{l}\textit{Not surprisingly,}\\ \textit{?Not astonishingly,}\end{array}\right\} \text{they were pleased with their efforts.}$$

Yet the two disjuncts are synonyms and both of the base adjectives can
be premodified by *not* in the possible source sentence:

$$\textit{It is not}\left\{\begin{array}{l}\textit{surprising}\\ \textit{astonishing}\end{array}\right\} \textit{(that)} \text{ they were pleased with their efforts.}$$

Enough is frequently used as a postmodifier of attitudinal disjuncts (cf. page 122). However, its meaning is quite different when it post-modifies the adjective bases of the disjuncts. We can contrast

> *Curiously enough,* he does not insist on his rights.

where *curiously enough* may be paraphrased as 'curious though it may seem', and

> *It is curious enough (that)* he does not insist on his rights.

where *curious enough* may be paraphrased 'sufficiently curious'.

(6) There is often the possibility of a specification of the range of an attitudinal disjunct (cf. §.5.2.4, pages 125ff.). Certain differences occur in this respect that are not paralleled by differences in transformational history. The range of *surprisingly* and its synonyms may only be specified in respect to the Subject of the clause to which they are related, whereas for other disjuncts there are no restrictions (cf. page 126). Yet there does not appear to be any difference in derivation between *surprisingly* and, for example, *annoyingly*. There is no difference, moreover, between the prepositional phrases corresponding to these that function as disjuncts:

> *To his father's surprise,* } John failed the exam.
> *To his father's annoyance,* }

Both may be related to a passive Subject:

> His father is { *surprised* } that John failed the exam.
> { *annoyed* }

Nevertheless, there is the distinction in acceptability between:

> **Surprisingly* } *for his father,* John failed the exam.
> *Annoyingly* }

10.3 Other data to be taken into account

(1) The members of one of the correspondence classes established on the basis of more than one correspondence, class [H] represented by *rightly* and *wisely*, have limitations on their co-occurrence potentialities. It seems, however, easier to apply semantic rules to account for the restrictions than to establish rules for sub-categorisation of verbs (cf. pages 154ff.).

(2) One feature has been shown to be capable of distinguishing between two major semantic groupings of attitudinal disjuncts, namely the acceptance or non-acceptance of the special use of *should* in a corresponding structure (cf. pages 98f., 212). This feature (which of course only applies if the disjunct has a corresponding structure) can presumably be incorporated in the transformational history of the two classes of attitudinal disjuncts.

Chapter 11

Conclusions

In the course of this book we have looked at sets of linguistic units that we have termed 'conjuncts' and 'disjuncts'. These have usually been treated as belonging to the class of adverbs. We have been primarily concerned with the ways in which they relate syntactically to features of the clause. Accordingly the analysis has included within its scope potential features. The units have been defined by their syntactic potentialities as contrasted with those of other units. Since many of them have homonyms with different functions, we have been compelled to take account of the differences between the homonyms.

Three diagnostic criteria were set up to distinguish conjuncts and disjuncts from adverbs having other functions: (1) their acceptability in initial position in an independent tone unit with certain nuclear tones when the clause is negated, (2) their inability to be the focus of clause interrogation, and (3) their inability to be the focus of clause negation (page 24). Adverbs thus separated were then assigned to two major classes on the basis of one criterion: whether they could serve as the response to a *yes-no* question together with *yes* or *no*. Those that could not serve as a response were classed as conjuncts, while those that could were classed as disjuncts (page 25). Disjuncts were in turn divided into two sub-classes, style disjuncts and attitudinal disjuncts (pages 81f., 94). Adverbs not assigned to the classes of conjuncts and disjuncts were termed 'adjuncts' (page 24).

It was found necessary to distinguish conjuncts that are immobile in initial position from other items with the same feature, in particular from conjunctions (pages 27ff.). Initial position, indeed, is the favoured position for both conjuncts and disjuncts (pages 78 and 191).

It has been noticed that other form-classes may have similar functions to conjuncts and disjuncts (cf. for conjuncts pages 46, 53f., 57, 58, 62, 69, 75, 77; for style disjuncts, §4.4, pages 90ff.; for attitudinal disjuncts, Chapter 9, pages 213ff.). Many of the examples that were brought share a morpheme with a conjunct or disjunct.

Most disjuncts may be given a formalised paraphrase, which was termed a 'correspondence' (page 7). The various types of correspondences were displayed for style disjuncts in §4.1 (pages 82f.) and for attitudinal disjuncts in §5.1 (pages 94ff.). Some conjuncts were also shown to have correspondences (pages 44, 47, 57, 59, 60).

Although the correspondence relationships were not treated in terms of transformational-generative grammar, some observations were made with respect to the formulation of tranformational rules to account for the relationships (Chapter 10). It was seen, in any case that a classification based on correspondence relationships does not coincide completely with one based on syntactic features (pages 227, 108ff.), nor does it coincide completely with a semantic classification (pages 211f.).

Equally, a semantic classification does not coincide with a syntactic classification. If we said, for example, that conjuncts were items that linked two clauses, we should have to class them semantically with conjunctions. As Sweet (1891, 143) puts it: 'The difference between half- and full conjunctions is that half-conjunctions connect logically only, not formally also, as full conjunctions do.'[1] A further example can be brought of a semantic criterion, this time for disjuncts, that would not coincide with a syntactic classification. Poldauf (1964, 251), in contrasting the differences between Czech and English in the ways they express 'the evaluation of the form of a communication', states that English more easily associates these expressions with suitable bits of the communication. As an example he cites *downright* in *That's downright nonsense*. This, however, would not be a disjunct in our classification, because (amongst other things) *downright* cannot be moved to initial position in an independent tone unit.

It has been demonstrated (cf. Chapter 6,) that we cannot rely merely on features that happen to be present for the classification we have proposed. We cannot distinguish between disjuncts or conjuncts and their homonyms solely by features of position or of intonation and punctuation, although for given items their function may be unambiguous in a given context if the items are in certain positions or are accompanied by certain intonation or punctuation features. In potentially ambiguous cases, the ambiguity is usually resolved by the context. In the course of speech we appear to distinguish between two or more functions on the basis of the probability of a particular semantic interpretation.

In an immediate-constituent analysis, it would be reasonable to make

---

[1] Sweet gives as examples of half-conjunctions the conjuncts *still* and *nevertheless*.

the first cut between the conjunct or disjunct and the rest of the clause (cf. Jacobson 1964, 15). This would account for the application of such terms as 'sentence modifier' or 'sentence adverb' to these items (cf. page 2). The term 'sentence adverbial' has been adopted by those writing within the framework of the theory of transformational-generative grammar (e.g. Katz and Postal 1964, 77 and Chomsky 1965, 102). However, the criteria by which the sentence adverbials may be distinguished from other adverbials has so far not been made explicit.

Chomsky refers to sentence adverbials incidentally when discussing a modified version of some of the first rules of the base:

(i) S → NP⁀Predicate-Phrase
(ii) Predicate-Phrase → Aux⁀VP (Place) (Time)

He has excluded Place and Time Adverbials from the Verb Phrase, but leaves open a decision whether these adverbials should be associated with the full Predicate-Phrase (as in his rewriting rule) or whether they should be associated with the Auxiliary or with 'Sentence Adverbials which form a 'pre-Sentence' unit in the underlying structure' (Chomsky 1965, 102). He is in doubt, accordingly, about whether the major distinction between adverbials should be binary or ternary. Earlier in the same work (Chomsky 1965, 72), he gives a rewriting rule which contains what we may presume is a sentence adverbial, though he does not name it as such:

S → Adverbial⁀NP⁀Aux⁀VP   (*Naturally, John will leave*)

This rule could be represented by a tree in which Adverbial would be directly dominated by S:

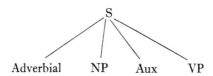

Writing within the framework of the theory of transformational-generative grammar, Kuroda suggests that *also* and *even* should be attached to the whole sentence in the basic representation (Kuroda 1966). He wishes to introduce the phrase-structure rule:

$$S \to \begin{Bmatrix} even \\ also \end{Bmatrix} \ NP \ \ VP$$

There would then be an optional attachment transformation to adjoin *even* and *also* to a particular clause constituent. It is curious that Kuroda does not mention the conjunct *also* in the course of his discussion (cf.

pages 49ff.), although he writes of *also* modifying the whole sentence (b) in the discourse represented by the pair of sentences:

(a) The storm destroyed his house.
(b) The flood *also* devastated his farm.

It is reasonable to assume that the conjunct *also* would likewise not be dominated by the nodes NP and VP. If we follow Kuroda's suggestion for the treatment of the adjunct *also*, there are two possible phrase-structure rules for a sentence with the conjunct *also*:

Also, the flood devastated his farm.

The first solution would be for the conjunct to be dominated by S. It would not, however, be like the adjunct, because there would not be an optional attachment transformation. The phrase structure rule would be:

S → (conjunct *also*) (adjunct *also*) NP VP

This is represented by the tree:

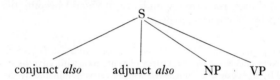

However, from the point of view of transformational-generative theory the distinction in the two functions of *also* is not adequately explained by such a tree-structure diagram. Another solution would be for the conjunct to be dominated by a node that dominates S:

X → (conjunct *also*) S

The analogous tree-representation would be:

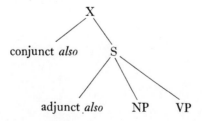

A similar problem of bracketing arises with other conjuncts, and indeed with disjuncts as well.

From a generative point of view, the questions raised in §**10.2** (pages 227ff.) also require to be considered in an analysis of grammatical categories and grammatical function. (See Chomsky 1965, 68ff. for a distinction between grammatical category and grammatical function.) We must assume, for example, that *usually* needs to be treated differently from the disjuncts in view of the difference in its syntactic features (cf. pages 178ff.). Such questions are best treated at length in the framework of a theoretical discussion, though they require a prior thorough description of the syntactic features of different classes of adjuncts in addition to the description of conjuncts and disjuncts in this study.[1]

Features in which a conjunct or disjunct differs from most other conjuncts or disjuncts respectively should be noted in the lexicon (e.g. *apparently*, page 118, and *surprisingly* and its synonyms, page 126). Conjuncts and disjuncts should be defined separately from their homonyms. Existing dictionaries often fail to mention (in particular) the disjunct in their definitions. For example, Webster's Third New International Dictionary defines *strangely* as 'in a strange manner', ignoring the disjunct *strangely*. It is usual for dictionaries to define the manner adjunct in a regularised way as '*in a(n)* adjective base *manner*'. Where a disjunct has a correspondence, it should become the practice to define it by its correspondence.

---

[1] A working paper by Jacobson 1968 has just come to hand. It discusses derived phrase-makers and the deep structures of sentences with adverbs immediately dominated by the node S as contrasted with adverbs dominated by the node VP. The paper arrived too late to be taken into account in this study.

Appendix

Tabulation of experimental data

Evidence derived from experiments with informants has been referred to in various parts of the book. It is convenient to assemble the results and display them in summary form.

The total number of informants for each Battery was:

Battery I   – 85
Battery II – 179
Battery III – 117

However, through a technical error, the results of only sixty-four informants could be used for the similarity tests given in Battery I.

Tables 16-30 display the results of compliance, evaluation, and similarity tests (cf. pages 11ff.). The Tables fall into three groups: (1) Tables 16-20 display the results of tests on the acceptability of an adverb immediately following the clause negative particle; (2) Tables 21-3 display the results of tests on the acceptability of an adverb in an interrogative form of the sentence or in initial position in that form of the sentence; (3) Tables 24-30 display the results of tests on the similarity between two instances of an adverb, one in initial position and the other placed elsewhere in the sentence.

A complete list of the tests in the three Batteries together with a discussion of aims in testing, techniques of presentation, and criteria and methods of scoring will be found in Greenbaum and Quirk (forthcoming).

TABLE 16 *Compliance test results: negative transformations*

BATTERY I   Compliance

he will /*possibly* become a tèacher#   23(27%)

he can /*probably* drive a càr#   4(5%)

he can /*certainly* drive a càr#   0

he can /*usually* write wèll#   51(60%)

BATTERY II

she has /*wisely* refused your òffer#   29(16%)

he has /*kindly* accepted our invitàtion#   35(20%)

I can /*fortunately* understand her mèssage#   19(11%)

he can /*often* explain what they mèan#   123(69%)

I can /*really* believe what they sày#   139(78%)

TABLE 17 *Compliance tests requiring negative transformations: types of non-compliance*

pre-V in test sentence	Total non-compliance	Types of non-compliance			Transposed to				
		Omission of item	Replacement of item	Transposition of item	pre-S	pre-aux.	pre-neg.	post-V	end
BATTERY I									
possibly	62(73%)	4(5%)	13(15%)	39(46%)	1(1%)	9(11%)	29(34%)	0	0
probably	81(95%)	2(2%)	1(1%)	77(91%)	7(8%)	54(64%)	14(16%)	0	2(2%)
certainly	85(100%)	2(2%)	0	83(98%)	4(5%)	66(78%)	13(15%)	0	0
usually	34(40%)	0	2(2%)	28(33%)	7(8%)	16(19%)	2(2%)	0	3(4%)
BATTERY II									
wisely	150(84%)	9(5%)	29(16%)	88(49%)	23(13%)	3(2%)	60(34%)	0	2(1%)
kindly	144(80%)	61(34%)	20(11%)	30(17%)	0	1(1%)	27(15%)	1(1%)	1(1%)
fortunately	160(89%)	7(4%)	111(62%)	37(21%)	20(11%)	8(4%)	8(4%)	0	1(1%)
often	56(31%)	0	4(2%)	26(15%)	10(6%)	13(7%)	1(1%)	2(1%)	0
really	40(22%)	6(3%)	2(1%)	25(14%)	0	23(13%)	2(1%)	0	0

TABLE 18 *Compliance tests requiring negative transformations: mode of negation – Battery II*

pre-V in test sentence	Ø	1	2	3	4	5	6	7	8
[i] *wisely*	12(7%)	125(70%)	11(6%)		15(8%)	14(8%)		1	
[ii] *kindly*	9(5%)	116(65%)			39(22%)	7(4%)	2	7(4%)	1
[iii] *fortunately*	6(3%)	62(35%)				111(62%)			
[iv] *often*	4(2%)	172(96%)		3(2%)					
[v] *really*	3(2%)	174(97%)							

KEY

Ø: no negation 1: clause negation 2: morphemic negation of pre-verb item 3: semantic negation of pre-verb item 4: semantic negation of verb 5: 1+2 6: 1+4 7: 2+4 8: 4+5

LEXICAL CHANGES

[i] 2 – *unwisely* [all instances]; 4 – *accepted; agreed to* [once]

[ii] 2 – *unkindly* [all instances]; 3 – *churlishly*; 4 – *refused; declined* [8 instances]; *rejected* [once]

[iii] 2 – *unfortunately* [all instances]

[iv] 3 – *never* [twice]; *rarely* [once]

TABLE 19 *Compliance tests requiring negative transformations: positions of morphemically negated items—Battery II*

	No. of times substitution is made	POSITION					
		pre-S	pre-aux.	pre-neg.	post-neg.	end	pre-V (no neg.)
wisely → *unwisely*	26(15%)	5(3%)	0	10(6%)	2(1%)	0	9(5%)
kindly → *unkindly*	14(8%)	1(1%)	0	3(2%)	3(2%)	0	7(4%)
fortunately → *unfortunately*	111(62%)	52(29%)	10(6%)	8(4%)	40(22%)	1(1%)	0

TABLE 20 *Evaluation tests: negated sentences*

BATTERY I	+	−	?
he /won't *possibly* become a tèacher #	12(14%)	60(71%)	13(15%)
he /can't *probably* drive a càr#	3(4%)	79(93%)	3(4%)
he /can't *certainly* drive a càr#	3(4%)	75(87%)	7(8%)
he /can't *usually* write wèll	44(52%)	24(28%)	15(18%)

BATTERY II			
she /hasn't *wisely* refused your òffer#	31(17%)	101(56%)	47(26%)
he /hasn't *kindly* accepted our invitàtion#	18(10%)	120(67%)	41(23%)
I /can't *fortunately* understand her mèssage#	24(13%)	96(54%)	59(33%)
he /can't *often* explain what they mèan#	162(90%)	5(3%)	12(7%)
I /can't *really* believe what they sày#	176(98%)	1(1%)	2(1%)

BATTERY III			
under/stăndably# they /didn't open the lètter#	110(94%)	2(2%)	5(4%)
re/lŭctantly# they /didn't insist on his resignàtion#	39(33%)	45(38%)	33(28%)

TABLE 21 *Compliance test results: interrogative transformations*

BATTERY I	Compliance
/*străngely*# they re/fuse to pày#	19(22%)
/*ăctually*# she /sat nèar him#	13(15%)
/*cĕrtainly*# the /car broke dòwn#	5(6%)
how/*ĕver*# he /started a new bùsiness#	14(16%)
to/*dăy*# the mu/seum was òpen#	3(4%)
/*sŭddenly*# he /opened the dòor#	1(1%)
/*mŭsically*# the /concert was a succèss#	20(24%)
confi/*dĕntially*# he is a /fòol#	72(85%)

BATTERY II	
/it's in the pàpers *surprisingly*#	42(23%)
he /*rightly* decided to make a wìll#	87(49%)
he will /*probably* stay làte#	105(59%)
they will /*possibly* leave èarly#	118(66%)
they will *per*/*haps* come sòon#	114(64%)
inci/*dĕntally*# /he is the chàirman#	122(68%)

9*

TABLE 22 *Compliance tests requiring interrogative transformations: types of non-compliance*

	Total non-compliance	Types of non-compliance		
		Omis-sion of item	Replace-ment of item	Trans-position of item
BATTERY I				
/strắngely# they re/fuse to pày#	66(78%)	34(40%)	14(16%)	13(15%)
/ăctually# she /sat nèar him#	72(85%)	5(6%)	2(2%)	60(71%)
/cĕrtainly# the /car broke dòwn#	80(94%)	26(31%)	11(13%)	41(48%)
how/ĕver# he /started a new bùsiness#	71(84%)	14(16%)	1(1%)	48(56%)
to/dăy# the mu/seum was òpen#	82(96%)	0	0	80(94%)
/sŭddenly# he /opened the dòor#	84(99%)	3(4%)	0	82(96%)
/mŭsically# the /concert was a succèss#	65(76%)	0	4(5%)	60(71%)
confi/dĕntially# he is a /fòol#	13(15%)	0	1(1%)	3(4%)
BATTERY II				
/it's in the pàpers *surprisingly*#	137(77%)	84(47%)	18(10%)	29(16%)
he /*rightly* decided to make a wìll#	92(51%)	42(23%)	18(10%)	17(9%)
he will /*probably* stay làte#	74(41%)	26(15%)	19(11%)	5(3%)
they will /*possibly* leave èarly#	61(34%)	12(6%)	27(15%)	7(4%)
they will per/haps come sòon#	65(36%)	16(9%)	6(3%)	30(17%)
inci/dĕntally# /he is the chàirman#	57(32%)	15(8%)	3(4%)	30(17%)

TABLE 23 *Evaluation tests: interrogative sentences*

BATTERY I	+	−	?
/*străngely*# /do they refuse to páy#	6(7%)	65(76%)	14(16%)
/*ăctually*# /did she sit néar him#	40(47%)	25(29%)	20(24%)
/*cĕrtainly*# /did the car break dówn#	1(1%)	72(85%)	12(14%)
how/*ĕver*# /did he start a new búsiness#	37(44%)	25(29%)	23(27%)
to/*dăy*# /was the museum ópen#	16(19%)	51(60%)	18(21%)
/*sŭddenly*# /did he open the dóor#	2(2%)	76(89%)	7(8%)
/*mŭsically*# /was the concert a succéss#	57(67%)	17(20%)	11(13%)
confi/*dĕntially*# /is he a fóol#	71(84%)	4(5%)	10(12%)

BATTERY II			
/is it in the pápers *surprisingly*#	10(6%)	132(74%)	37(21%)
/did he *rightly* decide to make a wíll#	108(60%)	27(15%)	44(25%)
/will he *probably* stay láte#	108(60%)	27(15%)	44(25%)
/will they *possibly* leave éarly#	120(67%)	18(10%)	41(23%)
/will they *perhaps* come sóon#	123(69%)	24(12%)	32(18%)
inci/*dĕntally*# /is he the cháirman#	167(93%)	4(2%)	8(4%)
/is he the cháirman *incidentally*#	136(75%)	23(13%)	20(11%)

TABLE 24 *Results of compliance tests on sentences with repeated items – Battery I*

Task required		Compliance
present	in/dèed# /some people indèed attempted it#	53(63%)
present	in/dèed# /many soldiers thòroughly hated it#	69(81%)
singular	/rèally# the /students rèally wòrk during the term#	71(84%)
singular	/frànkly# they were /really appalled by their lèader#	67(79%)
singular	/rèally# your /children absolutely hòwl every night#	71(84%)
singular	/cèrtainly# your /children cèrtainly disliked me#	72(85%)
singular	/cèrtainly# his /workers entìrely distrùsted him#	50(59%)
present	/hònestly# Mr /Jones honestly believed our stòry#	68(80%)
present	/hònestly# Mr /Jones honestly reported our stòry#	63(74%)
present	/pèrsonally# /I mysèlf# ap/pròved of the idea#	67(79%)
singular	/àlso# your /children also disliked me#	69(81%)
present	/neverthelèss# /some people neverthelèss attempted it#	60(71%)

TABLE 25 *Results of compliance tests on sentences with repeated items – Battery* II

Task required		Compliance
present	/pĕrsonally# /I pĕrsonally# ap/prŏved of the idea#	135(75%)
present	in/dĕed# /some people indĕed attempted it#	130(73%)
past	/ăctually# /some lectures are actually given before tèn#	129(72%)
past	/sŭrely# the /child surely apologises for his mistàkes#	98(55%)
past	/thĕrefore# /many seats are therefore booked a week befòre#	87(49%)
past	/sŭddenly# the /woman suddenly agrees to the plàn#	77(43%)

TABLE 26 *Results of evaluation tests on sentences with repeated items – Battery I*

	+	−	?
in|dĕed# |some people índeed attempted it#	8(9%)	60(71%)	17(20%)
in|dĕed# |many soldiers thoroughly hated it#	75(88%)	6(7%)	4(5%)
|rĕally# the |students réally wòrk during the term#	24(28%)	38(45%)	23(27%)
|frănkly# they were |really appalled by their léader#	71(83%)	3(4%)	11(13%)
|rĕally# your |children ábsolutely hòwl every night#	58(68%)	16(19%)	11(13%)
|cĕrtainly# your |children cértainly disliked me#	15(18%)	42(49%)	28(33%)
|cĕrtainly# his |workers entìrely distrùsted him#	55(65%)	16(19%)	14(16%)
|hŏnestly# |Mr Jones honestly believed our stòry#	22(26%)	39(46%)	24(28%)
|hŏnestly# |Mr Jones honestly reported our stòry#	29(34%)	39(46%)	17(20%)
|pĕrsonally# |I mysélf# ap|próved of the idea#	44(52%)	31(36%)	10(12%)
|ălso# your |children álso disliked me#	19(22%)	46(54%)	20(24%)
|nevertheléss# |some people nevertheléss attempted it#	11(13%)	53(62%)	21(25%)

TABLE 27 *Results of evaluation tests on sentences with repeated items – Battery II*

	+	–	?
|pěrsonally# |I pěrsonally# ap|proved of the idea#	15(8%)	131(73%)	33(18%)
in|děed# |some people indèed attempted it#	15(8%)	126(70%)	48(27%)
|àctually# |some lectures are *actually* given before tèn#	30(17%)	109(61%)	40(22%)
|sǔrely# the |child *surely* apologises for his mistàkes#	11(6%)	145(81%)	23(13%)
|thěrefore# |many seats are *therefore* booked a week befòre#	12(7%)	127(71%)	40(22%)
|sǔddenly# the |woman *suddenly* agrees to the plàn#	13(7%)	137(77%)	29(16%)

TABLE 28 *Results of similarity tests – Battery* I

	=	≠	?
{/hŏnestly# /Mr Jones reported our stòry# /Mr Jones *honestly* reported our stòry#	3(5%)	57(89%)	4(6%)
{/Mr Jones *honestly* believed our stòry# /hŏnestly# /Mr Jones believed our stòry#	8(12%)	46(72%)	10(16%)
{/rĕally# the /students wòrk during the term# the /students *réally* wòrk during the term#	12(19%)	47(73%)	5(8%)
{his /workers *entírely* distrùsted him# /cĕrtainly# his /workers distrùsted him#	19(30%)	33(52%)	12(19%)
{/ălso# your /children disliked me# your /children *álso* disliked me#	22(34%)	27(42%)	15(23%)
{they were /really appalled by their lèader# /frănkly# they were ap/palled by their lèader#	23(36%)	32(50%)	9(14%)
{your /children *cértainly* disliked me# /cĕrtainly# your /children disliked me#	26(41%)	19(30%)	19(30%)
{your /children *ábsolutely* hòwl every night# /rĕally# your /children hòwl every night#	27(42%)	24(38%)	13(20%)
{in/dĕed# /some people attèmpted it# /some people *indèed* attempted it#	30(47%)	17(27%)	17(27%)
{in/dĕed# /many soldiers hàted it# /many soldiers *thòroughly* hated it#	33(52%)	23(36%)	8(12%)
{/neverthelĕss# /some people attèmpted it# /some people *neverthelèss* attempted it#	53(83%)	7(11%)	4(6%)
{/personally# I ap/pròved of the idea# /I *mysĕlf#* ap/pròved of the idea#	58(91%)	4(6%)	2(3%)

TABLE 29 *Results of similarity tests – Battery* II

	=	≠	?
{ /some lectures are *actually* given before tèn# /*ăctually*# /some lectures are given before tèn#	40(23%)	100(56%)	39(22%)
{ /*rĕally*# your /children hòwl during the night# your /children *often* hòwl during the night#	45(25%)	90(50%)	44(25%)
{ /some people *indèed* attempted it# *in*/*dĕed*# /some people attèmpted it#	72(40%)	62(35%)	45(25%)
{ your /father *luckily* owns a càr# /*lŭckily*# your /father owns a càr#	88(49%)	59(33%)	32(18%)
{ the /child *surely* apologises for his mistàkes# /*sŭrely*# the /child apologises for his mistàkes#	107(60%)	46(26%)	26(14%)
{ /*pĕrsonally*# I ap/pròved of the idea# /I *pĕrsonally*# ap/pròved of the idea#	124(69%)	12(7%)	43(24%)
{ /*sŭddenly*# the /woman agrèes to the plan# the /woman *suddenly* agrèes to the plan#	150(84%)	8(4%)	21(12%)
{ /*thĕrefore*# /many seats are booked a week befòre# /many seats are *therefore* booked a week befòre#	156(87%)	12(7%)	11(6%)

TABLE 30 *Results of similarity tests – Battery* III

	=	≠	?
{ the /book was *unfortunately* dìfficult# { un/fŏrtunately# the /book was dìfficult#	29(25%)	51(44%)	37(32%)
{ the /test was *surprisingly* èasy# { sur/prĭsingly# the /test was èasy#	39(33%)	55(47%)	23(20%)
{ the /students *obviously* understood the lècture# { /ŏbviously# the /students understood the lècture#	57(49%)	29(25%)	31(26%)
{ sur/prĭsingly# your /father owns a càr# { your /father *surprisingly* owns a càr#	72(62%)	20(17%)	25(21%)
{ /lŭckily# the /game ends at sèven# { the /game *luckily* ends at sèven#	72(66%)	22(19%)	18(15%)
{ the /child *understandably* feels neglècted# { /understăndably# the /child feels neglècted#	96(82%)	10(9%)	11(9%)
{ /wĭsely# the /Minister insisted on a full repòrt# { the /Minister *wisely* insisted on a full repòrt#	104(89%)	5(4%)	8(7%)

Bibliography

Behre, F. (1955) *Meditative-Polemic 'Should' in Modern English 'That'-Clauses*. Stockholm

Bendix, E. H. (1966) *Componential Analysis of General Vocabulary. The Semantic Structure of a Set of Verbs in English, Hindi, and Japanese*. Bloomington, Indiana. (= Part II *International Journal of American Linguistics* **32**, no 2)

Bolinger, D. L. (1961a) *Generality, Gradience, and the All-or-None*. The Hague

(1961b) 'Syntactic Blends and Other Matters', *Language* **37**, 366-81

(1967) 'Adjectives in English: Attribution & Predication', *Lingua* **18**, 1-34

Borst, E. (1902) *Die Gradadverbien im Englischen* (= *Anglistische Forschungen*, Heft 10). Heidelberg

Chomsky, N. (1965) *Aspects of the Theory of Syntax*. Cambridge, Massachusetts

Curme, G. O. (1931) *Syntax* (= Curme, G. O. and Kurath, H., *A Grammar of the English Language* 3). Boston

(1935) *Parts of Speech and Accidence* (= Curme, G. O. and Kurath, H., *A Grammar of the English Language* 2). Boston

Crystal, D. (1966) 'Specification and English tenses', *Journal of Linguistics* **2**, 1-33

(1967) 'English', *Lingua* **17**, 24-56

Crystal, D. and Quirk, R. (1964) *Systems of Prosodic and Paralinguistic Features in English*. The Hague

Davies, E. C. (1967) 'Some Notes on English Clause Types', *Transactions of the Philological Society* 1-31. Oxford

Feldman, S. S. (1959) *Mannerisms of Speech and Gestures in Everyday Life*. New York

Francis, W. N. (1958) *The Structure of American English*. New York

Gleitman, L. R. (1965) 'Coordinating Conjunctions in English', *Language* **41**, 260-93

Godfrey, J. (1965) 'The Survey of English Usage', *English Language Teaching* **19**, 98-103

Greenbaum, S. (1969a) *Verb-Intensifier Collocations in English*. The Hague

(1969b) 'The Question of *But*', *Folia Linguistica*, III, 3/4

Greenbaum, S. and Quirk, R. (forthcoming) *The Elicitation of Language Data*

Halliday, M. A. K. (1963) 'The Tones of English', *Archivum Linguisticum* **15**, 1-28

(1967a) 'Notes on transitivity and theme in English, Part 1', *Journal of Linguistics* **3**, 37-81

(1967b) 'Notes on transitivity and theme in English, Part 2', *Journal of Linguistics* **3**, 199-244

Harris, Z. S. (1957) 'Co-occurrence and Transformation in Linguistic Structure', *Language* **33**, 283-340

Huddleston, R. (1967) 'More on the English Comparative', *Journal of Linguistics* **3**, 91-102

Hudson, R. A. (1967) 'Constituency in a Systemic Description of the English Clause', *Lingua* **18**, 225-50

Jacobson, S. (1964) *Adverbial Positions in English*, Stockholm

(1968) *The Placement of Preverbs in American English*, Introduction and Chapter I (mimeographed). Stockholm University

Jespersen, O. (1917) 'Negation in English and Other Languages', *Kgl. Danske Videnskabernes Selskab: Historisk-Filologiske Meddelelser* **1**, 5. Copenhagen. (Reprinted in *Selected Writings of Otto Jespersen* 3-151. London, Tokyo.)

(1924) *The Philosophy of Grammar*. London

(1937), *Linguistic Self-Criticism* (= *Society for Pure English Tract* 48). London

(1949) *A Modern English Grammar on Historical Principles* vol 7. London, Copenhagen

Katz, J. J. and Postal, P. M. (1964) *An Integrated Theory of Linguistic Description*. Cambridge, Massachusetts

Kirchner, G. (1955) *Gradadverbien: Restriktiva und Verwandtes im heutigen Englisch*. Halle

Klima, E. S. (1964) 'Negation in English' in *The Structure of Language*, ed Fodor, J. A. and Katz, J. J., 246-323. Englewood Cliffs, New Jersey

Kruisinga, E. (1932a) *A Handbook of Present-Day English* Part 2:2. (5th ed). Groningen

(1932b) *A Handbook of Present-Day English* Part 2:3. (5th ed). Groningen

Kuroda, S.-Y. (1966) *Attachment Transformations* (mimeographed). (= slightly expanded version of chapter 1 of MIT Dissertation, 1965, *Generative Grammatical Studies in the Japanese Language*)

(1967) *Notes on English Manner Adverbials* (mimeographed). University of California, San Diego

Lee, W. R. (1965) 'Preliminary Notes on *Also* and *Too*', *Philologica Pragensia* **8**, 255-60

Lees, R. B. (1960) 'A Multiply Ambiguous Adjectival Construction in English', *Language* **36**, 207-21
  (1963a) 'Analysis of the "Cleft Sentence" in English', *Zeitschrift für Phonetik, Sprachwissenschaft und Kommunikationsforschung* **16** (4), 371-88
  (1963b) *The Grammar of English Nominalizations*. Bloomington, Indiana
Longacre, R. E. (1964) *Grammar Discovery Procedures*. The Hague
Palmer, H. E. (1939) *A Grammar of Spoken English* (2nd ed). Cambridge
Palmer, F. R. (1965) *A Linguistic Study of the English Verb*. London
Poldauf, I. (1959) 'Further comments on Gustav Kirchner's *Gradadverbien*', *Philologica Pragensia* **2**, 1-6
  (1964) 'The Third Syntactical Plan', *Travaux Linguistiques de Prague* **1**, 241-55
Poutsma, H. (1926) *A Grammar of Late Modern English* Part 2:2. Groningen
  (1928) *A Grammar of Late Modern English* Part 1:1 (2nd ed). Groningen
Quirk, R. (1954) *The Concessive Relation in Old English Poetry*. New Haven
  (1960) 'Towards a Description of English Usage', *Transactions of the Philological Society* 1960, 40-61. Oxford
  (1965) 'Descriptive Statement and Serial Relationship', *Language* **41**, 205-17
  (1966) 'On English Usage', *Journal of the Royal Society of Arts* **114**, 837-51
Quirk, R. and Svartvik, J. (1966) *Investigating Linguistic Acceptability*. The Hague
Rensky, M. (1964) 'English Verbo-Nominal Phrases', *Travaux Linguistiques de Prague* **1**, 289-99
Spitzbardt, H. (1965) 'English adverbs of degree and their semantic fields', *Philologica Pragensia* **8**, 349-59
Stoffel, C. (1901) *Intensives and Down-toners* (= *Anglistische Forschungen*, Heft 1). Heidelberg
Storms, G. (1966) '*That*-clauses in Modern English', *English Studies* **47**, 249-70
Strang, B. M. H. (1962) *Modern English Structure*. London
Svartvik, J. (1966) *On Voice in the English Verb*. The Hague
Sweet, H. (1891) *A New English Grammar* Part 1. Oxford
  (1898) *A New English Grammar* Part 2. Oxford
Waldron, R. A. (1967) *Sense and Sense Development*. London
Zandvoort, R. W. (1962) *A Handbook of English Grammar* (2nd ed). London
Zimmer, K. E. (1964) *Affixal Negation in English and Other Languages* (= Supplement to *Word* **20**, no 2, Monograph no 5)

Index